# Generating Breakthrough New Product Ideas

D0710920

OTHER BEST SELLING BOOKS BY THE AUTHORS:

*Winning at New Products: Accelerating the
Process from Idea to Launch,* Third Edition
(authored by Robert G. Cooper)

*Product Leadership: Creating and Launching
Superior New Products*
(authored by Robert G. Cooper)

*Lean, Rapid, and Profitable New Product Development*
(authored by Robert G. Cooper and Scott J. Edgett)

*Product Development for the Service Sector*
(authored by Robert G. Cooper and Scott J. Edgett)

*Portfolio Management of New Products*
(authored by Robert G. Cooper, Scott J. Edgett and
Elko J. Kleinschmidt)

All books are available for online purchase at
www.stage-gate.com

# Generating Breakthrough New Product Ideas

## Feeding the Innovation Funnel

ROBERT G. COOPER
SCOTT J. EDGETT

**Product Development Institute Inc.**

Copyright © 2007 by Robert G. Cooper and Scott J. Edgett

Published by the Product Development Institute

All rights reserved.

No part of this publication may be reproduced, store in a retrieval system or transmitted in any form or by any means, electronic, mechanical, photocopying, recording or otherwise without the prior written permission of the publisher.

Printed in Canada

For more information on the concepts and tools introduced in this book, please visit the Product Development Institute Inc. at www.prod-dev.com.

Special discounts for bulk purchase are available to corporations, institutes and other organizations. For more information, please call 905-304-8798 or email info@prod-dev.com.

ISBN 978-0-9732827-2-6

First Printing, February 2007

Cover and Text Design by Laura Brady

Typeset in 11 point Abode Garamond

# CONTENTS

# CHAPTER 1

# The Quest for Breakthrough Ideas

> History is in essence a history of ideas.
> —H.G. WELLS, *The Outline of History*

Product innovations are the life blood of the modern corporation. Look at any major company doing well today – Apple, Procter & Gamble, Toyota, GE – and invariably you'll see a steady stream of successful new product launches. But product innovation is in trouble – R&D productivity is down: There is less bang for buck today; blockbuster or game-changing product innovations are absent in most firms' development portfolios; and increasingly there is pressure from the financial community to improve innovation results.

Fixing the shortage of blockbuster and game-changing product innovations is what this book is about. Many companies already have a solid idea-to-launch process or Stage-Gate®* system in place (see Exhibit 1.1).[1] That's an important part of the puzzle, because without an effective new product process, good new product concepts never reach the marketplace. But a solid idea-to-launch process is not enough: What many senior

---

\* Stage-Gate® is a registered trademark of the Product Development Institute Inc., see www.prod-dev.com.

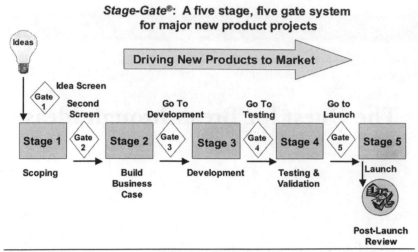

EXHIBIT 1.1 A typical Stage-Gate product innovation system is used by virtually every best performing company to drive their new product ideas through to successful market launches.

executives are realizing is that there is a *real shortage of strong, high-value ideas* and development projects entering and progressing through their development pipelines. In short, the process is robust enough, but the cupboard is bare – the *pipeline feed is dry.*

## Product Innovation is the Key Management Imperative

Companies around the world have emerged from a period of retrench-ment, cost-cutting and operational excellence, and are now focused on a vision of *sustained organic growth.* Senior executives and Wall Street have finally figured out that no company ever shrank its way to greatness. Rather, product and service innovation must be the engine for growth. As the Chairman and CEO of P&G put it so boldly:

"Innovation is a prerequisite for sustained growth. No other path to profitable growth can be sustained over time. Without continual innovation, markets stagnate, products become commodities and margins shrink."[2]

Innovation has become the hot button for chief executives everywhere, according to *Business Week*.[3] CEOs and business leaders around the world see increased competitiveness; they see challenges to their business models as they go forward; and they see many products and services being commoditized. They also see that all these roads and converging trends lead to innovation.

For many corporate executives, product innovation has become *the only game in town*; and if not the only game then it's certainly the most important one. The message is simple: Either you succeed at product innovation or you will fail as a business! That is, *innovate or die*! The ill-fated dot.com boom and bust was only the precursor to the rapid rise of innovation's role. Look around and witness those companies doing well today – Procter & Gamble whose new launches are setting sales and profit records in its industry; Apple with its iPod, which has created a whole new industry overnight; RIM (Research In Motion) whose BlackBerry is the coveted communications device in business today; Toyota with its hybrid Prius, which has raised the bar in engine technology; and Motorola whose ultra-thin Moto RAZR cell phone is in huge demand. And an analysis of data from Fortune's annual survey of the most admired companies in America reveals that "value as a long term investment" is closely linked to the "innovativeness of a company".

Product innovation is vital to the growth and prosperity of the modern corporation. New products now account for a major portion of companies' sales revenues annually in the U.S., at almost 30 percent of the top line of the profit and loss statement.[4] Even more astonishing is that the best performing companies see a remarkable 47.6 percent of annual sales coming from new products, and an astounding 49.1 percent of annual profits derived from new products. That's almost half of these companies' profits and sales coming from new products! Similar results are shown in a major global study of innovation, which reveals the impact that new products have on company sales broken down by industry (Exhibit 1.2).[5]

Check your industry and compare how your company fares. Again the top performers achieve almost half their sales from new products, but, in some industries, new products account for two-thirds of current sales!

The reasons for the current heavy emphasis on product innovation are evident. Globalization, the growth of outsourcing and off-shoring of not only manufacturing but R&D, rapidly changing markets and competitive environments, commoditization of existing products and the search for competitive advantage, and the quickening pace of technological change are but some of the drivers of innovation. Thus, expect to see product and service innovation play an even greater role in deciding corporate fortunes in the years ahead.

The key role of innovation has not gone unnoticed by the financial community, with Wall Street placing increased pressure on CEOs to deliver. Indeed, a Cheskin and Fitch survey revealed that almost half of CEOs view product innovation as *very critical to their business's future success*,[6] while a global Arthur D. Little survey showed that *enhancing innovation capabilities* is viewed by CEOs as the *number one lever* to increase corporate profitability and growth – see Exhibit 1.3.[7] Note that innovation is rated well ahead of cost-cutting in Exhibit 1.3, a traditional lever used by senior executives to increase profits. The message from the financial community is that *organic growth* based on product innovation is paramount.

## But It's Not So Easy

If generating a steady stream of innovative and profitable product innovations was as easy as some of the pundits make it out to be, then half the companies in America and Europe would be incredibly wealthy, and the others would be doing quite well. And there would be no need for searching for new best practices, nor for this book.

The fact is that product innovation performance is in trouble, in spite of all the hype from CEOs, the pundits and Wall Street. Corporations and nations continue to spend heavily on R&D, and yet productivity is

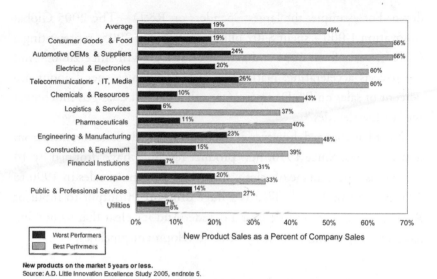

Worst Performers
Best Performers

New Product Sales as a Percent of Company Sales

**New products on the market 5 years or less.**
Source: A.D. Little Innovation Excellence Study 2005, endnote 5.

EXHIBIT 1.2 New products represent a huge percentage of company sales; this percent also varies greatly by industry. Note how much better the best performers are – 2.5 times higher new product sales on average.

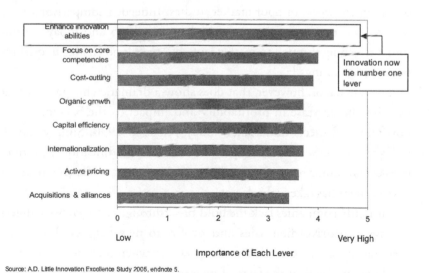

Innovation now the number one lever

Low                                    Very High

Importance of Each Lever

Source: A.D. Little Innovation Excellence Study 2005, endnote 5.

EXHIBIT 1.3 Of 8 key levers to increase corporate profitability and growth, CEOs identified innovation as the most important, and ahead of cost-cutting.

down. For example, the largest spenders on R&D – The 2005 Global Innovation 1,000 – spent $407 billion on R&D in 2005, representing a 6.0% increase from 2004 and a 4.2% annual growth since 2000.[8] And the pace is accelerating! Nationally, U.S. companies spend about 4.9 percent of sales on R&D, a percentage that has not changed much over the last few decades.[9]

What has changed, however, is the output, namely sales revenues from new products. Since 1990, new product revenues have dropped by 14 percent as a percentage of sales – from 32.6 percent of sales in 1990 to 28.0 percent in 2004.[10] That is a huge drop-off in output-to-input or R&D productivity in little over a decade. And it's clear that something has gone very wrong with many firms' development pipelines.

## Why is Productivity Down?

We looked at the many possible causes of this decrease in R&D or new product development (NPD) productivity.[11] There's no evidence that people are doing a worse job today: bad launches, deficient design and development work, or poor market studies. Indeed, a comparison of the quality of execution of key activities between 1985 and today – from initial screening through to market launch – reveals no change in quality-of-execution ratings.[12]

The one factor, however, that does show a dramatic change, and that explains the decrease in profitability and impact, is the balance in the portfolio of projects undertaken today versus in 1990. Simply stated, today's businesses are preoccupied with minor modifications, product tweaks and minor responses to salespeople's requests, while true product development has taken a back seat.

Currently companies lack the bold breakthroughs and game-changers necessary to drive their sales and profits to new heights. Too many corporations *are picking the low hanging fruit* when it comes to product development! Look at the facts, shown in Exhibit 1.4. Businesses undertook almost twice as many "new to world" or true innovation products in 1990 as they do today as a percentage of their development portfo-

Percentage Breakdown of Projects in the Development Portfolio

| Development Project Type | 1990[2] | 2004[1] | % Change from 1990 |
|---|---|---|---|
| New to world – true innovations | 20.4% | 11.5% | 43.6% decrease |
| New product lines to the company | 38.8 | 27.1 | 30.1% decrease |
| Additions to existing product line in company | 20.4 | 24.7 | 21.0% increase |
| Improvements & modifications to existing company products | 20.4 | 36.7 | 79.9% increase |
| Total | 100.0% | 100.0% | |

Sources: 1. Cooper-Edgett-Kleinschmidt benchmarking study, endnotes 12 & 13; and 2. Kleinschmidt & Cooper, endnote 13.

EXHIBIT 1.4 In the last 15 years, there has been a major shift in types of development projects undertaken to much less innovative and less venturesome projects.

lios, according to a major benchmarking study we undertook.[13] Now things are reversed. Today, businesses undertake almost twice as many minor projects – improvements, modifications and tweaks – as they did in 1990.

These trends are also evident in a study conducted by the Product Development Management Association (PDMA), which revealed that "the number of projects motivated by cost reduction, repositioning and incremental improvements has grown, while the percentage of major revisions, product-line additions, new to the firm and new-to-the-world projects has dropped."[14] For example, new-to-world and new-to-firm projects have decreased from 30 percent of the portfolio in 1995 to 25 percent in nine short years – a 17 percent decrease. This may explain why cycle times have decreased so dramatically, from 41.7 months to 24 months: Businesses simply are not undertaking the challenging, step-out and significant product innovations they once did; instead, they are focusing on incremental improvements which inherently take less time. This is an alarming trend in the composition of the portfolio – from venturesome projects to lower risk projects.

Astute executives in some businesses recognize the dangers. Our benchmarking study reveals that executives are indeed concerned about their portfolio of development projects, as shown in Exhibit 1.5.[15] The management in only 21.2 percent of businesses indicate that their development portfolios contain *enough high value-to-the-corporation projects*; but twice as many or 40.5 percent of businesses do not. And only 19.4 percent of business managements claim that their portfolio has the *right balance* between short term and long term projects; 38.0 percent do not.

## Top Performers Model the Way

What are the secrets to more successful and profitable innovation? To answer the questions, we identified best performing businesses in our benchmarking study – those top 20% of businesses that outperformed the rest in NPD on a variety of financial and time metrics. When one

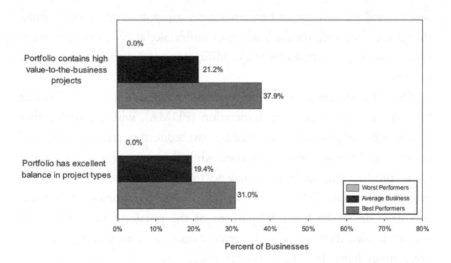

Source: Cooper-Edgett-Kleinschmidt benchmarking study, endnotes 12 & 13.

EXHIBIT 1.5 Development portfolios in most firms are substandard. But note how much better the best performers are, especially versus the worst performing businesses.

lowers the microscope on these best performers, a different portfolio picture emerges. For example, in Exhibit 1.5, best performing companies have higher value projects in their development pipelines, and a much better balance and mix of projects. The portfolio breakdown in Exhibit 1.6 reveals why:

- Best performers today have twice as many true innovations in their development pipelines (17.1 percent of their portfolios) than do worse performers (8.5 percent).
- But note how much things have changed: The average business in the mid 90s had an even higher proportion of innovations (20.4 percent) than today's best performers.
- Almost half the projects in worst performers' portfolios are small projects – tweaks, modifications and extensions (46.5 percent of the total portfolio), much more than is the case for best performers.

**Percentage of Projects in the Development Portfolio**

| Development Project Type | Best Performers 2004 | Worst Performers 2004 | Average Business 1990 |
|---|---|---|---|
| New to world – true innovations | 17.1% | 8.5% | 20.4% |
| New product lines to the company | 31.1 | 23.0 | 38.7 |
| Additions to existing product line in company | 25.8 | 22.0 | 20.5 |
| Improvements & modifications to existing company products | 26.0 | 46.5 | 20.4 |
| Total | 100.0% | 100.0% | 100.0% |

Sources: Cooper-Edgett-Kleinschmidt benchmarking, endnotes 12 & 13; also: Kleinschmidt & Cooper, endnote 13.

EXHIBIT 1.6 The development portfolios of top performers are far more innovative than portfolios of poor performers ... and similar to the portfolios of the "average company" 15 years ago.

One cannot prove that a certain portfolio mix of projects yields better performance, but the analysis is convincing. First, best performers have decidedly more innovative development portfolios – a higher proportion of true innovation projects and a lower proportion of minor projects. Second, years ago, the average company had an even better portfolio than today's best performers.

## Why the Shortage of Innovative Projects: Understanding the Root Causes

Before we leap forward to solutions, let's reflect on what's causing this portfolio shift.[16] In discussions with managers as part of several recent studies, we identify five main roadblocks to an innovative development portfolio.

### Roadblock #1 – speed demons and racing to market

The last decade or so has witnessed a preoccupation with reducing cycle time and on speeding new products to market. While cycle time reduction is an admirable goal, often the results of trying to reduce time-to-market have unexpected and negative consequences. For example, cutting corners on projects, dumbing-down projects, and poor team morale have all been blamed on excessive emphasis on cycle time reduction.[17]

One very negative result of this heavy emphasis on speed is that decision-makers tend to gravitate towards the smaller, low hanging fruit projects. The easiest way to reduce cycle time, but with negative consequences, is simply to select projects that are *fast and easy to do*. The result is not only a drop in cycle time, but also a deterioration of the quality of the portfolio of development projects.

## Roadblock #2 – reacting to customers' and salespeople's urgent requests

A parallel cause is the urgent response to a customer's or a salesperson's request for a new product. Often the product is not new at all, but merely a repackaged, slightly modified or tweaked product. Individually, these projects do not consume many resources; but collectively they can divert a large proportion of resources away from genuine product development.

These urgent sales requests must be handled: They are vital to keeping your sales force and your customers happy; they also keep your product line fresh and up-to-date. But if these projects begin to dominate your portfolio, then in the long run, your business is in trouble. Such urgent projects will devour the resources needed to develop genuine product innovations, blockbusters and new platforms for growth. As one executive noted:

> "Many of the smaller projects have to be done – they're needed to respond to a customer request. The trouble is… they consume almost all our development resources."

## Roadblock #3 – a resource crunch

The battle cry, "make the numbers" and "make the quarter", has led to serious resource deficiencies for many businesses' new product efforts. The financial goal has become "doing more with less"; and so executives fail to commit the necessary resources to product innovation, cutting vital technical and marketing staff.[18] Moreover, look at the hard research evidence in Exhibit 1.7:[19]

- Businesses are putting more projects through their development pipelines with no real increase in resources. The great majority have a poor balance between resources available and the number of projects underway; only 10.7 percent allocate enough resources to NPD projects to ensure that they are undertaken in a quality fashion.

- With too many projects underway, people are spread too thin (only 11.4 percent of businesses do not spread their people and resources across too many development projects).
- There is no focused effort: Project team members are spread over too many other activities and not focused enough on their product development projects. Only 21.9 percent of businesses achieve adequate resource focus.
- NPD projects suffer from a lack of resources from all functional areas. Only 31.4 percent of businesses have enough technical resources on projects. Marketing and Sales resources are even more deficient: In only 15.2 percent and 25.3 percent of businesses respectively are there enough Marketing and Sales resources available to projects.

This *resource crunch* has a direct impact on the nature of the portfolio that a business elects. Why? When resources are tight, managers take few chances – they choose the "sure bets", which are typically the smaller, closer-to-home projects. Here's a typical comment:

> "My business has a limited R&D budget. I can't afford to risk a major percentage of that budget on a handful of big projects. I've got to hedge my bets here, and pick the smaller and lower risk ones. If I had a larger R&D budget, then I might tackle some more venturesome projects . . ."

## Roadblock #4 – a lack of blockbuster, game-changing ideas

Perhaps the *most important and most challenging deficiency* is simply a dearth of innovative, creative and game-changing ideas. The pipeline is dry in too many companies. In our benchmarking study, for example, only 19 percent of businesses were judged to have a proficient ideation front-end to feed their development funnel, as shown in Exhibit 1.8. In the same exhibit, note that only one-third of companies work with lead or innovative customers to create their next breakthroughs.

**EXHIBIT 1.7** There is a resource crunch across the board in NPD – too many projects; and team members are spread too thinly and are unfocused, regardless of the functional department.

Corporations cannot achieve their aggressive innovation goals if they continue to focus on small, incremental development products and projects. The quest for competitive advantage and achieving significant increases in sales and profits though product development means that the portfolio of projects must change. For that to happen will require new, bold and innovative product ideas – some real game-changers and blockbuster ideas.

Note that best performers, to a certain extent, model the way here again. In Exhibit 1.8, twice as many best performers boast a well-oiled ideation phase and execute ideation proficiently when compared to the average firms. But even among best performers, there is much room for improvement. Similarly, 55 percent of best performers seek out innovative users and work with them to create innovative new product concepts. These are some hints that more effective ideation is indeed one of the solutions to what ails many companies' new product efforts.

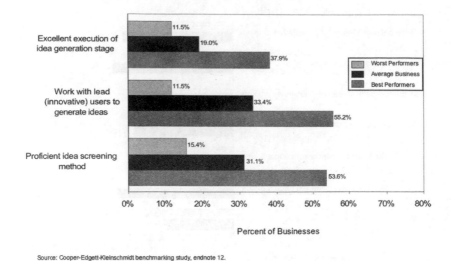

Source: Cooper-Edgett-Kleinschmidt benchmarking study, endnote 12.

EXHIBIT 1.8 Idea generation needs major improvements in most firms. Best performing businesses undertake much better and more proactive ideation.

## Roadblock #5 – the wrong project selection criteria

Less than one third of businesses were judged to utilize a first-rate idea screening, evaluation and selection methodology – see Exhibit 1.8. As any venture capitalist will attest, the ability to make the right investment decisions – to evaluate and select would-be projects early and when little information is known – is key to success. Yet most corporations use the wrong methods for screening innovative ideas, or no methods at all. By contrast, and by almost a two-to-one ratio, best performers use effective methods to screen and select new product ideas.

The most popular project selection and prioritization methods by far are financial tools: payback period, NPV and the productivity index. Financial techniques work very well for well-defined projects, such as modifications and extensions, where financial outcomes are predicable. But for step-out projects or early in the life of a project, applying such tools is likely to do more damage than good. Indeed, an Industrial Research Institute study revealed that for new product projects, those businesses that rigorously applied financial models as the main selection tool *ended up with the worst portfolios!*[20] An over-emphasis on financial criteria for project selection will drive the portfolio to smaller, lower risk projects, simply because their returns at first glance appear better, they are lower cost to do, and these projects are much more predicable.

## Remove the Roadblocks and Fix the Problems

If a steady stream of game-changing and innovative new product ideas and projects is the goal, then review the typical roadblocks above and find out what's standing in the way of innovation in your company. Then fix the blockages, namely:

- Back off the relentless pursuit of speed – remember, the goal is profitable product innovations, not fast execution of a bunch of projects that are low-value initiatives and low hanging fruit. As one executive at P&G noted: "Speed is dead at P&G… a decade of pursuing speed has caused us to do many stupid things!"
- Avoid a reactive mode to every sales force request and put a cap on the number of reactive projects you do.
- Put the necessary resources in place to enable innovation, and even create a ring-fenced and dedicated innovation team that does nothing but innovative projects.
- Create robust and high-value new product ideas to feed the funnel.
- Rethink how you evaluate, rate and rank projects – your project selection methods.

# The Need for a Proactive Idea Generation and Management System

A shortage of robust ideas plagues too many firms' product innovation efforts, but it takes roughly 100 ideas to yield one successful new product. So you must shovel a lot of earth to find a few diamonds! This is a huge

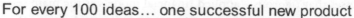

For every 100 ideas… one successful new product

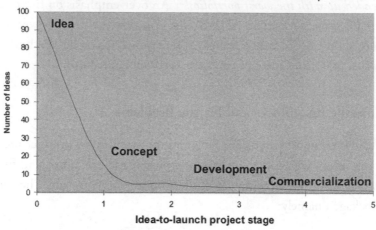

EXHIBIT 1.9 Many new ideas are required to create one major new product – there is a huge attrition rate.

attrition or fall-off rate, as shown in Exhibit 1.9. Given the importance of ideas as feed to the pipeline, together with this large attrition rate, what is needed is a *formal, systematic and professional idea generation and management approach* – one that generates and screens lots of ideas and good quality ones. Indeed, according to the Arthur D. Little study, of five best practices identified, idea management has the strongest impact on the increase in sales by new products (see Exhibit 1.10) – that is, having effective idea management results in an extra 7.2% of sales from new products.[21]

## Elements of an Effective Idea Management System

What are the most important elements of an effective idea management effort? First is creative employees that are actively involved in the ideation process (refer to Exhibit 1.11).[22] Some firms, such as Swarovski and Saint-Gobain, have developed comprehensive systems for engaging their employees in the ideation process and produce huge numbers of solid ideas this way.

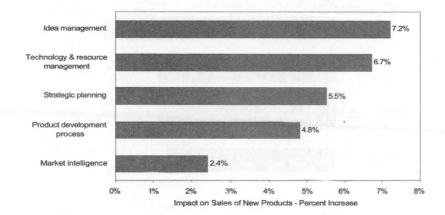

Source: Adapted from A.D. Little Innovation Excellence Study, 2005, endnote 5.

EXHIBIT 1.10 Of the five most important drivers of NPD performance, idea management has the highest positive impact on sales revenue.

Other key elements of about equal importance from the study in Exhibit 1.11 include:

*A systematic process to generate new ideas.* Good ideas are not just serendipitous or the result of chance. Yes, serendipitous and chance ideas can be fruitful ones. But ideas can also be made to happen. Increasingly companies are building systematic methods for generating ideas into the early stages of their idea-to-launch process. Much of this book is devoted to proactive methods for making new product ideas happen – the Discovery Stage of your product innovation process.

*Available time to generate new ideas.* When employees, even creative employees, are so busy that they can barely cope with the day-to-day work, don't expect them to be overly innovative and creative. One needs time to be creative and thoughtful, and not just at 4:30 on a Friday afternoon after a busy week.

*A method to select and evaluate new ideas.* Many companies lack an effective method to evaluate or rate and rank ideas. The traditional evaluation techniques don't work – for example financial tools – simply because ideas are too embryonic to be subjected to a rigorous financial

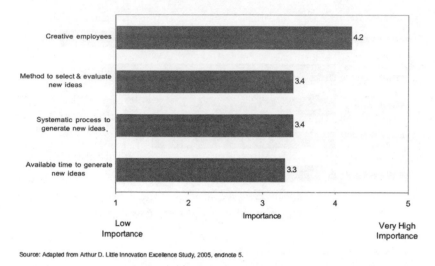

Source: Adapted from Arthur D. Little Innovation Excellence Study, 2005, endnote 5.

EXHIBIT 1.11 The most important factors in idea management are creative employees, a method to effectively select the best ideas, and a systematic process to generate ideas.

analysis; and it's almost impossible to undertake a reliable financial analysis on the most innovative of projects with so many unknowns. With a poor idea evaluation scheme in place, many excellent ideas will be killed, while ideas that are less innovative and with less potential will survive, simply because they are smaller, less innovative and less risky. Later in this book, we look at more effective ways to screen innovative ideas.

## Where to Begin?

Perhaps the first place to begin crafting an effective idea management system is by identifying potential sources of ideas: Where do the good ideas come from? Perhaps more important is the question: Where should they be coming from, and which valuable sources are you missing? Prolific or favorite idea sources may be evident in your company, but there is no conclusive evidence that ideas from any one source are the best. So think more broadly than the handful of traditional sources. Indeed many studies show that good ideas come from a broad range of sources, as shown in Exhibit 1.12. For example, external sources are almost as vital to ideation as are internal sources such as R&D and Marketing. As a result, for example, P&G has shifted its emphasis from internally-generated ideas and products to external, with the goal of at least 50 percent of new products coming from outside the company. Thus the notion of a "best source" and focusing only on it may be much too narrow.

When one expands the definition of innovation ideas to include new business models as well as new products and services, the mix and importance of sources shifts somewhat. Exhibit 1.13 shows the results from the latest IBM CEO global survey.[23] Here employees and external partners are the major sources, with traditional ideation sources, such as internal Sales and R&D units buried in the middle of the pack.

The point is that to drive innovation, your idea system must tap into a broad array of potential sources both inside and outside the company – employees, executives, customers, collaborators and partners, and even private inventors. No longer can you rely on a few people or a few departments to be the only source of innovation ideas. Ideation is now a

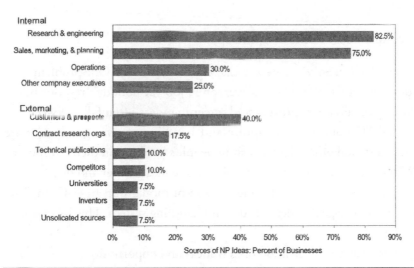

EXHIBIT 1.12 Traditional new product idea sources vary widely – these are the primary sources of new product ideas.

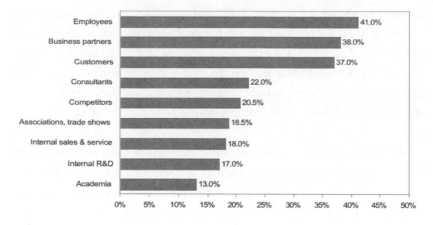

Source of Innovation Ideas: Percentage of Businesses

Source: IBM, *Expanding the Innovation Horizon: The Global CEO Study*, 2006, endnote 23.

EXHIBIT 1.13  Sources of all innovation ideas (includes new business models as well as new products and services) show new patterns with more emphasis on partners and employees, less on R&D and sales units.

business function or activity requiring the involvement of everyone in the business and even those external to, but affiliated with, your business.

## Create a Focal Point or I-Group

Next, establish an *idea person, focal point or idea group*. One problem with ideation is that it's viewed as everyone's job yet nobody's responsibility. And so the task of capturing and screening ideas often falls between the cracks. Without an idea capture and handling system, good ideas are often lost; and other ideas just sit in people's heads or on their computers. Without action, like grapes on a vine, these ideas wither and die.

Some companies call this idea person or focal group an "I-Group". Its role is to manage the idea capture and handling system. This I-Group…

- stimulates the creation of new ideas and opportunities
- captures ideas from inside and outside the company
- enhances and fleshes out ideas to the point where they can be evaluated

- secures a Go/Kill decision on the ideas
- and if Go, moves the ideas along – into the first steps of the product innovation process.

## Install a Formal Front End on Your Development Process

Here's how this front end of the innovation process, namely the idea capture and handling system, should work (see Exhibit 1.14). Compare this best practice process to what happens in your company.

Ideas from multiple sources are recorded on a standard idea submission form or template, either electronic or physical. These ideas are sent to the I-Group for a decision and action. Here, ideas are pre-screened, enhanced, massaged, incubated, combined and "visualized". The I-Group then present the fleshed-out ideas to a management committee, the Gate 1 screening group, for a Go/Kill decision. Of course, feedback is provided to the idea submitter or source.

Ideas that are killed or deemed too early are stored in the idea vault (also shown in Exhibit 1.14). This idea vault should be an electronic one,

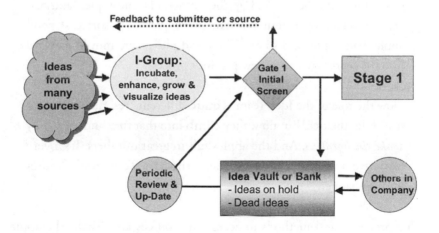

Exhibit 1.14 Install a systematic idea capture and handling process, complete with a focal point or I-Group, a Gate 1 screen to yield a Go/Kill decision, and an open-system Idea Vault.

and perhaps even an open system, where other employees are invited to review and improve ideas in the vault.

If the idea is given a Go decision at Gate 1, then the Gate 1 gatekeepers agree to a "go-forward" action plan, and commit the resources needed to move the idea though the next stage, namely Stage 1 or Scoping. And thus the idea transitions from a gleam in someone's eye into an early-stage development project – there is momentum and the project has begun its journey through the product innovation process.

### Establish the Communication Lines and Shake the Branches

A final step to creating an idea management system is to establish the flow lines, mechanisms, processes and events to encourage, and even to help create, ideas which then flow to the I-Group. As one executive described it:

> "Previously our Idea Team [a task force charged with gathering ideas and vetting them] viewed their role simply as this: They spread a net under the apple tree, and waited for the apples – the ideas – to fall. Once a month, they picked up the net with all the apples, and had an idea screening meeting where the apples were sorted – good apple, bad apple, and so on. The good ideas were moved forward into the first stage of our new product process.
>
> Now the role of the Idea Team is quite different. Yes, they still put a net under the tree. But now, they climb into that tree, and *vigorously shake the branches*. And the apples fall in great numbers. It's a very proactive and aggressive effort, and the Idea Team really 'causes ideas to happen'."

The processes and methods to access the sources and "shake the apple tree" are described in the chapters to follow – methods designed to access the sources and generate ideas both internal and external to the firm. Note that all ideas, regardless of the source, are fed into the I-Group for handling and initial vetting. This group becomes the on-ramp or entrance road to the innovation process.

## Make Your Company an Innovation Machine

The challenge is this: How do you generate, conceptualize and select winning new product ideas and opportunities, including some big ideas and game-changers? In this book, we outline methods and approaches to do so that are proven in top-performing companies. We begin with ways to help define your product innovation strategy in the next chapter. After all, from strategy, all else flows: Your innovation strategy defines the *hunting grounds* for new opportunities – what's in bounds and perhaps more important, what's out of bounds. The search fields are defined!

We continue with this strategic theme in Chapter 3, and look at various strategic approaches to anticipating the future and thereby identifying great innovation opportunities. These methods include developing peripheral vision, using scenario generation, and identifying and exploiting disruptive technologies.

The customer is a source of superb opportunities and ideas in many companies. Voice of Customer (VoC) methods have been developed and refined to the point where numerous best performing companies use them regularly to create innovative ideas. These are highlighted in Chapter 4, where we explore both newer methods such as crowdsourcing and lead user analysis and more traditional VoC ideation approaches such as ethnography.

Your external environment should be a limitless source of new product ideas, but are you seeing them? Seeking ideas from other sources outside the company is the topic of Chapter 5. Open innovation is heralded as the new wave in innovation, enabling your company to tap into creative minds around the world. We use P&G's "Connect + Develop" initiative as a model. Other externally-oriented methods are also explored, including patent mapping, competitive triggers, working with suppliers and leveraging creativity at universities.

Your own employees are potentially excellent sources of ideas. Toyota's employees submit an estimated 80,000 ideas annually! How many new product ideas do you get from your employees? Chapter 6 explores how to harness the creative ability of your entire organization through creativity events and active idea solicitation schemes.

Many companies engage in fundamental research and science projects. The rationale is that such fundamental projects should create the foundation for new opportunities and new ideas that could change the basis of competition. But often fundamental research results in little of value. Find out in Chapter 7 how leading firms harness the creative and scientific abilities of their scientific community to provide the feed to the product innovation process.

Finally in Chapter 8, we focus on picking the winners – how to screen and evaluate these ideas and early-stage opportunities. The challenge is difficult because innovative ideas are often fraught with uncertainty and unknowns, rendering traditional investment-and-evaluation techniques all but useless. Moreover these are early-stage opportunities when little information is available. But still a decision must be made. How effective you are at this may well decide the success of your business's total innovation effort.

So read on and find out how your business can increase the quality and value of ideas and opportunities for product innovation – how you can generate a steady stream of game-changing, robust and high-value new product ideas.

# CHAPTER 2

# A Product Innovation Strategy to Guide Your Idea Generation Effort

> I find the great thing in this world is not so much where
> we stand, as in which direction we are moving: To reach
> the port of heaven, we must sail sometimes with the
> wind and sometimes against it but we must sail, and not
> drift, and not lie at anchor.
>
> —OLIVER WENDELL HOLMES,
> *The Autocrat of the Breakfast Table, 1858.*

## Add a Strategic Discovery Stage

From strategy all else flows. Given the high attrition rate of new product ideas and concepts coupled with the difficulty in getting blockbuster ideas, *a strategically-driven idea generation system* is essential in order to feed the funnel with high value opportunities. Ideas are no longer the traditional serendipitous light bulb trigger to the process: While chance or serendipitous ideas – a clever idea that comes out of nowhere – have proven to be an effective route in the past, these by-chance ideas are harder and harder to come by, particularly in more mature industry sectors. Today idea generation must be strategic, systematic, managed and a vital part of the innovation process. Thus, replace the traditional serendipitous light bulb in your product innovation process with a new stage – Strategic Discovery – in your Stage-Gate process, as in Exhibit 2.1.

## Begin with Your Product Innovation Strategy

The best place to begin in your quest for great new opportunities is with the product innovation strategy for your business. This innovation strategy, among other things, defines the *arenas of strategic focus* – in short, the hunting grounds or "search fields" for idea generation – see Exhibit 2.2. This is important for idea and opportunity identification, because it specifies what is in bounds, and perhaps more important, what is out of bounds. This specification makes the quest for great new product ideas much more directed and focused, and thus more effective – you avoid the scatter-gun approach often found in traditional idea searches.

A second key role of your innovation strategy is to help *validate or screen ideas.* Creative organizations usually are able to generate far more opportunities and ideas than there are resources to execute them, and so screening and prioritization – picking the winners – becomes critical to winning. Many companies use scoring models and/or idea selection criteria to help cull out the losers and focus resources on the winners. But the first question in every such scorecard system is: Does the proposed

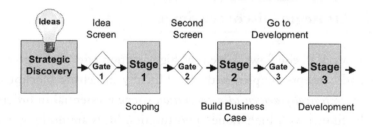

- Use this Strategic Discovery stage to hunt for blockbusters
  - Major revenue generators
  - Big new product ideas
  - Strategically-derived ideas

---

EXHIBIT 2.1 Add a "Strategic Discovery" stage to replace the traditional idea phase or "light bulb" in your product innovation process. Ensure that the search for ideas is strategically driven.

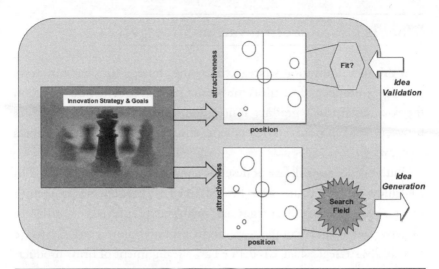

EXHIBIT 2.2 An articulated Innovation Strategy drives both the generation of ideas as well as the validation and screening of ideas.

product align with your strategy? And how important to your strategy is the idea? Without a well-defined innovation strategy in place, there are blank stares and shrugged shoulders around the screening meeting room, as the idea-screening group struggles to pick the best ideas without a definition of what is in bounds and what is out of bounds and what direction the business wants to move in.

This chapter begins with a look at the evidence in support of strategy – why it is important that you and your leadership team develop a product innovation strategy for your business. The components of an innovation strategy are then defined. Next, approaches to developing a product innovation strategy are outlined – approaches where you define and elect arenas of strategic thrust for your new product efforts and possible attack strategies.

## What Is a Product Innovation Strategy?

A product innovation strategy charts the strategy for your business's entire new product effort.[1] It is the master plan: It provides the direction for your enterprise's product innovation, and it is the essential link between your product development effort and your total business strategy.[2]

But how does one define or describe a product innovation strategy? In a business context, strategy has been defined as "the schemes whereby a firm's resources and advantages are managed (deployed) in order to surprise and surpass competitors or to exploit opportunities".[3] More specifically, strategic change is defined as "a realignment of firm's product-market environment".[4] Strategy is closely tied to product and market specification: Strategy is about choosing your markets to target, and choosing the products to target them with.[5]

Business strategy here refers to the business's overall strategy; and product innovation strategy is a component of that business strategy.[6] And by business and product innovation strategy, we do not mean a vaguely worded statement of intent, one that approaches a vision or mission statement. Rather we mean operational, action-specific strategies that include defined goals, arenas of strategic focus, deployment decisions and attack and entry plans.

### Why Have a Product Innovation Strategy At All?

Running a product innovation program without a strategy is like running a war without a military strategy. There's no rudder, there's no direction, and the results are often highly unsatisfactory. You simply drift.

A new product effort without a strategy will inevitably lead to a number of ad hoc decisions made independently of one another. New product and R&D projects are initiated solely on their own merits and with little regard to their fit into the grander scheme (portfolio management is all but impossible, for example). The result is that the business finds itself in unrelated or unwanted markets, products, and technologies: There is no focus.

One of the first studies into new product practices found that businesses that are most likely to succeed in the development and launch of new products are those that implement a company-specific approach, driven by business objectives and strategies, with a well-defined product innovation strategy at its core. The product innovation strategy was viewed as instrumental to the effective identification of market and product opportunities. Here is why having a product innovation strategy is tied to success:

"A product innovation strategy links the new product process to company objectives, and provides focus for idea or concept generation and for establishing appropriate screening criteria. The outcome of this strategy analysis is a set of strategic roles, used not to generate specific new product ideas, but to help identify markets for which new products will be developed. These market opportunities provide the set of product and market requirements from which new product ideas are generated. In addition, strategic roles provide guidelines for new product performance measurement criteria. Performance thresholds tied to strategic roles provide a more precise means of screening new product ideas."[7]

Ten best practices were identified by management in another study of 79 leading R&D organizations.[8] Near the top of the list is "use a formal development process", an endorsement of the use of stage-and-gate processes. Even higher on the list is "coordinate long-range business planning and R&D plans" – a call for a new product or R&D plan for the business that meshes with the business plan. Although adoption of these best practices varies widely by company, the study revealed that high performers tend to embrace these best practices more than do low performers.

Our major benchmarking study introduced in Chapter 1 reveals that having an articulated product innovation strategy for the business is one of the four important drivers of new product performance (Exhibit 2.3).[9] Businesses with a defined product innovation strategy – one that specifies goals and the role of new products, defines arenas of strategic thrust and their priorities, outlines a product roadmap, and has a longer term orientation – achieve better new product results: Their innovation efforts meet their new product sales and profit objectives; they have a much greater impact on the business; and they achieve higher success rates at launch.

## The Elements of a Product Innovation Strategy

Six ingredients of a solid product innovation strategy strongly distinguish the best performing businesses (see Exhibit 2.4).[10] These strategy elements provide insights into how to go about developing a product innovation strategy for your business and provide a basis for the ideal logical flow or "thought process" to guide your leadership team in developing an insightful product innovation strategy (see Exhibit 2.5 for the pathway or flow). Let's look at each of these elements, what they are and why they are so critical.[11]

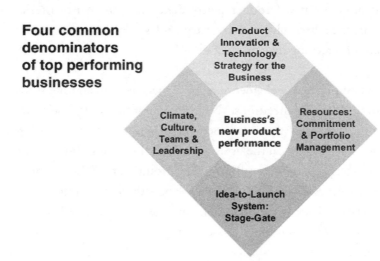

**Four common denominators of top performing businesses**

Product Innovation & Technology Strategy for the Business

Climate, Culture, Teams & Leadership

Business's new product performance

Resources: Commitment & Portfolio Management

Idea-to-Launch System: Stage-Gate

EXHIBIT 2.3 Top performing businesses in NPD have a clearly defined and articulated Product Innovation Strategy in place.

*1. Goals and role:* Begin with your goals! The business's product innovation strategy specifies the goals of the product innovation effort, and it
indicates the role that product innovation will play in helping the business
achieve its business objectives. It answers the question: How do new products and product innovation fit into your business's overall plan? A
statement such as "By the year 2011, 30 percent of our business's sales will
come from new products" is a typical goal. Performance goals can also be
stated, such as the desired number of major new product introductions,
expected success rates, and desired financial returns from new products.

This ingredient of strategy – having clear goals – would seem to be
fairly basic. What is surprising is how many businesses lack clear, written
goals for their overall new product effort. Note the mediocre scores in
Exhibit 2.4: Only 38.1 percent of businesses proficiently define such
NPD goals. By contrast, 51.7 percent of best performers do spell out their
NPD goals; and the worst performers are quite weak here with only 34.6
percent defining goals. Having clearly articulated NPD goals for your
business is thus a mandatory best practice.

Another key best practice is to ensure that the role of product innovation in achieving the business's goals is clear and communicated to all
(also in Exhibit 2.4). The whole point of having goals is so that everyone
involved in the activity has a common purpose – something to work
towards. Yet, far too often, personnel who work on new product projects
are not aware of their business's innovation objectives, or the role that new
products play in the total business objectives. What we witness here are
very mediocre practices: Only 46.3 percent of businesses define and
communicate the role of NPD in achieving their business goals. However,
58.6 percent of best performers do define this role (versus only 30.8
percent of the worst performers), and this element of an innovation
strategy is the most strongly correlated with product innovation performance. It's clearly a best practice.

*2. Arenas and strategic thrust:* Focus is the key to an effective strategy.
Your product innovation strategy specifies where you'll attack, or perhaps
more importantly, where you won't attack. Thus the concept of *strategic
arenas* is at the heart of a product innovation strategy – the markets,

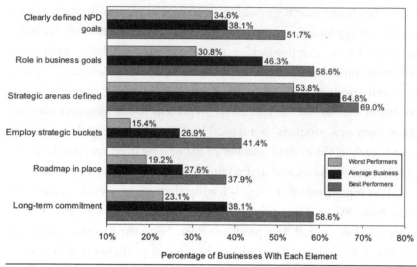

**EXHIBIT 2.4** The Innovation Strategy and its elements impact strongly on performance. Note how much more the best performers have each strategic element in place.

industry sectors, applications, product types or technologies on which your business will focus its new product efforts. The battlefields must be defined!

Here, businesses on average do a good job, with 64.8 percent identifying and designating strategic arenas in order to help focus their product innovation efforts (Exhibit 2.4). Best performers define strategic arenas more so than do worst performers: 69.0 percent versus 53.8 percent; and this strategy element is again strongly correlated with performance.

The specification of these arenas – what's "in bounds" and what's "out of bounds" – is fundamental to spelling out the direction or *strategic thrust* of the business's product innovation effort. It is the result of identifying and assessing innovation opportunities at the strategic level. Without arenas defined, the search for specific new product ideas or opportunities is unfocused. Over time, the portfolio of new product projects is likely to contain a lot of unrelated projects, in many different markets, technologies or product-types – a scatter-gun effort. And the results are predicable: a not-so-profitable innovation effort.

*Example:* One DuPont polymers business faced exactly this problem; much money spent on R&D, but no focus because there was no strategy or defined arenas. Senior management recognized the deficiency. Management first identified a number of possible arenas (product-market-technology areas) which might be "in bounds"; assessed each in terms of their market attractiveness and the opportunity for leveraging the business's core competencies; selected several arenas; and then began to focus their new product initiatives within these chosen arenas.

*3. Attack strategy and entry strategy:* The issue of *how to attack* each strategic arena should also be part of your business's product innovation strategy. For example, the strategy may be to be the industry innovator, the first to market with new products; or the attack strategy may be to be a "fast follower", rapidly copying and improving upon competitive entries. Other strategies might focus on being low cost, a differentiator, or a niche player; strategies may also emphasize certain strengths, core competencies or product attributes or advantages. Additionally, entry

EXHIBIT 2.5 The major steps in defining your Product Innovation Strategy begin with defining the goals for NPD for your business.

plans should be outlined and can include internal product development, licensing, joint ventures, and even acquisitions of other firms.

**4. Deployment – spending commitments, priorities and strategic buckets:** Strategy becomes real when you start spending money! Your product innovation strategy must deal with how much to spend on product innovation; and it should indicate the relative emphasis, or strategic priorities, accorded each arena of strategic focus. Thus an important facet is *resource commitment and allocation.* Ear-marking buckets of resources (funds or person-days targeted at different strategic arenas or project types) helps to ensure the strategic alignment of innovation with your business goals.[12]

Many best-in-class companies use the concept of *strategic buckets* to help in this deployment decision. But the use of strategic buckets is a decidedly weak area overall with only 26.9 percent of businesses doing this well. Using strategic buckets is clearly a best practice, with 41.4 percent of best performers employing this strategic buckets approach (and only 15.4 percent of worst performers).

**5. The strategic product roadmap – the major initiatives and platform developments:** A strategic roadmap is an effective way to map out a series of major initiatives in an attack plan. A roadmap is simply a management group's view of how to get where they want to go or to achieve their desired objective.[13]

The product innovation strategy should map out the planned assaults – major new product initiatives and their timing – that are required in order to succeed in a certain market or sector in the form of a *strategic product roadmap.* This roadmap may also specify the platform developments required for these new products. Additionally, the development or acquisition of new technologies may be mapped out in the form of a technology roadmap.

The use of roadmaps is a weak area generally, with only 27.6 percent of businesses developing product roadmaps proficiently. About twice as many best performers (37.9 percent) use product roadmaps than do worst performers (19.2 percent).

Once these five strategy steps are completed, management can then deal with the next level of decision making: translating strategy into reality, namely the tactical decisions.

*6. Tactical – individual project selection:* Tactical decisions focus on individual projects, but obviously follow from the strategic decisions. They address the question: What specific new product projects should you do? And what resources should be allocated to each: What are their relative priorities? Even when a strategic product roadmap has been sketched out strategically (above), it tends to be conceptual and directional; one still must look at each and every project and decide whether or not it is really a Go. And while resource spending splits (buckets), decided above, are useful directional guides, Go decisions on specific projects must still be made. More on these tactical decisions and picking the right projects in Chapter 8.

## Setting Goals for Your Product Innovation Effort

Defining goals for your product innovation strategy is essential, but your goals must be SMART:

- *Specific:* Your innovation goals should be very clear and concrete. For example, "In the year 2010, our business's innovation goal is new product sales of $40 million annually".
- *Measurable:* Goals must be operational and measurable so that they can be used as benchmarks against which to measure performance.
- *Actionable:* Goals must be a call to action to everyone in the organization, and not some vaguely-worded statement of vision or philosophy. An example of a poor goal is: "To be a recognized leader in innovation in our industry" – it's vague, not specific, not measurable and not actionable. But "To launch five major new products worth $10 million each in the next five years" is a solid actionable innovation goal.

- *Realistic:* Goals must be "stretch goals" but, most important, achievable. There is no sense stating a goal, such as "we plan to triple our sales from new products" that everyone in your organization knows is unattainable; but at the same time, goals should be a stretch.
- *Time-frame:* Goals must have a time-frame and specify clearly when the goal is to be met.

Additionally your product innovation goals should tie the business's innovation initiatives tightly to its business strategy.

## Typical Product Innovation Goals

Product innovation goals for your business usually focus on the role that your business's new product effort will play in achieving your overall business goals. Some examples:

- The percentage of your business's sales in Year 3 that will be derived from new products introduced in that three-year period. (Three years is a generally accepted time span in which to define a product as "new," although given today's pace, two years may be more appropriate for many businesses; businesses in slower industries often use five years).
- The absolute sales – dollars in Year 3 from new products – rather than percentages.
- The percentage of your business's profits in Year 3 that will be derived from new products introduced in that time span. Again, absolute dollars can be used instead of percentages.
- The strategic role, such as defending market share, exploiting a new technology, establishing a foothold in a new market, opening up a new technological or market window of opportunity, capitalizing on a strength or resource, or diversifying into higher-growth areas.
- The number of new products to be introduced. For example, "over the next five years, we plan to launch ten major new products". Here a "major new product" must be defined.

*Example:* One general manager in a mature manufacturing business has a very clear product innovation goal: "fifteen in five", which translates into fifteen major new product introductions over the next five years. And this simply-stated goal has become the battle cry of everyone within his business, and has provided a very clear and measurable purpose for the organization.

## How to Set Your Business's Product Innovation Goals

Goal setting usually begins with a strategic planning exercise for the entire business. The business's growth and profit goals are decided, along with the business's overall strategy. These business goals and thrusts then are translated into product innovation goals, often via *gap analysis*.

In gap analysis, you create two plots:

- What you desire your business's sales (or profits) to be over the next 3-5 years, based on your overall business goals.
- What the expected sales (or profits) will likely be, assuming the current product lines and status quo strategy. This amounts to making forecasts of current products and lines, and their life cycle curves.

Usually there is a gap between the two projections. And this gap must be filled by: new products, new markets, new businesses, market development, or market share increases. The goals are decided for each of these efforts, including product development. The chart in Exhibit 2.6 shows how to translate overall growth goals into goals for new products (versus goals for other sources of growth) and then drills down into specific sales goals by project type, product line and market segments.

*Example:* Lucent Technologies maps out sales projections from current products and product categories. From this exercise, Lucent's management is able to spot shortfalls, which leads to the need for new products to fill the gaps, and hence defines their goals for new products for the business.[14]

EXHIBIT 2.6 Use a strategic framework like this to define NPD sales goals, cascading down to new product sales goals by project types, markets and product lines.

## Defining Target Arenas for Your Business

The specification of strategic arenas or battlefields provides an important guide to your product innovation efforts. As George Day notes, "What is needed is a strategy statement that specifies those areas where development is to proceed and identifies (perhaps by exclusion) those areas that are off limits."[15] The arenas provide direction for resource commitment and deployment. They guide the search for new product ideas and help in idea screening and project selection. Finally, delineation of where the business wishes to focus its new product efforts is critical to long-term planning, particularly for resource and skills acquisition.

Defining the target arenas answers the question: On what business, product, market, or technology areas should your business focus its new product efforts? The general approach or thought process we recommend is shown in Exhibit 2.7:

1. Strategic analysis – assessing your marketplace as well as your own company.
2. Developing a comprehensive list of possible arenas to focus on.
3. Paring the list down – assessing the opportunities to yield a choice of the target arenas.

Once target arenas have been defined, the hunt for significant opportunities and major development initiatives can begin, as you drill down into the selected arenas, searching for unmet needs, customer problems, emerging areas and profit voids that offer potential for profit.

## Step 1 – Strategic Analysis

The purpose here is to identify promising areas – markets, technologies or product areas – which might become candidate arenas for you to focus your product innovation efforts. Key actions include:

- *Market and industry assessment:* This is an externally focused analysis, where you assess possible markets and technologies, gain

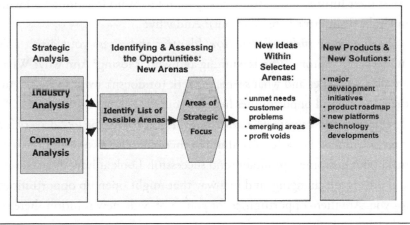

EXHIBIT 2.7 Follow this thought process to define and select your Strategic Arenas – areas where you should focus your hunt for new product opportunities and breakthrough ideas.

insights into their relative attractiveness and potential, and identify potential threats and opportunities.

- *Company analysis:* This is an internally-focused company analysis where the goal is to pinpoint your core competencies and strengths that can be leveraged to advantage.

## Assess Your Industry and Market – Here's How

*Undertake a market and industry trend analysis:* Analyze your markets (how large and profitable are they?), estimate future trends and forecast market size and shifts. Look at qualitative trends that are occurring: Spell out a scenario (or alternate scenarios) of where your market and industry are headed. Look for possible disruptions in your industry and in your customer's industry. And look for opportunities (or threats) that can be exploited.

*Undertake a segmentation analysis:* What are the various types of customers and users in your marketplace? How are they different? How large is each segment and what is the future for each? Are there opportunities to differentially access or appeal to each segment?

*Map your value chain:* Identify the key players, including rivals, and assess their futures and possible changing roles. Who is gaining and who might be disintermediated (cut out)? And why?

*Look at your industry structure:* Identify and assess your direct and indirect competitors. Who is winning and who is losing? And why? What are their strategies and what seems to work (or doesn't work so well)? Are there lessons and opportunities here for you?

*Uncover your customers' industry drivers:* Identify the key drivers for your customers. Look for any shifts in these drivers. Assess what factors make your customers profitable and successful. Look at how these factors and drivers are changing, and in a way that might open up opportunities for you. Are there opportunities for you to provide new solutions here to help your customers?

*Pinpoint where the profits are to be found:* Look for pools of profits in your industry and in your value chain (and why your business may be missing its fair share of profits). For example, develop profit pool maps and market maps that illustrate who makes the money in your industry, market or value chain.

*Example:* A major manufacturer of high-end synthetic kitchen countertops undertook an analysis of its downstream value chain. Numerous players are involved in the installation of countertops: the manufacturer, the fabrication shop, the kitchen designer, the retailer and the installer. To its surprise, the manufacturer discovered that the bulk of the profits were going to other members of the value chain. For example, the fabricator not only cuts the countertop to size, but often adds edging in the form of multiple layers, which is then machined to a contoured edge – a highly desired feature for high-end installations, but also very pricey. Strategically the manufacturer made a commitment to get control of the distribution channel, obtain its fair share of the profit pool, and also introduce new molded products to move some of the fabricator value-add to the manufacturer.

**Look for niches or holes in the marketplace:** Identify areas that may be underserved or have been missed altogether. Use Porter's Five Forces model to assess the attractiveness of these areas, checking...

- the strength of suppliers
- the strength and intensity of potential competitors (rivals)
- the power of the customers
- the ease that players can enter and exit the arena
- the threat of substitutes.[16]

This strategic analysis should not only identify possible new opportunities – arenas that are emerging and on which your business might focus; it also provides quality data so important to evaluating and selecting the right arenas.

*Assess the impact of disruptive technologies:* Identify potential disruptive technologies and radical or step-change innovations. But what is a disruptive technology? Most new technologies result in improved performance, which can come from incremental innovations, or from those that are more radical in character. Most technological advances in industry are sustaining, but: "Occasionally disruptive technologies emerge: innovations that result in worse performance, at least in the near term".[17] These innovations may be inferior to the existing technology when measured on traditional performance metrics, but they bring a new performance dimension or a new value proposition to the market. Assess whether each represents an opportunity (or a threat) for your business, and what can, and should, you do about this technology?

## Identify Your Core Competencies

The next component of this strategic analysis is an internal assessment, namely looking at your own business and identifying points of leverage. The adage "attack from a position of strength" rings true in product innovation. Many studies repeat the message: Leveraging your strengths and competencies increases new product success rates and profitability.[18] So take a hard look at your business, and undertake a core competencies assessment.

A company's core competency is defined as something it can do better than its competitors. A core competency is critical to achieving competitive advantage and enabling the firm to create new products and services. According to Prahalad and Hamel, a core competency has three characteristics:[19]

- It provides potential access to a wide variety of markets
- It should make a significant contribution to the perceived customer benefits
- It should be difficult for competitors to imitate.

This means looking at strengths and weaknesses in all facets of your business, and relative to your competitors – see Exhibit 2.8 for an example:

- Your marketing and sales force strengths, brand name, relationships with customers, distribution, sales force and technical support strengths
- Your products and their technology – product quality and design, unique or proprietary technologies, trade secrets and patents
- Your operations or production capabilities, capacities and technology.

Assess yourself on each item, especially relative to your direct and indirect competitors. Then identify areas where you are better than the rest: your core or distinctive competencies. These are your strengths, so look for arenas that can leverage these to your advantage.

| Competitor (Market Share) | Strengths & Weaknesses | Core Competency | Strategic Goals | Customer-perceived Value Proposition |
|---|---|---|---|---|
| Our company (%) | | | | |
| Competitor A | | | | |
| Competitor B | | | | |
| Competitor C | | | | |
| Competitor D | | | | |

Source: Albright R.E., endnote 14.

EXHIBIT 2.8  This sample chart is a guide to assessing your Core Competencies versus your competitors'.

## Step 2 – Defining the Arenas… But What Is a Strategic Arena?

Your industry, business, market and company assessments (above) are all instrumental in helping to identify and define potential arenas on which to focus. For example, your market analysis will identify new market segments or emerging needs that represent a new arena. Similarly your value chain and industry assessments should also reveal new opportunities and new arenas. And when undertaking your core competencies assessment, be sure to look for adjacencies – adjacent markets, product types or technologies that you might exploit and where you could leverage your existing strengths.

Before moving forward, however, first think for a moment about how to define a "strategic arena". Is it a market? Or a product category? Or a technology? Or all of these? Building a product-market matrix, with the dimensions labeled "products" and "markets", helps to identify and define new business arenas and is a recommended approach – see Exhibit 2.9.[20] Markets and the products that can be developed in response to needs in these markets define the opportunities for exploitation – the arenas.

> *Example:* Telenor, the Norwegian telephone system, uses a product-market matrix to help visualize strategic choices, and to define arenas on which to focus its new product efforts. One dimension of the matrix is market segments: Home Office; Medium Business; Residential; and so on (Exhibit 2.9). The other dimension is the product offering or product categories: voice, data, Internet, wireless, etc. The five by five matrix identifies 25 cells or possible arenas; some are ruled out immediately as non-feasible. The remaining cells are evaluated, and priorities are established. The top priority or "star" arenas are singled out for more intensive product development efforts.

This matrix approach can be taken one step further by noting that a business is defined in terms of *three* dimensions:[21]

1. *Customer groups served.* For a computer manufacturer, customer groups might include banks, manufacturers, universities, hospitals, retailers, etc.
2. *Customer functions served.* These might include hardware, support and services, software applications, etc.
3. *Technologies utilized.* For hardware data storage this would be digital platforms using technology like flash drives and optical media.

The result is a three-dimensional diagram, with new product arenas defined in this three-dimensional space.

Finally, a study of innovation charters points to several ways in which managers define new product arenas in practice.[22] For example, for a pump manufacturer the arenas might be by:

- Product-type (e.g. high pressure industrial pumps)
- End-user activity (e.g. plants or factories that process chemicals or liquids)

| Markets | Voice | Data | Internet | Wireless | Long Distance |
|---|---|---|---|---|---|
| Small Home Office | | | ★ | ★ | ★ |
| Medium Business | | ★ | | ★ | |
| Large Business | | ★ | | ★ | |
| Multinationals | | ★ | | ★ | ★ |
| Residential | ★ | | | ★ | |

**Products**

- The axis of the diagram are "Products" and "Markets." Each cell represents a potential strategic arena.

- Arenas are assessed for their potential and the company's business position. Stars designate top-priority arenas – where new product efforts will be focused.

EXHIBIT 2.9 Create a Product-Market Matrix, showing your products across the top and markets down the side. Each cell represents a potential strategic arena for you to consider and perhaps target your NPD effort.

- Type of technology employed (e.g. rotary hydraulic, centrifugal pump technology)
- End-user group (e.g. oil refineries).

A review of these and other schemes for defining a business arena reveals that a single-dimension approach is likely too narrow. A two- or three-dimensional approach, variants of Exhibit 2.9, probably will suit most business contexts.[23] For example, a new product arena can be defined in terms of three key dimensions:

1. *Who:* the customer group to be served (markets or market segments)
2. *What:* the application (or customer need to be satisfied)
3. *How:* the technology required to design, develop, and produce products for the arena.

These three dimensions – who, what, and how – provide a useful starting point to describe new product arenas. Sometimes, the last two dimensions – what and how – can be combined into a single dimension, product type.

### Defining Arenas: An Illustration

Let's look more closely at some of the details of this process of searching for and prioritizing arenas. A two- or three-dimensional diagram can be used for this search and evaluation. You might also use the product-market matrix in Exhibit 2.9, or any other convenient dimensions that define arenas for your business. Here, we use the three dimensions of customer groups, applications, and technologies, which are shown as the X, Y, and Z axes of the diagram (Exhibit 2.10). Home base is located, and then other opportunities are identified by moving away from home base in terms of other (but related) customer groups, applications, and technologies.

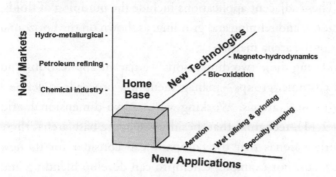

- "Home Base" or the current business is current markets served, current technologies employed, and current applications – shown as a cube.
- One can move away from home base in any direction – new markets, new technologies, and new applications for the business.

EXHIBIT 2.10  Our illustration company, Chempro, uses a three-dimensional map – markets, applications and technologies – to define possible Strategic Arenas.

*Illustration:* Chempro is a medium-sized manufacturer of mixing and agitation process equipment for the pulp and paper industry. The company's major strength is its ability to design and manufacture rotary hydraulic mixers – equipment much like a huge kitchen mixer. The market served is the pulp and paper industry. The application is agitation and blending of liquids and slurries. The company's current or home base is shown as the cube in Exhibit 2.10.

What new product arenas exist for the company? Clearly, the home base is one of these, and indeed the firm is active in seeking new product ideas for agitation equipment in the pulp and paper field. Most of these opportunities, however, are limited to modifications and improvements.

One direction that senior management can take is to develop new products aimed at nearby but new customer groups – adjacent markets. These adjacent customer groups include the chemical, petroleum-refining, and hydro-metallurgical markets. The options are shown on the vertical axis of Exhibit 2.10.

Similarly, new products in related or adjacent applications can be sought. These adjacent applications include the pumping of fluids, fluid aeration, and refining and grinding, as shown on the horizontal or X axis of the arena matrix.

Considering these two dimensions – adjacent applications and adjacent customer groups – management now proceeds to define a number of new arenas. Working with a two-dimensional grid (Exhibit 2.11), recognize that, besides the home base arena, there are 13 other arenas that the company can consider for its new product focus. For example, Chempro can develop blending and agitation equipment (same application) aimed at the chemical or petroleum industries (new customer groups). Alternatively, the business can develop aeration devices (new application) targeted at its current customers, namely pulp and paper companies. Each of these possibilities represents a new arena for Chempro.

Chempro might also be able to change its third dimension by moving from its home base of rotary hydraulic technology to adjacent or somewhat familiar technologies. If the alternatives are super-imposed along the third dimension atop the matrix, the result is a much larger number of possible arenas. Possible alternative arenas along the "new technologies" axis include magneto-hydrodynamic pumps and agitators for a variety of end-user groups, bio-oxidation reactors for the food industry, and many others.

Chempro management simplified their choices by deciding that their current technology was already a strength, and that venturing into new technologies was unwise and too expensive for this mid-sized firm. Thus the arena choice boiled down to two dimensions, markets and applications, as shown in Exhibit 2.11 (note the similarity to the product-market matrix of Exhibit 2.9).

## Selecting the Right Arenas

The task now is to narrow down the many possible arenas to a target set that will become the focus of the business's innovation strategy. To a certain extent, a pre-screening of these arenas has already occurred: the

| | Pulp & Paper (home base) | Chemical Process Industry | Petroleum Refining | Hydro-Metallurgical |
|---|---|---|---|---|
| **Agitation & Blending** | *HOME BASE: Agitators & blender for P&P industry* | Chemical mixers & blenders | Blenders for petroleum storage tanks | Hydro metallurgy mixers, agitators |
| **Aeration** | Surface aerators for P&P: waste treatment | Aerators for chemical waste treatment plants | Aerators for petroleum waste treatment plants | Aerators for floatation cells |
| **Wet Refining & Grinding** | Pulper, repulpers & refiners | | | Wet refining equipment |
| **Specialty Pumping** | High density paper stock pumps | Specialty chemical pumps | Specialty petroleum pumps | Slurry pumps |

(left margin label) **Applications**

EXHIBIT 2.11 Chempro's management reduces its arena choices to two dimensions – markets and applications – and defines 13 possible arenas in addition to home base.

arenas have been identified as being adjacent to the base business on at least one of the three dimensions.

The choice of the right arenas is based upon two main criteria that have been identified in our studies of successful new product strategies. These criteria are *arena attractiveness* and *business strength* (see the Strategic Map in Exhibit 2.12).

*Arena attractiveness:* This strategic dimension captures how attractive the external opportunities are within that arena. Is this strategic arena an oasis – lush and fertile with ample opportunities for profitable new products? Or is it a sterile wasteland, offering few opportunities for innovation and growth? This dimension, arena attractiveness, consists of:

- *Market attractiveness:* the size, growth, and competitive situation of the arena market
- *Technological opportunities:* the degree to which technological and new product opportunities exist within the arena.

In practice, arena attractiveness is a composite index constructed by rating the arena on a number of detailed criteria that capture market

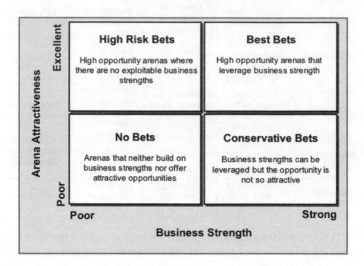

**EXHIBIT 2.12** Evaluate each arena on two main dimensions – arena attractiveness and your business strength. Locate each of your possible arenas into one of the four quadrants on this Strategic Map.

growth, size and the potential for new products in that arena. Typically, the leadership team of the business scores each arena on these criteria; and scores are added to yield an *index of arena attractiveness*. Arenas that feature large, growing, and high-potential markets, limited or weak competition, good margins earned by others, dynamic technologies, many new product introductions, and positive technological elasticity (large bang for R&D buck spent[*]) score high on the arena attractiveness dimension.

*Business strength:* The other strategic dimension focuses on your business's ability to successfully exploit the arena. In other words, what does your business bring to the table that suggests that you will be successful in

---

[*] Technological elasticity captures the slope of the technology S-curve: the curve that plots product performance versus development money spent to achieve this. Technology elasticity answers the question: will a dollar spent on product development in this arena yield products with significant performance advantages?

this arena? The ability to leverage your business's resources and skills to your advantage in the new arena is a key concept here. Business strength is again a composite dimension or index, consisting of three factors:

- Ability to leverage your business's technological (development and operations) competencies
- Ability to leverage your marketing and sales competencies
- Ability for a strategic leverage: the potential to achieve product advantage and product differentiation.

Arenas that build on the business's core competencies, that fit well the business's marketing and technological strengths and resources, and that offer the business a solid opportunity to gain product advantage or achieve product differentiation, are the ones that score high on the business strength dimension.

## Mapping the Strategic Arenas

How the various arenas score on the two criteria can be shown pictorially in the Strategic Map of Exhibit 2.12. Arena attractiveness is shown as the vertical or north-south dimension, and business strength as the horizontal or east-west axis. The result is a four-quadrant diagram, not unlike traditional business portfolio models, but with different dimensions and different components to each dimension.

Each quadrant represents a different type of opportunity:

- The arenas shown in the upper-right sector, that feature high arena attractiveness and business strength, are clearly the most desirable. These are called the "best bets".
- Diagonally opposite (in the lower left sector) are the "low-low" arenas – those arenas that neither build on the business's strengths nor offer attractive external opportunities. These are the "no bets".
- The "high-risk bets" are in the upper left sector. They represent high-opportunity arenas where the business has no exploitable strengths.

- Finally, the lower right sector houses the "conservative bets" – arenas where the business can utilize its strengths to advantage, but where the external opportunity is not so attractive. These opportunities can be pursued at little risk, but offer limited returns.

Using such a map, senior management can eliminate certain arenas outright (those in the "no bet" quadrant), and select a reasonable balance of arenas from the other three quadrants. The "good bets" are usually the top-priority ones.

*Assessing the arenas at Chempro:* Next, the 13 new arenas plus the home base defined in Exhibit 2.11 are rated by senior management on the two key dimensions of arena attractiveness and business strength. A list of rating questions is employed, with each arena rated on each question. The ratings are added, and both a *business strength* and *arena attractiveness index* are computed for each of the 14 possible arenas. Using these two indexes for each arena, the 14

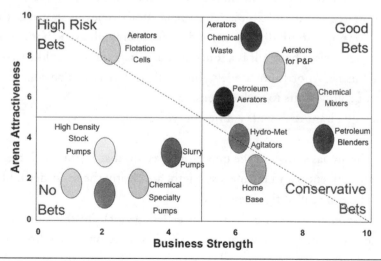

EXHIBIT 2.13 Chempro's Strategic Map with its possible arenas plotted. Management rates each arena on a number of questions to create the 0-10 indexes for the two dimensions, Arena Attractiveness & Business Strength.

arenas are plotted as bubbles on an X-Y grid. The results for Chempro are shown in Exhibit 2.13.

## Selecting the Arenas

The choice of arenas depends on the risk-return values of management. Selecting only those arenas in the top half of the arena assessment diagram – the good bets and the high-risk bets – emphasizes the attractiveness of the external opportunity. This choice places no weight at all on the business-strength dimension: It is a high-return, but a higher risk strategy. The other extreme is selecting only those arenas on the right of the horizontal, the good bets and conservative bets. This is a low-risk, lower return strategy – a selection of only those arenas in which the company possesses a good business position. Ideally, one looks for a combination of the two.

> *At Chempro:* Six arenas are rated positively on both dimensions. In order to quantify or rank-order the arenas, a cutoff diagonal line is drawn on Exhibit 2.13 (the dashed line). Arenas to the right of and above this line are positive; those to the left and below are negative. The distance of each arena from that line is measured: the greater the distance, the more desirable the arena. Based on this exercise, three good bets and one conservative bet are defined as target arenas for Chempro:
> - Aerators for the chemical industry (waste water treatment)
> - Blenders for the petroleum industry
> - Agitators and mixers for the chemical industry
> - Surface aerators for the pulp and paper industry.
>
> Management decides to continue seeking new products in the home base arena as well.

The arenas are decided. These arenas are the areas of focus for your NPD or R&D efforts, and define the "search fields" for new products. Now everyone in the business – marketing, sales force, R&D, senior

**Discovery Stage**

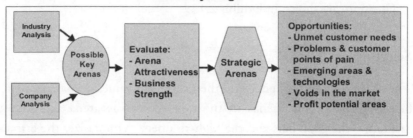

- Once your Strategic Arenas are decided, you can begin your hunt for new product opportunities and ideas in a focused way.
- Engage everyone in the business to uncover unmet needs, customer problems, emerging areas and technologies, voids in the marketplace and areas that promise profit.

EXHIBIT 2.14 With Arenas decided, now identify major new product opportunities and potential game-changer new product projects.

management, and all employees – can begin the hunt for new product opportunities in a *focused fashion*, as shown in Exhibit 2.14. *Ideation or Discovery can begin in earnest.*

## Your Product Roadmap

Developing a product roadmap is a logical extension of your product innovation strategy. What is a roadmap? It is simply management's view of how to get where they want to go or to achieve their desired objective.[24] The product roadmap is a useful tool that helps the senior management ensure that the capabilities to achieve their objective are in place when needed. Because the roadmap often includes place-marks for a number of future development projects, it can thus be thought of as a form of strategic ideation – a translation of strategy into a list of specific projects. The roadmap answers the question: Given your product innovation strategy, what major new products, platforms and technologies do you need to develop or acquire?

Your *strategic product roadmap* defines your major new product and platform developments along a timeline. An example is in Exhibit 2.15 for Chempro. Here the product roadmap not only maps out the various major product introductions and their timing, it also defines the platforms and platform extensions needed to develop these new products (see text box for a definition of "platform").

The *technology roadmap* is derived from the product roadmap, but also specifies how you will get there. That is, it lays out the technologies and technological competencies that are needed in order to implement (develop and source) the products and platforms in the product roadmap. The technology roadmap is a logical extension of the product roadmap and is closely linked to it. At Lucent Technologies, the two are combined into a product-technology roadmap as a tool to help management link

## Platforms: A Base From Which to Operate

Many businesses now look to platforms as a way to think about strategic thrusts in product development. The original definition of a platform was very much product based. The PDMA handbook defines a platform product to be "design and components that are shared by a set of products in a product family. From this platform, numerous derivatives can be designed". Thus Chrysler's engine-transmission from its K-car was a platform that spawned other vehicles, including the famous Chrysler minivan.

The concept of platforms has since been broadened to include technological capabilities. For example, ExxonMobil's Metallocene platform is simply a catalyst which has yielded an entirely new generation of polymers. Thus a platform is like an oil drilling platform in the ocean, which you invest heavily in. From this platform, you can drill many holes, relatively quickly and at low cost.

The definition of platforms has also been broadened to include marketing or branding concepts as well as technological capabilities. For example, some consider 3M's Post-It Notes™ to be a marketing platform, which has created many individual products.

business strategy, product plans and technology development.[25] (Note: In some industries the "technology roadmap" is the term used to portray technology forecast for the industry. We use the term the way it was originally intended, namely as a mapping of the major technology initiatives that are planned by your business.)

Most often, the specification of projects on your product roadmap is fairly general and high-level: for example, designations such as "a low carb beer for the Atkins diet market" or "ceramic coated tooling for the aerospace industry" or "low power petroleum blenders" as in Exhibit 2.15, are often the way these projects are shown on the product roadmap timeline. That is, place-marks for projects "yet to be precisely defined" are the norm: The roadmap is meant to be directional and strategic, but not provide detailed product and project definitions. As each project progresses through your idea-to-launch process, however, increasingly the project and product becomes specified and defined.

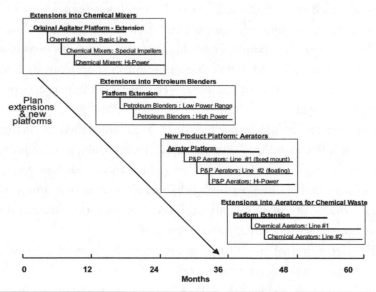

EXHIBIT 2.15 Chempro management translates their Strategic Arenas exercise into a timed sequence of major development initiatives in the form of a Product Roadmap.

## How to Develop Your Strategic Product Roadmap

The development of a product roadmap flows logically from your product innovation strategy. Delineating the major initiatives required as part of your product roadmap is a multifaceted task and includes the following inputs from your strategy development, as shown in Exhibit 2.16.

*Strategic assessment:* Translate your product innovation strategy into specific development initiatives. When you denote a strategic arena as top priority – for example, waste treatment equipment and aerators for the pulp and paper industry, as in Chempro's case – this leads logically to a list of those products and projects that are necessary to enter and be successful in that arena.

> *Example:* A major health products company identified "wound care" as a priority strategic arena (the company already sold a few products in this health-care sector, but was a minor player). However, once "wound care" was made a top priority arena, the specific products one needed to be a major player in this sector became evident; and the development programs to generate these products fell into a logical sequence in a product roadmap.

*Portfolio review of existing company products:* Take a hard look at your current product offerings, and decide which are tired and should be pruned, and which should be replaced. Forecasts of your products' life cycles often reveal the need and timing for replacement products, or perhaps even a new platform. Additionally, gaps in the product line are identified. In this way, insert place-marks in your product roadmap for these required developments.

*Competitive analysis:* Where are your products and product lines relative to your competitors? Here, assess your competitors' current and probable future offerings, where they have advantage, and assess your gaps. Anticipate their product roadmap and what new products they will introduce and their timing. This exercise often points to the need for new products either immediately or in the foreseeable future.

*Technology trend assessment:* Look at your technology forecast and identify what new technologies and platform developments will be required or available, and their timing. For example, the advent of each new cell-phone technology signals a number of development projects within cell-phone manufacturing firms, and also within service providers.

*Market trends assessment:* Look at your market forecast, and review major market trends and shifts. In this exercise, often you are able to pinpoint specific initiatives that you must undertake in response to these evident trends; for example, in the food industry, the development of a line of nutriceutical 'good-for-you' foods.

## Include Platform Developments in Your Roadmap

New and existing platforms are often defined in the strategic product roadmap. For example, having identified certain markets as strategic arenas, and in order to win in these market arenas, certain new technology platforms may be envisioned.[26]

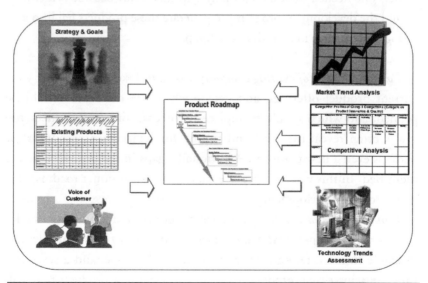

EXHIBIT 2.16 A Product Roadmap outlines the major development initiatives into the future. Developing a Roadmap requires many inputs, some of which are shown here.

*Chempro's roadmap:* Chempro's management translated their strategy into the product roadmap in Exhibit 2.15. Their roadmap outlines the major new product projects and platforms (and timing), needed to successfully attack the designated strategic arenas.[27] For example, top priority is given to extension of the current platform – agitators and mixers – to both the chemical and petroleum industries. A new platform is envisioned as the next major initiative after extension possibilities are exhausted: Priority is thus given to the development of a family of high efficiency surface aerators based on this new platform and targeted initially at the pulp and paper industry. Next, extending this new platform into chemical waste treatment is mapped out in the roadmap... and so on, as shown in the roadmap in Exhibit 2.15.

## Putting Your Product Innovation Strategy to Work

### Discovery: Searching for Product Ideas

Developing a product innovation and technology strategy and generating great new product ideas overlap considerably – and so they should! We call this the *Strategic Discovery* Stage of the product innovation process in Exhibit 2.1. Indeed progressive companies build in a heavy dose of strategy development into their Discovery Stage: The search for major new product ideas begins with a strategic analysis of your marketplace (or your customer's industry) coupled with a core competencies assessment of your own business. The goal: looking for opportunities in the form of gaps, discontinuities, emerging arenas, new technologies, new platforms and unarticulated needs.

Your product innovation strategy helps to energize the Discovery Stage. For example, undertaking the various assessments – industry, market, technology, value chain and core competencies – is almost certain to identify new opportunities in the form of new markets, new products and perhaps even new businesses to consider – *strategic ideation*. This exercise is also a major input into the development of a strategic product roadmap, as in Exhibit 2.15.

Additionally, specifying your new product arenas (Exhibit 2.13) provides guidance to your ongoing idea search effort. Armed with a knowledge of the arenas the business wishes to target, those charged with seeking new product ideas now have a clear definition of where to search: the hunting grounds are defined. Moreover, it becomes feasible to implement formal search programs – seeking unmet customer needs and undertaking voice of customer research; initiating fundamental scientific research; focusing idea suggestion schemes, sales force programs and creativity sessions; and all the other methods highlighted later in this book – to generate new product ideas. The search for ideas is more efficient, generating product ideas that are consistent with the business's focus.

*Example:* In Chempro's case, all personnel, from the president to sales trainees, gained a clear view of which new product arenas the company wished to concentrate on. First, the strategic exercise identified some "must do" projects, which are outlined in the product roadmap (Exhibit 2.15). But the new insights also made it possible for good new product ideas in the designated arenas to pour in from everyone in the company.

## More Effective Project Selection

The most critical criterion for selecting new product projects to invest in is whether the project is aligned with and supports your business's strategy. A clear delineation of your business's new product arenas provides the criterion essential to answer this "strategic alignment" question. Either the new product proposal under consideration fits into one of the designated arenas, or it does not. And your strategic product roadmap, which defines place-marks for strategic projects, also provides directional guidance to the selection of specific development projects. The result is more effective and efficient project screening and investment decisions. Precious management time and resources are not wasted on new product proposals that may seem attractive on their own merits, but simply do not mesh with the long-term strategy or direction of the business.

# Strategic Inputs to Ideation –
# Forecasting the Future

Plans are nothing. Planning is everything.

DWIGHT D. EISENHOWER,

*US General and Supreme Allied
Commander D-Day, 1945*

Three strategic approaches are examined in this chapter that are invaluable inputs to your ideation and discovery effort. Strategic ideation requires that the business leadership team have the correct view or vision of the future. In effect, they must be crystal ball gazers – able to integrate existing information and trends and to accurately forecast what the future will look like. If successful, then they are much more effective at envisioning what new products or new services will be required by the business.

This ability to forecast the future state of your industry, market or world is no easy task. Indeed senior executives and planning groups in countless organizations seem adept at *consistently missing the mark* when it comes to future forecasts: AT&T's inability to recognize the impact that the Internet would have on telephony; IBM's reluctance to invest more heavily in the PC business in the early days; the inability of Kodak and Polaroid to recognize early enough the threat of digital camera technology; and the U.S. automobile industry's focus on big gas-guzzling

63

SUVs when the rest of the world is moving to energy efficiency.

While there is no magic formula designed to accurately predict the future, and thus what new products you should develop, three strategic methods or approaches should help. They are:

1. Developing peripheral vision
2. Assessing the impact of disruptive technologies
3. Using scenarios generation to envision the future.

Each is described in this chapter.

## 1. Develop Peripheral Vision

The biggest dangers are the ones that you don't see coming argue Day and Shoemaker, who make a strong case for *developing peripheral vision* in your company[1]. Too many companies are simply blindsided by events and issues that they did not anticipate or did not understand their potential impact. For example, most companies failed to recognize the major impact that the Internet would have on the way business is done today, and even worse, failed to act early enough. Even Microsoft underestimated the speed of adoption of the Internet. Similarly, many North American and European companies failed to take seriously the low cost yet proficient manufacturing capabilities in China and the IT development skills in India and, as a result did not formulate global outsourcing and off-shoring strategies. The companies now face unbeatable competition from those in their industries that did take action and implement an effective off-shore development and manufacturing strategy in time.

Understanding these threats and anticipating the opportunities requires strong peripheral vision. If you can see a threat coming before your competitors do, and take appropriate action first, you *flip that threat into an opportunity*. But too many companies seem too focused on the here-and-now and on their day-to-day and short term issues, so that when major shifts occur in the marketplace or their industry, they are caught totally unaware and unprepared.

In a major survey of corporate strategists, two-thirds indicated that their companies had been surprised by up to three high-impact competitive events within the last five years.[2] And 97 percent of these firms *lack a formal early-warning system!* A typical example of a leading firm that lacked the necessary early-warning system is Mattel, and its failure to recognize that pre-teen girls were maturing at a much earlier age than they used to. These pre-teens were quickly outgrowing the traditional Barbie Doll, and shifting their wants to more urban-modern dolls such as Bratz.[3] Similarly, Lego, once considered a most creative company, has failed to deal with the fact that boys also grow up much faster and stop playing with blocks and construction sets at a much earlier age than they used to. True, Lego made an attempt to pro-act by introducing computer-aided Lego sets, but they were too expensive and not on target for the audience and their moms and dads.

Another once innovative company, DuPont, lost sight of what was happening around it. After creating market after market for decades in the polymers field – Nylon, Dacron, Lycra, Teflon – it failed to recognize and act on the threat of slowing markets and low cost polymers from offshore.[4] Instead of dealing with the threat, DuPont retreated from these mature businesses, which lead to under-utilization of its production capacity, higher costs and eventually even greater vulnerability.

By contrast, Apple Computer's management over the years seems to have a good sense and broad perspective of where the world is heading. Interestingly, Apple is not a huge spender on R&D: for example, Apple's 2004 R&D-to-sales ratio of 5.9 percent trails the computer industry average of 7.6 percent, and its $489 million spend is a fraction of its larger competitors.[5] But by rigorously focusing its development resources on a short list of projects with the greatest potential, the company created an innovation machine that eventually produced the iMac, iBook, iPod, and iTunes.

## Define the Need for Peripheral Vision in Your Company

Not every company requires peripheral vision to the same extent. When assessing the need to establish a peripheral vision group or specific peripheral vision capability, three factors to consider that point to a strong need for peripheral vision are:

- The nature of your strategy
- The complexity of your external environment
- The volatility of your external environment.[6]

*Nature of your strategy:* If your business strategy is very aggressive and growth oriented; if there is a heavy emphasis on product innovation and on reinvention of your business; if it is a broad or global strategy (as opposed to a narrow or niche strategy); and if you have many different businesses to integrate, then chances are having a strong peripheral vision capability is mandatory for your company.

*Complexity of your environment:* If your industry is characterized by many and complex market segments, long and complex distribution channels, and many competitors with competition from many sources, then your peripheral vision must be strong. Similarly, if your industry is highly visible publicly, dependant on the global economy, features many or changing regulations, and is dependant on government funding, again, your industry is complex and hence your business is more vulnerable to being blindsided.

*Volatility of your environment:* If your company has had a number of surprises in the last few years; if your market forecasts – both quantitative and qualitative trends – have missed the mark and been wrong; if the speed and nature of technological change in your industry is unpredictable, and if there is a high potential for disruptions in your industry, then you face a highly volatile environment – strong peripheral vision is key. Similarly, if your industry is sensitive to social changes; if the number of growth opportunities facing your company or industry has increased; if your competitors are aggressive and hostile; and your customers and channel system extremely powerful, then volatility is even higher. All these drivers point to the need for a more systematic peripheral vision capability.

## Scan the External Environment

The key to an effective scanning effort is to look in the right places and ask the right questions. For example, examining competitive actions is often a good place to begin. The key question is: Which of your competitors seems to be ahead of the wave – which is able to anticipate market trends and needs, and act before the rest of the industry? A second area of focus is your own company – looking at your own historical strategies, and identifying those blind spots that you've had in the past. A list of questions suggested by Day and Shoemaker is shown in Exhibit 3.1. This list provides the framework for the scanning effort. But how does one translate these into opportunities for new products?

---

**Key Questions in Developing Peripheral Vision**

1. Who in your industry picks up on advance warnings and acts on them?
2. What have been your blind spots in the past?
   - What's happening now?
3. Is there a relevant analogy from another industry?
   - Example: Will nanotechnology run into the same environmental resistance that plagued Genetically Modified Food technology?
4. What important signals are you rationalizing away?
   - Example: Coors' failure to deal with low carb diets
5. What are peripheral customers (adjacent markets, former customers) and non-direct competitors saying?
6. What are your mavericks in your own company trying to tell you?
7. What new futures could really hurt (or help) you?
8. What emerging technologies could change the game?
9. Is there an unthinkable scenario of the future?
   - Example: Enron's financial collapse after so much praise from the financial community

Adapted from: Day & Shoemaker endnote 1.

---

EXHIBIT 3.1 When scanning the environment – seeking peripheral vision – look in the right places and ask the right questions.

## Undertake an Impact of Opportunities and Threats Assessment – an IOTA

The point of the scanning effort is not just about identifying potential threats, danger signals or shifting market conditions. Rather, the peripheral vision and scanning exercise is designed to identify new opportunities that could result in new products, new services and potentially new businesses. For those of you with an engineering background, you will recognize that this *impacts analysis* is similar to a FMEA – failure modes effects analysis – which is used to identify risks and actions needed in product design.

The first step in your impact of opportunities and threats assessment (or IOTA) is to list the key issues, trends, events, threats, dangers and disruptions identified in your peripheral vision or scanning efforts. That's the second column in Exhibit 3.2. Next estimate the likelihood and timing of this event, trend, threat or disruption – columns 3 and 4 of Exhibit 3.2. Next characterize the impact – the "so what": What is the

| Area of focus for Peripheral Vision Scanning | List: Threats, major changes & trends, disruptions, danger signals, key issues & events | How likely? | How imminent (timing)? | Impact – so what? | What opportunities: new products, new services, new businesses, new business models |
|---|---|---|---|---|---|
| Market changes & shifts – your customers | | | | | |
| Changes in your competitors & their strategies | | | | | |
| Changes in members of your value chain (e.g. retailers, dealers) | | | | | |
| Technology changes & disruptions | | | | | |
| Legislative & political changes, events, dangers | | | | | |
| Social & demographic trends, changes | | | | | |
| Economic changes, threats, dangers | | | | | |

EXHIBIT 3.2 Undertake an IOTA – an Impact of Opportunities & Threats Analysis. Use this IOTA template for translating the results of your peripheral vision scanning effort into opportunities.

impact on your business if this threat, disruption or event occurs? – column 5. Finally, identify the *action implications* – answer the question: What do you do about this event, trend, threat or disruption – what opportunities, new products, services or new businesses?

In order to help identify the action implications, try a brainstorming session comprised of marketing, technical and business development people. Brainstorm around each major event, trend, threat and disruption, beginning first with those that are the most imminent, have the highest likelihood of occurring, and have the greatest potential impact (columns 2-5).

> *Example:* Suppose you are in the brewing business, and see the significant threats of a much heavier emphasis on a healthy lifestyle in the next generation of consumers. This major shift represents a double threat, because it means less consumption of alcohol, and also less intake of carbohydrates... very bad news for a traditional brewer.
>
> The brainstorming session is structured to deal with the following challenge question: "Given this trend towards a healthier lifestyle – fewer carbs and less alcoholic beverages consumed – what new products or services can we think up that could capitalize on this trend?" The group brainstorms and generates numerous possibilities, for example obvious ideas such as a low carb beer, or low calorie beer. But they also generate some less obvious ideas such as fruit-juice based alcoholic beverages, or yogurt-based alcoholic beverages – ideas somewhat consistent with the healthiness trends. The group also generates more out-of-the-box ideas such as nutraceutical beverages – beverages that are good for you, yet have a dose of alcohol or beneficial red wine in them; or beverages with other stimulants, such as caffeine, such as nutraceutical teas with a medicinal or "good for you" claim.

Often the threats and disruptions yield such obvious conclusions and point to clearly needed actions that make brainstorming unnecessary. But regardless of how you generate the ideas, this IOTA exercise is key to translating your scanning and peripheral vision effort into action implications and specific new product or new business ideas and opportunities.

## What Might Have Been

One might speculate about what would have happened in the case of two companies mentioned above – Mattel and Lego – who were both blind-sided by the same disruption or threat, namely boys and girls growing up much faster today. First, both managements would have been aware of the threat and its potential damaging impact. Lego's management in Denmark was indeed very aware of the threat, and they did take action by launching computer-based Lego building products aimed at more sophisticated and computer-savvy boys and their parents. It is not that clear whether Mattel's management was sufficiently tuned into the same threat facing their business. But even in the case of Lego, one questions whether the response was sufficiently robust, adequate and timely – apparently not, because the company has fallen on tougher times. Perhaps a more thorough IOTA analysis would have helped Lego to generate multiple possible options, more creatively and with greater market appeal.

## 2. Exploit Disruptive Technologies

Periodically, an industry witnesses a technological change or radical innovation so disruptive that it changes the basis of competition and the face of that industry.[7] These disruptions do not happen every day in any one industry but, when they do occur, they have the potential to create *huge threats to the dominant firms* in an industry, and *great opportunities* for others. The last century has seen many such disruptions; digital watches which almost destroyed the Swiss watch industry but created a new industry in Japan; the hand-held calculator, which devastated the makers of mechanical calculating devices; the ball-point pen, the Xerox machine or photocopier, and the jet engine – all of which created great dislocations in their respective industries. More recent examples include the digital camera, the cell phone, and the Internet.

One reason why such disruptive technologies are so dangerous is that when they occur, the dominant firms before the discontinuity are most often *no longer the dominant firms after.* Recent research shows that in almost every industry, the leading firms faced with a period of discontinuous change fail to maintain their market leadership position in the new technological era[8,9]. These large firms are replaced by newer, faster and more agile firms that take the needed action in time. That's what happened in every technology disruption example cited above, except for the jet engine (where Pratt & Whitney, now a United Technologies company, successfully made the transition to the new technology).

This *tyranny of success* – the factors that made firms successful in the first place then sows the seeds of defeat in the future – is a worldwide dilemma. It is exemplified by recent struggles of firms such as Xerox in the United States, Michelin in France, Philips in Holland, Siemens in Germany, and Nissan in Japan.[10] The unseen danger is that the successful firm becomes large, dominant, complacent and set in its ways, and thus becomes unable or unwilling to react to new changes and disruptions in its industry.

This theory of radical, step-change innovation was first enunciated by MIT professors in the 1960s[11] and later popularized by Foster in *The Attacker's Advantage,*[12] and more recently by Christensen in *The Innovators Dilemma.*[13] The chart in Exhibit 3.3, showing the original technology and then the disruptive technology, is a useful way to portray the effects and threats.[14]

What makes disruptive technologies even more dangerous is that that *they are also stealthy* – they often occur almost unnoticed. Usually, the first few products that are built on the new technology are *inferior in performance* to the products using the existing and dominant technology. For example, the first cell phones were terrible when compared to the traditional land line – so heavy and cumbersome it was like speaking into a brick. And the first digital cameras actually produced a poorer picture (lower resolution) than traditional 35mm film cameras, and were

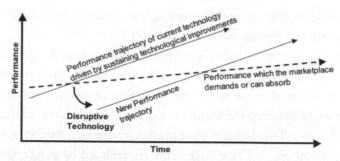

- The current technology sees many incremental improvements, and eventually exceeds what is demanded by the marketplace on the traditional performance dimension.
- By contrast, the new and disruptive technology often falls below acceptable performance limits when measured on the traditional performance metrics.
- But it delivers much better performance on a new performance metric (not shown) that might be valued by a minority of users. And it improves over time on traditional performance metrics.

Source: Adapted from Christensen, endnote 13; & Getz, endnote 14.

EXHIBIT 3.3  The disruptive technology under-performs the current technology initially, and thus its impact is often underestimated.

considered inferior products by most camera users. But for a handful of users – most notably those who wanted the picture in digital format so that they could modify or electronically transmit the photo – there was new value in the digital camera.

The fact that initial products are inferior means that when industry experts and strategists assess the new technology, they conclude that the products have poor performance and therefore do not take the technology seriously; or when market research studies are done, the studies conclude that a great majority of users agree that the product is unsatisfactory, and hence the technology has no future.

The strategists, industry experts and market researchers are wrong, of course, because they focused on the wrong potential users and asked the wrong questions. There is always a sub-group of users – a niche or tiny segment of *early adopters* – who are willing to put up with the negative performance of the new product in return for the one advantage that the new technology offers. In short, they see value in one feature or functionality of the products based on the new technology. For example, while most people dismissed digital cameras as yielding poor pictures, not having enough picture capacity, and being user-unfriendly, a minority of users thought they were great! Real estate agents, for example, were not interested in creating award-winning pictures, but fell in love with the ability to digitize a picture of a property so that they could then show it to their clients on their computer.

## Understand and Watch for the Different Types of Disruptions

One problem with assessing the future of radical innovations and disruptive technologies is that forecasters and strategists tend to lump all types of disruptions into the same pot. A careful analysis of past disruptions shows that there are indeed different types of discontinuities, and one should be aware of these types when assessing their future impacts. Paap and Katz outline three types of disruptions to be aware of:[15]

*1. The old technology matures:* This is probably the most familiar type of substitution. Here, your existing or old technology is no longer able to keep up with your customers' requirements, and a *newer technology simply does the job better*. The shift from dial-up Internet to broadband is an example. The customer's needs – convenience and ease-of-use, reliability, speed – have not changed, but broadband simply does a better job of satisfying existing needs than does dial-up.

Most businesses monitor their technology landscapes for clues that their existing technology is becoming obsolete, but they often fail to see the signs in time, or do not take action in time, thus losing out to the disruption.

*2. The old driver matures:* Most of the examples cited to describe disruptive technologies fall into this category. In an effort to follow the voice of the customer, suppliers often focus solely on their current technology to better meet customer demands or drivers. However, at a certain point, customers *no longer value increased performance* on that performance dimension, because what they now have is "good enough".

When that happens, *a new driver emerges* usually from the needs the customer may already have, but which have not been well articulated thus far. The new driver may be a new functional requirement once performance enhancements have reached their limits on traditional drivers or functions required. An example is the addition of the ability to take, store and transmit pictures on a cell phone; this is a new functional requirement for many users once the traditional drivers – size, weight, talk time, appearance – have been met.

An added challenge is that customers are often unaware that they do not need more of the old drivers or functionality until they can actually see, touch, feel and play with a product that incorporates the new functionality and which addresses one of the customer's unarticulated, unspoken needs. Thus companies that simply ask their customer what they want or need in the next generation of products often miss the next wave of innovation.

*3. The environment changes:* This situation is rarer but occurs when a totally new need emerges, not just a driver from an existing albeit unarticulated need. This can result from major changes in the economic or regulatory environment, the development of a new technology that allows the customer to do new things, or major shifts in your customer goals or preferences. For example, the development of a practical technology to produce ethanol as a fuel combined with changes in the economy (higher oil prices) and new energy-conservation regulations may create disruptions in the automotive engine industry in some countries – for example, the popularization of ethanol-powered cars, or perhaps even the use of fuel cells in cars (as they run better on alcohol than they do on gasoline).

## Estimating the Impact of Disruptive Technologies

The ability to correctly predict the impact and timing of such disruptive technologies is a key source of opportunities for new and game-changing products and new businesses. If you can anticipate the future, then you can be much more astute at identifying potential new products and services for which there will be a high demand. Apple is a company that has repeatedly shown that it understands the dynamics of innovation and disruptions, and continues to introduce technologies that eventually become standard, despite the lack of strong customer requests when first introduced.[16]

Disruptive technologies do present difficult challenges in terms of industry trend analysis simply because so many technologies fizzle out, yet others go on to create a major shift in the marketplace. Often it is difficult to predict which way the technology will go... boom or bust? Indeed, the entire theory of radical innovation or disruptive technology theory has been criticized as being more useful for *analysis of the past* or historic phenomena than for predicting the future. Whatever happened to the much-touted car turbine engine which Chrysler spent so heavily on? The turbine, along with the Wankel engine, was supposed to be the future of automotive power. Instead we still have the traditional internal combustion piston engine (which has been around for more than a century); and now the hybrid engine (which came out of nowhere). The one thing that is certain in forecasting the size of impact of the disruptive technology and the magnitude of the opportunity is this: The forecast will be wrong, and often by orders of magnitude.

So, how does one estimate impact and potential in the case of a disruptive technology? There is no easy solution, but here are some ways we have seen companies try to identify potential technology disruptions that hone in on better quantitative estimates of the impact or potential of the disruptive technology.

*Understand the dynamics of innovation and substitution:* There are reasons that new technologies emerge. There is an unmet customer need (existing, but sometimes unspoken) and the technology in use is not able to meet that need; or there is a new customer need, perhaps the result of shifts in the external environment. *Understand the causes* – the needs and the shifts or changes taking place – and then assess whether or not the new technology is likely to satisfy that need and go on to become a dominant force in the marketplace.

*Continually monitor the outside technology landscape in your own industry:* And be sure to monitor the technologies in those industries that are working on related problems. Identify those technologies that can or might address your current customers' drivers or solve their problems better than your own technology does.

*Start with the customers' needs:* If technology planning is to anticipate disruptive technologies, it must not start with technology but begin with customer needs. And it must assess how current customer needs will evolve, identifying unmet and unarticulated needs; and how these needs will evolve into new drivers. You must understand *what the customer sees as having value* – the value of achieving increased performance on existing drivers or functions, as well as the value of new functionality. Further, be sure to identify alternate technologies that might be better suited to deliver the new features and functionality.

*Look beyond what the customers ask for:* Do not ignore your customers. But do not simply focus on what they are asking for or demanding. Focus on their unmet, unspoken and unarticulated needs. In this way, you identify the new drivers and new functionality sought – tomorrows' dominant product or technology – that will emerge when the old functions and drivers reach their limit of value to the customer.

*Look beyond the mainstream:* Be aware that in the case of disruptive technologies, the initial application is not likely to be the mainstream market.[17] It pays to focus on market niches or applications that are often outside the mainstream, where the new product's particular strengths are appreciated (and its weaknesses can be tolerated). Recall that early adopters are usually not the mainstream market! The trick is to identify the handful of potential customers *who stand to benefit the most from the new solution*, and to determine what proportion will convert to the new solution.

*Do field work:* When a new technology does show signs of emerging, send the entire project team into the field for face-to-face discussions with early adopters and potential users. Let *team members learn first-hand* about the various potential applications of the product or new technology, and the users' potential for adoption. The better the entire project team understands potential applications, market segments, and exactly what features and performance each user seeks, the better the team can converge on the target market and make estimates of market potential.

***Get something in front of the customer:*** Customers do not know what they are looking for until they see it, touch it or experience it. So when testing reaction to a new concept based on a new technology, be sure to *expose the customers to something* – a protocept, virtual prototype, a crude mock-up, or a representation of the product or service. Merely asking people what they are looking for will not tell you much; equally, describing new concept or technology in words and asking for the customers' reactions to it is rather sterile, because the customers will not understand the concept or technology until they experience the product and its benefits. When Corel, the marketers of WordPerfect software, once the dominant word processing software and based on a DOS operating system, undertook a market study to ask users what they were looking for, no one asked for a Windows version of the software, simply because most users had no idea of what Windows was or could do. It was not until Microsoft introduced Word in a Windows format that users really understood the benefits – and that was the end of Corel's WordPerfect for many users.

***Examine how customers solve their problem now:*** There are very few totally new markets in the world. Usually there is something to benchmark. Even in the case of dramatic breakthroughs, such as the first jet engine or the introduction of xerographic photocopying, there was an "existing market". Potential users were solving their problem in some other way, albeit not very well. In offices, people used carbon paper, Gestetner machines and Kodak's wet photographic process for making copies. The military, the first target users of jet engines, were using piston engines at the time. Take a close look at the existing market or current solutions; and *understand how people employ the current solution* – their use system; and then probe users' needs, wants, preference, likes and dislikes regarding the current solution.

***Examine parallel markets:*** By observing what happened in similar or parallel markets, one often gains *insights to the rates of adoption, and* *perhaps barriers to adoption*, of the new technology. For example, look at the life cycle curves and adoption curves of similar innovative products or radical technologies introduced previously. This approach is particularly applicable where there has been a steady stream of innovative technologies over several decades, for example in the home entertainment field: Technologies such as VHS, CDs, DVDs; Digital TV and HDTV have all followed certain patterns, with the adoption rates of some being faster than others. Look at the adoption curves and understand the reasons for fast adoption, or the barriers to adoption. Often these insights from similar or parallel markets have direct applicability to the new market or new technology under investigation.

*Try differing scenarios:* Create varying views of the future, much like the scenario generation methodology to be described later in this chapter. You might label the different scenarios as "best case" and "worst case"; or "fast adoption" and "slow adoption". Create quite a few scenarios, and for each one consider the decisions you would make if that particular scenario came true. For example, under the "worst case" scenario, would you still proceed with investing in the new technology?

*Apply non-traditional project evaluation methods:* Perhaps the most difficult recommendation is to evaluate new or disruptive technology investments differently than traditional or sustaining new product projects. One reason that dominant firms often fail to transition to the new or disruptive technologies is that they simply *do not make the necessary investment decisions early enough*. Such companies usually are financially-driven, and new investment must proceed through the traditional financial evaluation procedures and criteria. And these financial criteria and techniques are almost certain to kill the investment in the new technology, for two reasons:

- There are too many unknowns and uncertainties: When risks and probabilities are factored in, the financial returns from the new technology investment invariably look poor.
- The new technology will cannibalize the firm's existing products and obsolete its existing production facilities. Few companies, with

an investment already made in the old technology, are willing to write it off for the sake of a new and uncertain technology!

In Chapter 8, new approaches for evaluating uncertain, risky and future-oriented projects and investments are outlined – methods that are much better suited to assessing investment decisions on new and disruptive technologies.

---

# 3. Employ Scenario Generation to Envision the Future

---

One of the most significant strategic decisions in recent years was made when AT&T turned down a free offer to take control of the Internet.[18,19] In the late 1980s, the National Science Foundation (U.S. government) wanted to withdraw from its role of administering the Internet, and offered AT&T a free monopoly position. But AT&T had a mental map of the future, namely a scenario or picture of the future where their centrally-switched technology would remain dominant. The notion of a packet-switched technology (what the Internet uses) would never work. The technical experts at AT&T concluded that the Internet was insignificant for telephony and had no commercial significance in any other context.

What AT&T should have done – and indeed what your company should do – is to develop alternate scenarios of the future. Yes, develop the scenario of the "official" or expected future… in AT&T's case, with centrally switched architecture remaining dominant. But develop an alternate scenario too – in this case, an alternative in which new markets for Internet services and new kinds of telephony challenge the dominant AT&T architecture, namely decentralized or packet switching. Such a scenario at minimum would have given decision-makers a sense of the Internet's potential, and may have led them to consider alternate courses of action.

Developing alternate scenarios also helps decision-makers to become much more sensitive to signals of change. As Schwartz, who advocates the use of scenarios in planning, declares: "What has not been foreseen is unlikely to be seen in time". For example, AT&T executives, by defining the alternative scenario, might have been more alert when increasing numbers of users began to go on the web, when web pages began to mushroom, and when PC sales to home users grew by leaps and bounds in the early 90s.

Developing alternate scenarios of the future usually involves senior people taking part in extensive discussions and work sessions – we outline the thought process in Exhibit 3.4. Since your purpose is to arrive at new product opportunities, restrict the discussion to scenarios that are relevant to the business, and deal with the external (or extended market) environment. For a bank, this might be: Describe the future of financial and related markets, and the financial industry as a whole.

### Steps in the Scenarios Method

- Develop a scenario of the "official future"
- Be sure to develop alternate scenarios too:
  - Worst case
  - Case that defies traditional assumptions
- Identify the primary decisions that must be made
- Identify potential sign posts along the way of the various scenarios
  - "What has not been foreseen is unlikely to be seen in time"
- Develop new product strategies (e.g. a list of ideas or a roadmap) assuming alternate scenarios
  - Assign just a small probability that these alternate scenarios might occur
  - Then reconsider your decisions

Source: Adapted from Schwartz endnote 18.

EXHIBIT 3.4 The Scenarios method helps to envision different views of the future and is a solid basis for creating novel product and service ideas, and even new business models.

## Ask the Right Questions

Questions to work on include:

1. What is the best future scenario? Try to describe in as great detail as possible what your company's world will look like, given the best case external environment assumptions.

2. What is the worst possible scenario of the future for your company's external environment? Or perhaps the most unexpected case or scenario?

3. What are some relevant dimensions that characterize these scenarios (for example, in AT&T's case, a relevant dimension was "centralized versus decentralized switching": The best scenario was at one end – namely centralized; the worst case was at the other – decentralized or packet-switching dominant).

Then identify the primary decisions that management faces. In order to identify new product opportunities from scenarios analysis, the questions are: Should you launch a new business or new product? Or should you invest in a new technology or new technology platform? Or what types of new products should you be seriously looking at? Scenarios are utilized by imagining that one or another future scenario will be true, and assessing the consequences of making each investment decision, assuming each alternate future.

Finally, markers or signals of each scenario occurring should be identified, so that managers can spot telltale signs over the next months or years as to which way the world is moving. For example, one banking scenario is that there will be no bank branches in the future – that bricks and mortar will be history. Telltale signals over the next decade may be: the number of new e-banks launched, the proportion of users in various age groups moving to e-banking and the development of new Internet devices that make the Internet more portable (for example, portable and wireless devices linked to the Internet that can handle financial transactions). If such trends or devices gain rapid momentum, then look for 100 percent branchless banking around the corner.

## The Greatest Business Mistake in History

In 1980, IBM developed its view of the future of the PC. An IBM study predicted the potential market, and concluded that 275,000 PCs would be in use by 1990. As a result, very generous contracts were signed with Intel and Microsoft to build and design key components for PCs. By 1990, the installed base had reached 60 million PCs, and it became apparent that the study foresaw only one future, causing IBM to transfer an enormous amount of wealth to two new companies that eventually became formidable competitors.

The point is that if alternate scenarios of the future had been generated – the official future, and another future that saw PCs in every home – and if a tiny probability had been allowed for this alternate future, then IBM would have altered its decisions to better protect its interests. And as PCs increased in popularity in the early 1980s, IBM management would have been tipped off that the alternate future, and not the official future, was indeed coming true, and IBM would have been better prepared for it.

## The Value of Scenarios – an Illustration

A major pet food manufacturer is attempting to identify new product opportunities over the longer term. Scenario generation is the method used. Here's how it works:

Three cross-functional teams are formed:

*Team A: the "official view" of the future.* This team develops a picture of the future world of pet food based on traditional assumptions and forecasts. For example, assume that people will continue to have dogs and cats as pets much as they have had for generations; and continue to purchase dog food and cat food as always.

*Team B: The worse case scenario.* What is the worse case scenario for a pet food supplier? Simple: that demographics will take their toll on the industry. The postwar baby-boomers have driven every market in the U.S. since 1955; and now they are entering retirement. These boomers are in good health and are often financially well-off. So what do they do (unlike their parents when they retired)? They travel; and/or they buy condominiums in warmer parts of the country. Look at the boom in real estate in Florida and Arizona! And what's the last thing people with condos or people who travel want – pets! So expect a decline in pet ownership – especially larger pets – as the boomers reach retirement.

*Team C: The most unusual or unexpected case.* Here's one – people today like to express themselves in unusual ways: blue colored hair, weird clothing, tattoos and body piecing are examples. So it will be with their pets! Expect the pets of the future to be weird: a pet snake, or iguana or alligator!

Each team has one month to paint a picture – develop a scenario – of what the future of the pet world will look like under these three different sets of assumptions. The teams then reconvene and present their respective pictures.

Next challenge: Given that the world will be as Team A, or Team B, or Team C describes it, the groups brainstorm some possible new products or services that the company could or would develop.

For example, imagine brainstorming and assume the Team B scenario of the future – fewer pets, smaller pets. What new products or new services would you dream up? Some examples include: pet hotels; rent-a-pet services in vacation-destinations; electronic pets (these already exist in Japan but for a different reason); pet baby-sitting services; travel snacks and travel food for pets; pet shipping services; automatic food dispensers for stay-at-home cats, and so on.

Finally, identify the sign-posts or markers that foretell whether Scenario A, B or C is occurring. For example, instead of just monitoring the population of dogs and cats, start measuring how many retirees are acquiring new pets; or how big these pets are. If the first boomers hitting age 60 start showing a downward trend regarding pet ownership, then get set for Scenario B!

**Summary – The Value of Scenarios**

When attempting to define new product opportunities, be sure to try scenario generation as a way of thinking beyond the normal view. Develop scenarios of the future. But do more than just developing the most likely scenario or your "official scenario". Develop *alternate scenarios* – best case, worse case, and unexpected case.

Then imagine that each alternate scenario were to come true – how would it alter your strategy and new product decisions? And what would be the financial consequences of making decisions assuming the official scenario, if indeed one of the alternate scenarios were to come true (as both IBM's and AT&T's did!).

Assign just a small probability to these alternate scenarios occurring, and reconsider your new product investment decisions! And move ahead with techniques to uncover imaginative ideas, given that each scenario – official and alternate – occurs.

---

# Watch for the Signals, Then Act!

Too many companies are blindsided or stunned into inaction by events and trends in their external environments. Sometimes senior management simply does not see the events and discontinuities coming because they have no early warning system. We make a strong case in this chapter for developing *peripheral vision*, and outline the types of questions that you should be asking. *Disruptive technology* has become a popular term in today's management circles; but it is not a new concept and certainly not a new phenomenon. We offer insights into the different types of technological discontinuities and also a number of ways of identifying potential disruptions and of gauging the likely impact. Finally, the *value of scenario generation* was outlined as yet another approach for trying to anticipate the future.

All three are useful and complementary methods that are key to helping you and your business anticipate and be prepared for the future.

But merely identifying and understanding the threats or opportunities is not enough. Some companies are fully aware of the major threats and discontinuities they are facing. However, like a deer paralyzed by a car's headlights, they seem frozen in place and unable to take action. Perhaps management lacks the imagination and simply is not able to dream up the appropriate set of responses – for example, the right new products or services, or a new business model – in order to deal with the threat or discontinuity. Or perhaps they are lulled into a sense of complacency by their own past successes and simply underestimated the threat.

The point is that seeing the threat or potential disruption is not enough. You must identity the right response or actions – for example, what new products or services, or what new platforms, businesses or business models does that threat or disruption point to or demand – and then take action and move forward.

The rest of the book is more tactical in nature, and outlines specific methods for generating ideas in light of some of the strategic threats, issues and opportunities identified in this and the last chapter. For example, the next chapter gets into tactical techniques that are designed to identify new product ideas based on a number of voice of customer approaches – approaches that when married to the strategic methods outlined in the current chapter, promise a rich feed of new product ideas for your development pipeline.

# Using Voice of Customer to Generate Blockbuster Ideas

> You can't just ask customers what they want and then try
> to give that to them. By the time you get it built, they'll
> want something new.
>
> STEVE JOBS (1955– )
> *Co-founder & former chairman of Apple Computer Inc.*

Your customer has your next new product idea! Voice of Customer (VoC) research is a powerful technique that has been proven to yield robust new product and new service ideas.[1] But most companies still do not undertake this essential VoC work – they do not understand how to do it well, nor are they willing to commit the necessary time and effort to undertake proper VoC work. On the other hand, if a steady stream of big new product winners is the goal, then VoC is well worth the effort! Still other companies think that they are doing voice of customer research. But they get it wrong – they confuse "voice of the salesman" or "voice of the Product Manager" with genuine voice of customer research. So let's drill down and gain insights into how to exploit VoC to feed the development funnel with solid product ideas.

This chapter shows why VoC is so critical to generating a steady stream of great new product and new service ideas. It also deals with some of the misconceptions about VoC – what VoC is and what it is not. And finally we outline proven methodologies for conducting VoC in order to generate ideas for your business.

## Why VoC Is So Vital

The *number one key to success and profitability* in product innovation is developing and delivering a unique, superior and differentiated product; a product with new and unique benefits for the customer; and a new product that boasts a compelling value proposition for the user. Countless studies have found this.[2] Note that "product superiority" is defined very much in the eye of the customer or user. For example, in Exhibit 4.1, look how top performing businesses understand the role of product superiority, differentiation and the need for a compelling value proposition:[3]

- Best performers understand what the customer sees as a benefit and value, and deliver important benefits to customers in their new products – by a four-to-one ratio when compared to poor performers
- Best performers' new products offer unique benefits to customers not available in competitive products
- Their products offer the customer or user better value for money – there is a compelling value proposition built in
- New products from best performers are superior to competitive products in terms of meeting customers' needs
- And they feature superior quality, however the customer defines quality.

Developing such unique and differentiated products is not so easy, however. On occasion, blockbuster products come from a technological breakthrough – from new science or invention. But this is rare. Most often, such differentiated and unique products are the result of gaining unique insights into customers' and users' *unmet, unspoken* and often *unarticulated needs*. Note how many of the items in Exhibit 4.1 – where the best performers really excel – require an intimate knowledge of the customer or user, insights into their unmet needs, what they see as value or a benefit, and what they perceive as a "superior product".

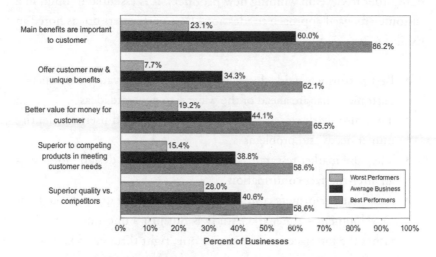

EXHIBIT 4.1 Best performing businesses emphasize product advantage – they conceive, develop and launch unique superior products featuring unique customer benefits with a compelling value proposition for the user.

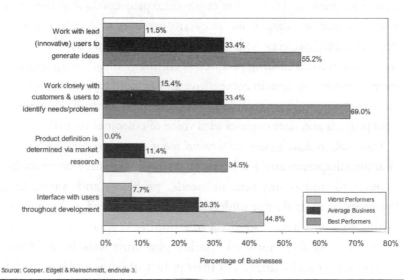

Source: Cooper, Edgett & Kleinschmidt, endnote 3.

EXHIBIT 4.2 In order to develop unique superior products, best performers emphasize VoC – they work with customers and users to define unmet and unarticulated needs to conceive winning new products.

In order to develop winning new products, it is essential to build in a customer-focused approach to ideation. Best performers do, as noted in Exhibit 4.2:

- Best performers work closely with lead and innovative customers – customers that are ahead of the wave – to generate ideas
- They also work closely with their customers and users to identify unmet needs and problems
- They use market research as an input to product design, not just as an after-the-fact confirmation
- And best performers continue to interface with users throughout Development – the market study is not just a one-time snap shot; rather the interface is a continuing one, right through to launch.

We often hear from executives, who profess to be customer oriented, that customer ideas are often small ideas – tweaks, modifications, and extensions. That's probably true, but what they are doing here *is not voice of customer research*. These are sales response projects done at the request of a customer or salesperson. They are reactive, and indeed they are typically small projects with limited potential, and involve a minor modification to an existing product. A company must do these types of projects in order to remain competitive and to keep its product line fresh and responsive to short term requests. But don't confuse these reactive small projects and sales requests with voice of customer research!

True VoC research goes *far beyond what customers say they want*, or what the salesperson asks for. It means getting inside the customers' head in order to understand genuine needs, problems and wants. Often customers or users do not understand what they need or have trouble putting this into words, so direct questioning – what do you want or need? – usually does not work. Rather you must walk in their shoes, understand their challenges and their points of pain, and gain insights into what their real needs are – both spoken and unspoken.

## What Voice of Customer Research Is Not

VoC work is *not* your Product Manager speaking on behalf of the customer – "here's what our customer wants this year… go develop it". While Product Managers are no doubt quite knowledgeable about their markets and clients and provide a useful data point, do not rely on the Product Manager's voice alone! They are not the customer; and do not speak for the customer. When you only listen to internal people, you get biased, filtered and often incorrect information!

Nor should listening to the voice of the salesperson be confused with true VoC work. They are probably very knowledgeable about their clients, but salespeople, like any of us, have built in biases and filters. Salespeople are often biased by a recency effect – the last three customers they talked to and what they asked for. Salespeople are also primarily interested in getting the order, and thus often make many requests on behalf of their clients for new products and services that lead to short term results – minor modifications and tweaks – to secure the sale.

VoC is also not about going to the customer's premise to solve a crisis problem – a product breakdown or serious quality problem. Engineering people talk about a visit to a customer site on a trouble-shooting or technical service emergency, and refer to the visit as "voice of customer". Not so! While a technical person can often learn a lot about the customer on such a trouble-shooting visit, the visit is too focused, narrow and pressured to be taken for a thoughtful VoC visit. Further, the right questions are not asked, VoC is research! And it must be conducted as a rigorous research study, not as a response to a product problem crisis.

VoC is also not the same as asking customers or users what they want in the next new product. Often customers are not aware of what is technically feasible, nor are they encouraged to think broadly and creativity. Thus asking customers what they want in a new product is likely to result in a rather obvious list of small, incremental improvements, or even a description of a competitive product's features. This line of direct questioning will not usually lead to game-changing ideas.

*Illustration:* Picture yourself at a New York City subway station interviewing commuters, asking them what they want in their rapid transit system. Chances are, you'll get a list of well-known items – more frequent service, more reliable service, better air conditioning, more security and cleaner subway cars. But you will not get the ideas for breakthrough concepts of urban mass transit envisioned over the next 10-30 years, such as monorails, maglev vehicles or personal transport pods.

Finally, VoC is not the same as early-stage concept testing. Managers sometimes confuse VoC work with concept testing or proposition testing. For example, your business runs focus groups with customers or users, and tests multiple product concepts at these group sessions. Feedback is sought: customer interest, liking and purchase intent. Or your sales force conducts an early stage product test with a mock-up or virtual prototype – a "show and tell" session with a number of clients designed to gauge customer interest in a new product.

Your marketing and salespeople may call these initiatives voice of the customer work. Not so. These concept tests are valuable research, but they are not VoC; rather they are confirmatory studies. In both examples cited, you and your people did most of the talking: You presented the product concepts in the focus groups; or your salespeople did "show and tell" presentations, complete with virtual prototypes, doing what they do best – talking. But there was precious little listening going on, so not much real voice of customer insights were gained.

In real VoC work, you present nothing – no concepts, nor virtual prototypes or mockups. Instead, you ask, you probe and you listen. You ask open ended questions such as:

• Tell me about your job?
• When you lie in bed at night and think about using this product, what really keeps you awake – what annoys you the most?
• Is this the only way you can think of doing this… is there a better way?

- Why did you say you wanted that feature… what does that feature let you do?

## Why Voice of Customer Works

Customers or users buy products generally for one, or both, of two reasons:

1. To solve a problem
2. To seek a benefit.

For example, some people buy an automobile principally because of its reliability – they fear breakdowns and maintenance costs. These buyers have had serious maintenance problems and costs in the past, and they view reliability and longevity issues as problems to be solved. By contrast, others buy cars because they are fun, sporty or sexy; these car buyers are seeking a benefit from their purchase – a new or better image, or a fun experience when driving.

Both purchase reasons – solving problems and seeking benefits – are viable sources of new product ideas. Smart businesses pursue both routes when they seek new product opportunities:

- They find big problems and then employ their technical skills to find big solutions
- Or they seek out what major benefits consumers desire in a product – why people buy the product in the first place – and then strive to deliver that benefit more effectively than the competition.

Voice of the customer work is instrumental in understanding both customer problems and benefits or values sought by customers. But sometimes the problems encountered or benefit sought by customers are not obvious or even well-understood by the customer. Customers often do not know their needs, or have trouble putting them into words. So it takes some probing and clever questioning to uncover these insights.

## Some Principles of Voice of Customer

The key principles in VoC are straightforward. First, it is necessary to understand customer value – what the customer sees as value, not what your scientists and engineers think. Next, probe for benefits sought and customer problems or points of pain. Focus on the customer's unspoken, unarticulated and often hidden needs. That is, you must go beyond what customers say they want, customer requests or a list of product specifications. The word "why" is as important as the word "what".

VoC work must be face-to-face – touching real customers. And it should involve the entire project team in order to promote learning first hand, and should take place at multiple customer sites (not just with a single lead user). Additionally, VoC work should be done early: the highest impact customer studies are those done near the beginning of projects.

Finally, there must be constant customer involvement throughout the entire development process – this is not just a one time snap-shot, but a continuing study or interactions – from idea development though the early stage concept work, and right into testing and validation of the product.

# VoC Methods

There are six major approaches to undertaking VoC work to generate new product and new service opportunities:

1. Focus group problem detection sessions
2. Brainstorming group events with customers
3. Customer visits with in-depth interviews
4. Camping out or ethnography
5. Lead user analysis
6. Crowdsourcing using online or IT-based approaches.

## 1. Use Focus Groups to Define the Big Problems

Find big problems and look for big solutions! This method requires that you gather a group of customers or prospects to sit in a problem detection session.

*Illustration:* A manufacturer of lawn-and-garden tractors invites a group of small tractor owners to a Saturday morning event at a local rural hotel. Demonstration tractors are in the parking lot for the invitees to play with, ride on, and make comments about. Company people mingle through the crowd, listen and take notes.

*Hint:* Always have sample products – yours and your competitors' – on display as customers gather for the event. Customers are encouraged to interact with the products, make comments and get in the right mood. Your own people can also mix with the customers to listen, probe and gain insights. Use video cameras too!

Then the focus group moderator moves the 12-person customer group into a meeting room, and begins the focus group discussion with a broad non-threatening question: "Introduce yourself and tell us about your lawn tractor". The idea behind focus groups is to start very broadly and then to narrow down and focus on specific issues that arise.

The next question is: "Think of the last time you used your tractor and something bad happened to you – please tell us about it." As the discussion questions become more narrow, issues begin to arise and are discussed at great length. Whenever a hot issue or serious problem arises, the moderator focuses or drills down into the issue – he directs the discussion there. But solutions are not sought, merely problems identified and defined.

Meanwhile in another room, watching the proceedings on closed-circuit TV, is a group of company people, in this case, design engineers and some marketing people. Once the problems are identified by the customer focus group, the company room shifts into a brainstorming mode. Solutions are proposed and sketched on flip charts.

Next the proposed solutions, one flip-chart sheet at a time, are taken into the customer focus group room for discussion and evaluation. Here the tractor owners rip the conceptual solutions apart, and, in so doing, devastate the design engineers still watching all this on TV. And more problems and issues are raised. Armed with this new information and feedback, the design engineers continue brainstorming, and come up with even better solutions.

And round and round the process goes – from the brainstorming group to the focus group and then back again. It's a series of iterations, until an ideal solution is proposed – one that the designers think is feasible, and which the customers agree that they like.

## 2. Invite Your Customers to an Innovation Day with Brainstorming Sessions

Brainstorming can be used with customer groups. In this method, you assemble a group of customers, mix them with your own people, and undertake a series of brainstorming and inverse brainstorming exercises.

Brainstorming is a popular, although frequently misused, technique that with some training anyone can lead. The theory is that under the right set of circumstances, even normally uncreative people can become quite creative as long as the barriers to creativity are removed. The greatest barriers are criticism and peer pressure to conform. So in a brainstorming session, the rule is simple: Any idea is a good one; and no criticism of any kind is allowed. More on how to conduct a brainstorming session in Chapter 6.

By contrast, *inverse brainstorming* is exactly the opposite. Here the group tries to be super-critical: Your group takes a product or solution and brainstorms to uncover everything that is wrong with it: They find all the creative ways they can to attack and destroy the product. In this way, numerous deficiencies and problems, including many unknown ones, are detected.

> *Example:* C&K, an ITT business unit, manufactures a complete range of industrial switches – for example, the on-off switch found on your printer, laptop or desk-top computer. The head of the business hosts a "customer day" on innovation. Salespeople work diligently to ensure that knowledgeable and key customers attend: from the automotive industry, the computers and servers sector, industrial equipment manufacturers; and the lab and scientific equipment industry. Guest speakers are invited to provide enlightening talks on the innovation topic, so that customers receive good value for the day. As part of the day, two group sessions are held:
>
> *Session I:* Attendees are split into groups by market segment or industry, and assigned the challenge question: "What's wrong with switches in your sector or in your equipment?" Also included on each team are company people – technical and marketing – from C&K. This inverse brainstorming session identifies many problems with switches: the fact that, with servers becoming smaller each year, switches occupy too much space on the servers; or that seat belt switches in autos – the switch that turns that light off on your dashboard when you buckle up – are problematic because they take so much wear and tear. Each of the four teams reports back a long list of very creative ways in which the current products and solutions are deficient.
>
> *Session II:* Later in the day, the same teams are asked to identify the three greatest problems or deficiencies identified in the inverse brainstorming session, and then to brainstorm for about 30 minutes on each major problem. Here the rules of brainstorming are applied – no criticism allowed! At the end, the teams quickly identify the best ideas, and report back a short list.

One idea in response to the problematic seat belt switch is a switch with no moving parts – one that relies on a magnetic field. As this book is being written, C&K and a major auto OEM are working together to replace the electro-mechanical seat belt switch with a magnetic one – a huge potential for C&K.

*Pros and Cons of Group Methods:* Groups are a cost-effective and time-efficient way to tap into the voice of the customer, and thus see much use in, for example, consumer goods markets. Here, focus groups are mostly used for concept testing, but what we recommend is that they also be used for VoC problem detection leading to idea generation. Formal brainstorming groups with customers – both inverse and traditional brainstorming – are used less frequently, but our experience is that they have merit, especially when dealing with knowledgeable customers (for example, business or professional customers), as illustrated in the C&K case.

Group discussions involving 8-12 people are often much more animated, insightful, creative and provocative than an interview involving just two or three people, simply because one group member feeds off another group member's comments, and the conversation and energy level build. Groups also have the advantage that, although the sample size is small, with care, a reasonably representative group of customers can be assembled fairly easily. Additionally, much of the leg work can be outsourced to a market research firm.

There are several words of caution about groups, however. The sample size of group attendees is obviously quite limited, and may not be totally representative of your market. The small size also makes drawing quantitative conclusions all but impossible. In business-to-business situations, it is often more difficult to assemble a group of customers from different geographies, although a trade show venue can be used. One must also be careful not to invite competitors to the same session. Another potential drawback is potential biases in the group discussion, for example, that one strong and dominant person sways the entire group to a certain conclusion. Had that person not attended, the group would have reached quite a different end point. Finally, group effectiveness is dependent to large extent on the skill and neutrality of the group moderator or facilitator; a biased or ineffective moderator will direct the group to an invalid conclusion, or no profound conclusions at all.

## 3. Use Customer Visits and Conduct In-Depth Interviews

In-depth interviews are an effective way to gain insights into customers' and user's unmet and unspoken needs. A program of customer visits typically involves visiting at least a dozen customers or sites in a planned and systematic program. A combination of face-to-face guided discussion with customers and users, and a walk-through the product-use area, works best.[4] Customer visits with in-depth interviews are an excellent tool for new product, service, or market creation and are highly recommended as a way to learn more about customer needs, wants and sources of satisfaction and dissatisfaction.

In practice, customer sites are identified, and agreement with the customer for such a visit is obtained. For a business customer, try to arrange for a small group of the customer's people to be available – the key purchase influencers. Your typical interview team is three people from your company, and is cross-functional – marketing, sales and technical. Be sure to involve your technical people so that they can acquire face-to-face learning also (rather than receiving the information second hand and filtered). Besides, *marketing is too important to be left to Marketing people!*

Do the interviews yourself, and don't outsource this research. Outsourcing the interviews means the research company gets the benefit of first-hand learning, and you get a rather sterile report of the results. The only exception is where you bring in a market research firm to help you design the study, and to train and help your people to do the interviews and interpret the data.

When conducting the interviews, use a structured and well-crafted conversation guide. This guide lays out the questions and topics, ensures consistency across interviews, completeness, and also provides a place to record answers. Probe for needs, functions and benefits sought – not features; and make sure that the questions are provocative, stimulating and effective. The best questions tend to be *indirect and inferential,* and include questions that identify likes, dislikes, problems, pain points, and unmet needs. A sample list of 20 questions and topics is provided in Exhibits 4.3 and 4.4.

## The First 11 Questions in The Interview

1. What is the application? How do you (the customer or user) use the product (describe your use system)?
2. How do you solve the problem now? Or what product (make or brand) do you buy or use now? Why?
3. If you had a choice, what product (brand or make) would you buy now? Why that one?
4. What's really important to you in making a purchase decision for these types of products (your criteria)?
5. How do currently available (competitive) products rate on these criteria?
6. Which product (or solution) would you rate as best on each of the things that you said are important?
7. Which product is worst on each? Why?
8. What are the biggest problems you face in this application? What are your real points of pain? Why? Can you think of any possible solutions to these major problems that you face?
9. What do you like most about current products for this application? Why? (try to be specific about which competitive product)
10. What do you dislike about these products (or current solution)? Why?
11. What problems do you have with these products? What really annoys you? What pet peeves do you have? Why?

EXHIBIT 4.3 Here are the first 11 of 20 questions that form the basis for a typical interview guide for VoC customer visits with in-depth interviews. Modify them as needed to suit your market and customers.

## The Next Nine Questions in the Interview

**Features:**
12. What new features and attributes or improved performance are you looking for in a new product here?
13. Why did you mention that feature/performance? Why is that feature/performance important to you?
14. What does that feature/performance let you do?
15. Does the feature/performance item cause you problems now? Why? What doesn't work well about that feature/performance item?
16. What works well about the feature/performance item?
17. What trade-offs do you have among various features and performance characteristics?

**Economics & the Future:**
18. How does this product impact on your bottom line (impact on your costs or profits)?
19. What changes or trends in the future might impact on your needs & requirements for this product & application?
20. Do you have any other suggestions for what's needed in a new product or new solution?

EXHIBIT 4.4 These nine VoC questions deal with features and why they are important, along with broader economic and future-oriented topics.

Once the interview is complete, you and your interview team should do a walk-about; spend time with the customer where the product is actually used. Often, by watching people use, misuse and abuse the product, you gain further insights into unmet needs.

*Example:* Smart-Pump 2000 was an ill-fated project that was spawned by a single customer request. The customer asked the Goulds Pumps' salesman: "Why don't you folks build an intelligent pump – one that can sense its own operating environment, and adjust its mode of operation to minimize wear and tear, minimize pump downtime, and maximize pump life?" A great idea, and it sailed through the Idea Gate and on into Development with little or no further customer research as the Smart-Pump 2000 project. The final product consisted of an intelligent pump with multiple sensors located both upstream and downstream measuring pressure, flow and temperature; these sensors were connected to a microprocessor which controlled a variable speed motor. The pump could adjust its speed in response to different operating conditions and thereby reduce wear and maintenance.

Smart Pump was launched with great fanfare in 2001 and proved to be a huge dud. The smart technology was brilliant, but the value proposition and product were weak.

All was not lost however. Sensing that the technology was indeed solid, Goulds' management had another try. By this time, however, Goulds' technical and marketing people had been through extensive training on VoC, and employed the technique on the new Smart Pump project. Teams of three people – technical, sales and marketing – undertook in-depth interviews at key users, and also undertook walk-throughs of customer facilities where pumps were used.

Their conclusions: While pump maintenance was an issue, it was not an overriding one. The customers' major pain point, however, was electrical power costs. These pumps, often high horsepower, run flat out and consume lots of power. What the visit teams also observed was that beside each pump is a flow valve – often in the half-closed position. "That's how we control the volume or flow," explained users.

To the Goulds team, this was absurd: "It's like driving a car with one's foot to the floor on the accelerator and then using the hand-brake to control the speed... very inefficient." The new Smart Pump was obvious: a much simpler version of the original Smart Pump, with a senor downstream and upstream to measure flow demand and supply, a simple microprocessor, and a variable speed drive. When demand is low, the pump slows down, and significant electrical power is saved. In a new installation, there is not even a need for a valve – the pump is the flow controller. In a retrofit installation, Smart Pump pays for itself in less than a year in power savings.

The product has been a huge success, but it was only through VoC work, and in particular the observation and walk-about facet of the visits, that the "aha" leading to the breakthrough was discovered.

*Pros and Cons of Customer Visits with In-Depth Interviews:* In-depth customer interviews have a number of strengths as a VoC technique. Because customer visits are a field research technique, they are valuable for gaining insight into the customer's world. Additionally, closer relationships can be developed with the customer. And because the interview structure is flexible and the questions open-ended, they allow the opportunity for surprises which might not be gained by other tools such as quantitative research. Finally, using cross-functional interview teams promotes a shared vision and understanding of what customers need and expect.

The greatest weakness of a customer visits program is problems with the interviewers themselves: the potential for interviewer bias; and few insights gained due to interviewers who do not listen well or do not probe well. A second weakness is the limited sample size due to visit costs, which precludes drawing quantitative conclusions and presenting statistical results. Finally, this method does require heavy resource commitments, both time and money, for traveling.

## 4. Camp Out with Your Customers – Employ Ethnography

If you want to study gorillas, a couple of focus groups with gorillas, an e-mail survey and a few interviews probably won't be enough. You must buy a tent and move into their village site – and *camp out with them*. And so it is with gaining real customer insights: You must move into their home, office or business and spend time observing and gaining insights. This anthropological style of research has been used by leading companies to uncover unmet needs and new product opportunities. It's called "camping out", "fly-on-the-wall" or "day-in-the-life-of" research. The formal term is "ethnography".

> *Example:* Dracger Safety is a major German manufacturer of safety, emergency and firefighting equipment. One of their product lines is breathalyzer testing devices used by police forces to test alcohol levels in suspected drunk drivers. A new product line in Europe was the goal, but the project needed direction and lacked blockbuster ideas.
>
> Two VoC study teams were formed and, after some training on how to do ethnographic research, the teams began their camping out exercises in England and Sweden. In both countries, the teams spent time at police stations, conducting interviews with police officers and their supervisors. But the real learning and aha's came from their nighttime vigils – the camping out exercise – where the VoC teams worked beside the police officers as they ran their night-time road-side spot checks on drivers. These learnings provided the key to a new product with significant competitive advantage.
>
> For example, the British VoC team soon realized how difficult a job the police officers had in maintaining order and control over a carload full of exuberant young drinkers fresh from the nearby pub. The police order to the suspected drunks is always: "Remain in the car!" The breathalyzer test device is passed through the driver's window by the officer (who wears latex gloves for fear of HIV), and the driver is commanded to blow into the mouthpiece. It takes two minutes to get a full reading.

Meanwhile the other officer has pulled over another car, so now there are two carloads of drunks to manage. Quite clearly, the police officers are somewhat intimidated by the task of crowd control – they're outnumbered, and many of the lads in the cars are twice the size and half the age of the officers (who incidentally do not carry guns). Note that officers never admitted to intimidation during the formal daytime interviews!

One solution the team came up with to overcome the problem of crowd control and intimidation was to speed up the process. The goal became to substantially reduce the two minute wait-time for test results that was creating the queue. And they did achieve this by developing a ten second test device.

A second observation was that because of the dials on the U.K. version of the instrument, it could only be used on right-hand-side drivers in the U.K. Thus, when a car from France or Germany, driving in the U.K., was pulled over (a left-hand-side driver) the police could not conduct the test. And they had no option but to simply wave the car through. This behavior was never revealed to their supervisors nor in the formal interviews. The solution was to design an ambidextrous testing instrument – an arm with the mouthpiece attached that could be swung over the top of the test device depending on whether a right-hand or left-hand side drive car was pulled over.

You get the idea. These are but two out of ten novel ideas that made the new Draeger product line a huge success. Each idea is not a breakthrough, but when all ten new benefits are added up, the new product was indeed a blockbuster and absolutely delighted police forces.

If you are in a business-to-business market, a powerful additional facet of ethnography is to observe and map out the customer's work flow, noting how they use your product as part of their work. Mapping the customer's workflow can be done using Value Stream Analysis, where you look at each step of the customer's work flow, identify value-added and non-value-added elements, and then seek improvements. In so doing, look for ways to offer new solutions and new products to help the customer.

*Pros and Cons of Camping Out or Ethnography:* Ethnography is a relatively new method for identifying unmet needs, although this general type of research – cultural anthropology – has been around for decades. The main advantage is the depth of knowledge that you gain. Properly undertaken, such research can probe and uncover insights, needs, behaviors and opportunities in much greater depth and far more profoundly than any of the other methods.

The main disadvantage is exactly that – because it is so deep, it also takes much time and is expensive. On the other hand, look at the payoffs! Also, the time can be reduced by shortening the length of visit – for example, to several days or even one day per customer site. For example, Fluke, a manufacturer of hand-held instruments, spends about one day per customer site in their "day-in-the-life-of" research. Proxy methods can also be used, for example, Johnsonville Sausage, a major U.S. food producer, installed video cameras in kitchens to observe householders as they cooked meals, looking for new opportunities for sausages.

Another word of warning is that this observational method relies very much on the skill of the researcher or observer. If your people lack observation and listening skills, or are poor at drawing inferences and integrating information, then the method loses effectiveness. Just because a person has an MBA or an Engineering degree does not make them a first-rate cultural anthropologist – it does take some talent and training.

### 5. Work with Your Lead or Innovative Customers

If you work with average customers, you'll get average ideas. But, if you identify a select group of *innovative* or *lead users*, and work closely with them, then expect much more innovative new products. It is an approach that Eric Von Hippel of MIT pioneered years ago, and has more recently gained prominence at 3M as a key tool for uncovering innovative new product ideas.[5]

Research by Von Hippel reveals that many commercially important products are initially thought of and even prototyped by users rather than manufactures. He also found that such products tend to be developed by "lead users" – companies, organizations or individuals that are well ahead of market trends and even have needs that go far beyond the average user. The trick is to track down lead users, who are, by definition, rare.

The lead user process has four main steps:[6]

1. *Laying the foundation:* identify the target market and company goals for innovations in this market (seeking buy-in of the stakeholders).
2. *Determining the trends:* talk to people in the field – people who have a broad view of emerging technologies and leading edge applications.
3. *Identifying lead users* – a networking process: project team members begin by briefly explaining their quest to people with apparent expertise on the subject, for example, research professionals or people who have written about the topic. They then ask for a referral to someone who has even more relevant knowledge. According to Von Hippel, it's usually not long before the team reaches the lead users at the leading edge of the target market. Based on what they learn, teams begin to shape preliminary product ideas and to assess their business potential.
4. *Developing the breakthroughs:* The team begins this phase by hosting a workshop with lead users and key in-house technical and marketing people. Participants work in small groups, then as a whole, to define final product concepts.

3M has adopted the approach and has used the lead user process to develop innovations in fields from new medical products through to telecom systems, as have other firms:[7]

*Example:* At Hilti, a leading European company in the demolition, fastening and concrete drilling equipment business, lead user analysis is extensively used. First, lead users are identified – leading edge, innovative customers in the construction or demolition field.

Hilti's direct sales force provides guidance here. Hilti's Innovation Management department then invites a group of these lead users for a weekend retreat – they watch and they listen, attempting to understand lead users' problems. Suggestions and possible solutions from lead users are fashioned into tentative new product concepts. Hilti management claims that this lead user technique has been used with great success across a wide variety of product groups within the company.

*Pros and Cons of Lead User Analysis:* The main advantage of the lead user method is that you are working with a select group of customers in terms of their innovativeness and creativity. And when you work with bright and creative people, the hope is that the end result – the ideas and opportunities identified – will be much above average too. Once these lead users have been identified and assembled at a workshop, the methods used in the workshop are much the same as those described in the group approaches above, so they have the same advantages and disadvantages.

One challenge is identifying lead users. Using referrals is one approach, but can be tedious and problematic. 3M management indicate that they survey customers, and ask questions about whether or not the customer modified the product. Hilti uses the same approach:

*Example:* In one Hilti project to develop a new line of pipe hangers (brackets to suspend pipes from a concrete ceiling), plumbers and installers were surveyed. The key question was: "Have you ever modified a pipe hanger – cut it, bent it, shaped it, or added to it?" The standard response was: "No. I use them the way they come out of the shipping box". But for a handful of users, the response was: "Yes, I have this favorite trick… let me tell you about it". These and other questions were instrumental in identifying innovative and creative plumbers who were then invited to a weekend retreat, and via a series of group exercises, conceived and designed an entire new and revolutionary line of pipe hangers.

## 6. Try Crowdsourcing – A New Source of Ideas

If you use a product a lot, have you ever thought that you could design it better than the manufacturer did? Most of us believe that. Every business has a subset of customers who think they are more clever than the company's product designers – customers that think that they could do a better job of designing the product than the company does. So why not let them?[8]

Crowdsourcing is a new form of *user-centered innovation* where manufacturers rely on customers, not just to define their needs, but to define the products or enhancements to meet them.[9] "Crowdsourcing" is the unofficial name of this IT-enabled trend whereby companies get unpaid or low-paid amateurs to design products, create ideas, and generate content mostly just for the fun of it. Crowdsourcing relies on would-be customers' willingness to hand over their ideas to the company, either cheaply or for free, in order to see them go into production. The use of customers as idea generators is made possible by ever-spreading, ever-cheaper IT to bring people outside the company into the design process. Create a web page and then ask people to contribute!

What is the motivation for customers to spend so much time creating ideas and designs all for free? It's the same motivation that caused thousands of techies to create and develop open-source software and receive no payment – software such Linux, the operating system available virtually for free. They do it for the satisfaction, for the fun, and perhaps for fame, but certainly not for fortune! This same motivation causes would-be artists to create spectacular graffiti drawings on building walls, or many talented people to contribute their time and knowledge to creating Wikipedia, the do-it-yourself encyclopedia. But unlike the bottom-up, ad-hoc communities that develop open-source software, graffiti artwork, Wikipedia, or even better windsurfing gear, crowdsourced work is *managed and owned by a single company* that sells the results.

*Example:* Threadless is a Chicago-based T-shirt maker whose design process consists entirely of an online contest. Each week the company receives hundreds of submissions from amateur and professional artists. Threadless posts these to its website, where anyone who signs up can give each shirt a score. The four to six highest-rated designs each week are put into production, but only after enough customers have pre-ordered the design to ensure it will not be a money-loser.

Each week's winners get $2,000 in cash and prizes. The real motivation is the chance to have their work seen and potentially worn in public, as Threadless puts the designer's name on the label of each shirt. For designers, it is a creative outlet; for customers, it's a wider range of choices. And from Threadless' point of view, the company doesn't have to hire a design staff, and only commits financially to shirts with proven, pre-ordered, appeal. It is not a revolution – it's risk reduction.[10]

Most companies' products are much more complicated than designing T-shirts. The method can be expanded, however, to promote ideation of somewhat more complex products:

*Another example:* The Japanese specialty furniture retailer, Muji, solicits novel and radical product furniture design ideas from a member base of roughly half a million people through its community site, Muji.net. On the site, Muji asks members to pre-evaluate the designs. The short list of highest-ranked ideas is given to professional designers, who develop the production-grade specifications.

Like Threadless, Muji then tests the market by soliciting customer pre-orders rather than conducting a focus group or survey, or using other traditional market research methodology. Simply put, if 300 customers pre-order an item online, it goes into production.

Muji.net also has a page boasting about its customers' greatest hits:

- A lamp that fits near the head of a bed where there's no power socket
- Wall shelves for renters that can be hung without using nails

- A small cubical beanbag chair that can be used in different positions.

Ironically, this customer-suggested cubical beanbag chair outsold the rest of Muji's models by fifty times![11]

Threadless and Muji fit customer designers into their businesses in quite different ways. Threadless' entire design and approval process is outsourced to the crowd. By contrast, Muji taps the crowd for ideas and feedback to come up with a few innovative products, yet keeps professional designers in the loop; moreover Muji does not rely on outside ideas for its entire product line.

As design software and IT improves, it will only get easier and cheaper for outsiders to create and submit ideas, technology and even professional quality product specs that once required expensive in-house work. For example, SAP, the German software giant, has a web page that its users can log onto and preview new software concepts, vote for or against them, and make suggestions for improvement. Procter & Gamble's new "Connect + Develop" initiative comes very close to soliciting ideas, products and technology from anyone in the world (more on P&G's "Connect + Develop" in Chapter 5). The point is that that these crowdsourcing methods are here now, and some leading firms are already employing them – so look for more and more companies, maybe even yours, to find ways to tap the creative abilities and wisdom of the crowd.

*Pros and Cons of Crowdsourcing:* It is really too soon to tell how effective crowdsourcing is. On the plus side, the method promises to be a huge source of creative ideas because it can tap into a much wider audience than traditional research methods do. Audience biases may be a problem, however: The audience is clearly limited to those who log on and take the time to participate, so may not be representative of your mainstream market. On the other hand, these folks are a self-selected group, and may be more creative and knowledgeable than your typical customers.

Another issue is that the method seems to be limited so far to relatively simple products. It's hard to imagine an industrial customer logging on and designing or conceiving a new lab instrument or a new motor control... or is it? Dell's customers in effect design their computers online by assembling available components. The online design software is available to do that today, and it gets better every year.

## If You're Not Doing VoC...

...then you are missing some major innovation opportunities. This chapter has outlined six different VoC methods designed to generate robust or game-changing new product ideas. They are summarized in Exhibit 4.5. Most businesses today are not employing these methods yet, or are not using them correctly or consistently. You have seen the examples of how these methods work and how they are implemented. And you've seen the results. Best performing businesses are reaping the benefits of using VoC to generate great new product ideas to feed their development funnel. So review the six methods above, and then pick the one or ones that best suit your need and budget. Then do it!

| VoC Method & Example | Description |
|---|---|
| 1. Focus groups to define big problems with solutions iterations. *Example: lawn tractors* | Run a focus group session on customers to identify problems, issues & points of pain. Company people watch the brainstorming session from another room. They then brainstorm solutions to the problems, which are taken back to the focus group. These solutions are voted on and discussed by the customer focus group; improvements are sought. The iterative process continues until the ideal concept is defined. |
| 2. Brainstorming event with customers. *Example: C&K Switches* | Invite customers for an Innovation Day that includes a set of inverse brainstorming and regular brainstorming sessions. Mix company people with the customer groups. In inverse brainstorming, find creative ways to destroy the product. Then pick the three major weaknesses, and employ traditional brainstorming to arrive at novel solutions. |
| 3. In-depth interviews via customer visits: *Example: Smart Pump* | Define cross-functional interview teams, visit key customers & conduct in-depth interviews with customer groups. Use an interview guide that includes indirect & inferential questions to help customers articulate their needs, likes, dislikes and desires. Also, build in a walk-through the customer facility to see use, abuse and misuse of the product first hand. |
| 4. Camping out: ethnography *Example: Draeger breathalyzer* | Identify customer sites and camp out with customers, spending at least a full day – usually longer – at their workplace or home. Watch them use the product; understand their use system and work flow; and look for innovation opportunities. |
| 5. Working with lead or innovative customers: *Example: Hilti* | Identify particularly innovative customers – those ahead of the wave. Then work with them to create innovative ideas. Host a workshop and invite them. Have attendees work first in small teams to help define problems, benefits sought and new solutions and ideas. Then move to a large group setting to refine and finalize the design. |
| 6. Crowdsourcing: *Examples: Threadless & Muji* | Invite your customers to suggest ideas, create content and even help design your new products. Use IT and a web page to enable them to log on and submit ideas and designs. Send the ideas out to other customers via IT for an evaluation. Pick the best and then move forward. |

EXHIBIT 4.5  Here's a summary of the six main VoC methods to generate new product and new service ideas. Pick one or more that best suits you and move forward.

# CHAPTER 5

# Getting Ideas From Outside the Company

*Open Innovation and External Sources of Innovative Ideas*

> The human mind treats a new idea the same way the
> body treats a strange protein; it rejects it.
> —P. B. MEDAWAR (1915–1987)
> *British anatomist; Nobel Prize in Medicine 1960*

At this moment, you can bet that there is a scientist, a small business entrepreneur or a private inventor with the seeds of your next great new product... or maybe the product that could put you out of business. The trouble is, this person does not work for your company. Closing the door to the outside world cuts off a huge potential source of ideas and innovation. Yet most companies do just that! This chapter focuses on getting ideas from outside your organization. We outline the potential of "open innovation", provide examples of how leading companies have implemented the approach, and share one in-depth case study or illustration at Procter & Gamble. Other external sources are also explored in this chapter including competitors, patent mapping, trade shows and universities.

## Open Innovation

Major corporations face a major threat – the fact that their own internal R&D has not been the engine of innovation in their industries, and that they have missed opportunity after opportunity. Indeed many of the breakthrough ideas over the last decades have come from outside major corporations.[1] IBM sat by and watched as others innovated with mini-computers, workstations, PCs and Palm computers; P&G failed to launch a major new consumer brand for almost 20 years (although they are now back in the innovation game with a new business model); Merck watched Pfizer seize the lead in the drug industry by marketing compounds that were usually licensed from other companies' laboratories; American Express watched others create the Cash Management Account, the debit card, and Internet payment systems; and AT&T witnessed microwave relay transmission, global positioning systems, satellite transmission, and packet switching technologies emerge far from its Bell Labs.[2] Some of the reasons why dominant firms seem to lack peripheral vision or fail to act on disruptive technologies were outlined in the last chapter. Open innovation is one solution to this failure to see and act in time.

"Not all of the smart people in your industry work for you," argues Chesbrough, who notes that too much invention and innovation take place outside of your walls to ignore it.[3] Many ideas, inventions and innovations come from smaller, entrepreneurial start-ups funded by venture capitalists.[4] Many of these create breakthrough technologies, ideas and new business models to disrupt established categories and markets. Thus competitive advantage now often comes from leveraging the discoveries of others. And the implication of that trend is unavoidable: "You cannot meet your growth objectives if you ignore all of the smart people out there who are not on your payroll".[5]

Does your organization suffer too much from NIH – the "not invented here" syndrome? Leading companies have recognized the need for *open innovation* – for a healthy balance between internally and externally generated ideas and new products. And they have put in place the processes, IT support, teams and culture to *leverage external partners and alliances* in the quest for new ideas, inventions and innovations from outside the firm. The goals of open innovation are to create new products in untapped white spaces, to gain access to new technologies, to create more value from internally generated technologies, and to speed development projects.

## Taking Corrective Action

Those companies that originally missed the boat are now acting quickly to become more externally focused. P&G's new Connect + Develop initiative is an ambitious and multi-faceted program to open up the company's innovation efforts and needs to the world; its goal is to generate 50 percent of the company's ideas or projects from sources external to the company. IBM now actively monitors the open software community and has more programmers working on Java and Linux software than any other company.[6] Merck has created a corporate venture capital program to invest in companies to streamline its drug development process, and has boosted its licensing of externally developed compounds. American Express now brings corporate expense planning solutions to its customers, many of which started outside the company.

Note that not every company is like IBM, AT&T and American Express. Indeed, many well-run companies did not miss out and have been actively engaged in externally-oriented innovation for some time. For example, Air Products and Chemicals' formal open innovation effort began in 1995 when their Corporate Technology Partnerships group was created in order to centralize the company's external technology efforts and to implement best practices across the company.[7] But long before 1995, each Air Products business unit was active in technology partnering. And while Merck sat on the sidelines, Pfizer was active in external licensing, both in- and out-licensing. Disney has worked in partnerships with outside firms for years to conceive new methods (its invisible garbage-handling system in Disney World); new communications systems (innovative telephone switching); and even new materials (bridge decking made from old auto tires).

## What's Different About Open Innovation?

Innovation via partnering with external firms and people has been around for decades – joint ventures, venture groups in large corporations, licensing arrangements and even venture nurturing. Open innovation is simply *a broader concept* that includes not only these traditional partnering models, but *all types of collaborative or partnering* activities and with a wider range of partners than in the past. Early work in this field is attributed to professors at MIT: For example, Ed Roberts' "newness framework" in Exhibit 5.1, which showed the types of innovation and collaboration models that are likely to work best under different circumstances, was published in the 1980s and is still a standard.[8] Exhibit 5.2 provides definitions of the types of partnering and external relationships common in product innovation.[9]

**Technologies Embodied in the Products**

| | | Base | New, familiar | New, unfamiliar |
|---|---|---|---|---|
| **Market Targeted by the Products** | **New, unfamiliar** | Joint Ventures | Venture Capital or Venture Nurturing or Educational Acquisitions | Venture Capital or Venture Nurturing or Educational Acquisitions |
| | **New, familiar** | Internal Market Development or Acquisitions (or Joint Ventures) | Internal Ventures or Acquisitions or Licensing | Venture Capital or Venture Nurturing or Educational Acquisitions |
| | **Base** | Internal Base Developments (or Acquisitions) | Internal Product Development or Acquisitions or Licensing | Joint Ventures (large firm with small firm) |

Source: Roberts & Berry, endnote 8.

EXHIBIT 5.1 The MIT newness framework shows the types of collaborative and external efforts that work best for different degrees of technological and market newness.

| Licensing – in and out | A formal legal agreement where one firm sells IP, technology or a product for use or sale by another firm, usually for a fixed fee and royalty. |
|---|---|
| Joint venture | A formal legal arrangement between partners in a joint development and/or business initiative. Risks and rewards are negotiated and shared formally. |
| Co-development | Working with outside partners in the development of new products and/or services. Can be a subset of joint venturing or open innovation initiative. May include peer-to-peer or supplier/customer co-development. |
| Open innovation | Collaborative development which includes the broad concepts of leveraging all external sources of ideas, technology and innovation to drive internal growth. Also entails the spin-off and outsourcing of unused intellectual property. |
| Collaborative innovation | Similar to open innovation and co-development, but can also include formal networks or consortia that come together in an alliance to study common issues and/or develop new products and services. |
| Open source | Derived from the term used in the software development industry, where informally structured collaborations take place (usually without ownership or remuneration) to create a shared outcome from which all can benefit. Similar to crowdsourcing described in Chapter 4, but not owned by any one corporation. |
| Educational acquisition | Where a large firm purchases a small high technology firm in order to learn more about a technology, acquire the technology, and/or to gain a first entry at low cost. |
| Venture capital & venture nurturing | Where the firm invests capital in a smaller, usually high technology firm and takes an ownership position. In the nurturing model, management in the large firm plays an active role in managing the smaller firm, playing a mentoring or nurturing role. |

EXHIBIT 5.2 A diversity of models exist for engaging external development partners.

In the traditional or *closed innovation model,* inputs come from both internal and external sources – customer inputs, marketing ideas, marketplace information or strategic planning inputs. Then, the R&D organization proceeds with the tasks of inventing, evolving and perfecting technologies for further development, immediately or at a later date.[10] The traditional funnel portrays the normal development process (Exhibit 5.3): Here, large numbers of ideas and concepts are narrowed down to the ones that best fit that company's needs at that time. The focus is on internal development of technologies and products for commercialization by the company. Technologies and innovations that are not used or needed immediately are put on-the-shelf for possible use at a later date.

*Example:* It was these technologies on-the-shelf that has led to so much criticism of Xerox for its failure to commercialize many inventions it had in the computer field. While the shareholders of Xerox did not benefit, others did! Employees who worked on promising technologies left to form start-up companies, many of which,

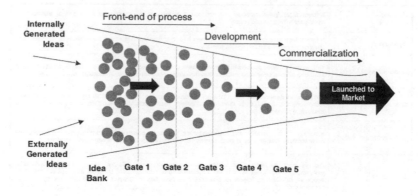

**EXHIBIT 5.3** In traditional product innovation, a funnel portrays the process. Ideas from inside and outside the company are screened through a series of culling points (gates) and are developed and commercialized by the company.

such as 3Com and Adobe, achieved huge success. In fact, the market capitalization of Xerox's spin-offs exceeded that of Xerox itself.[11]

By contrast, in open innovation, *companies look inside-out and outside-in, across all three aspects of the innovation process,* including ideation, development and commercialization. In doing so, much more value is created and realized throughout the process – see Exhibit 5.4. For example:[12]

- *Ideation or Discovery Stage:* Here, not only do companies look externally for customer problems to be solved or unmet needs to be satisfied, but now also to inventors, start-ups, small entrepreneurial firms, partners, and other sources of available technologies that can be used as a basis for internal or joint development.
- *Development Stage:* Established companies seek help in solving technology and development problems from scientists external to the corporation; and they acquire external innovations that have already become productized or even commercialized by others. Also, in this Development Stage, companies out-license or sell technologies and

intellectual property that are internally developed but are determined to be outside the core business.

- *Launch or commercialization stage:* Companies sell or out-license already commercialized products where more value can be realized elsewhere; or they in-license – they acquire already commercialized products that provide immediate sources of new growth for the company.

*Example:* Kimberly-Clark's "Insight Driven Innovation" is an open innovation initiative that employs multiple linkages to a number of partners in order to leverage the expertise and capabilities of others.[13] These partners include:

- Venture capital partners
- Contract manufacturers
- Co-branding and co-marketing partners
- Co-distribution partners

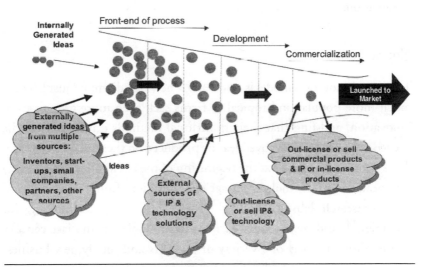

EXHIBIT 5.4  In open innovation, ideas, technology and products come from external sources; the product may be developed or marketed with a partner, or the developed technology may be licensed out.

- External brokers
- In-licensing and out-licensing partners
- Joint development partners.

Kimberly-Clark's effort stems from a realization that a larger pipeline of new product ideas was necessary in order to drive continued growth and to compete in their dynamic marketplace. The ultimate goal of the company is to leverage external partners in order to accelerate development, enhance the power of the company's existing brands, access external manufacturing capabilities, gain access to new and unique technologies, and create new categories in untapped white spaces.

*A Kimberly-Clark partnering example:* Huggies Little Swimmers is a new category of disposable swim-pants for babies and young children created by Kimberly-Clark some years ago. In 2006, in the spirit of open innovation and working with partner SunHealth Solutions, free UV sensors are now offered with Little Swimmers. The sensor allows parents to monitor the child's exposure to UV-B radiation.

## Not So New

The open innovation model is not really a new paradigm; it's just become much more popular and topical as firms seek even more growth from innovation, and find that their traditional methods cannot deliver the needed volumes of innovative ideas or products. So there are lots of precedents here. As far back as at the beginning of the twentieth century many European companies took advantage of innovations from universities and public research labs (organic chemistry and x-ray technology, for example).[14] And many complex new technologies in the last century required the interplay of a variety of partners and totally new business models (electricity supply, nuclear energy and air transportation). Additionally, many companies licensed their technologies (for example, to Japanese companies after WW II).

Nor is the traditional model of innovation dead – firms doing internal R&D work using the funnel approach. Indeed, many companies are very successful at designing and developing new products largely through internal efforts. Moreover, such firms have been diligent over the years at working with partners on collaborative efforts when appropriate, and will continue to do so in the future. Even at P&G, which is placing such a heavy emphasis on open innovation through its Connect + Develop effort, there is still a huge push behind internal development efforts;[15] and the company continues to perfect methods such as their SIMPL idea-to-launch process, and their Initiatives Diamond model for internal developments.[16]

## Why the Shift in Paradigm Now?

The sudden interest and growth in open innovation is based on several multi-fold trends in innovation that have converged in the early part of this century:[17]

- First, the huge pressures from shareholders and senior management to drive innovation began in the 1990s. Expectations for rapid growth through innovation had been created during the dot.com boom, and the innovation game was in play. Aggressive innovation goals were set, and astute managements realized that these goals could not be achieved with the traditional models and approaches. New sources of innovation would be required, so they began to look for new sources outside the firm.

- After some years of arrogance in larger corporations, it finally dawned on many executives that a lot of the truly innovative work and great breakthroughs do not come from the large, dominant firms in an industry, but from smaller and mid-sized entrepreneurial firms. This truth had been in evidence for some decades, but the dot.com boom of the 90s and the parallel bio-tech boom, both smaller-company driven, made this truth all the more evident – small entrepreneurial firms lead!

- Additionally, universities, government labs and institutions had become increasingly interested in commercializing their science and inventions. This was becoming big business for the university and the non-profit lab, both of which were somewhat strapped for cash – no longer is the university or public lab just interested in curiosity-based research, they want a revenue stream!

- Also in the nineties, many large companies, such as IBM and Eli Lily, were beginning to experiment with the new concept of open innovation, leveraging one another's and even competitors' innovation assets, technology and IP. They modeled the way.

- At the same time, there was a huge increase in the availability of outsourced RD&E capabilities, particularly in developing countries such as India and China. This trend to off-shoring and outsourcing has been accelerated by the widespread availability of inexpensive communications and also by situations, such as the Y2K crisis in 1999, where U.S. firms were forced to go off-shore to India for IT talent.[18] In a similar vein and from a U.S. perceptive, the fact that there is a reduced inflow of scientific talent to the U.S., and that the rest of the world has surpassed the U.S. in science education and doctoral degrees granted, has hastened the quest for off-shore talent.

- Finally, the Internet made it possible for everyone to connect with everyone and very easily – regardless of whether you were a scientist in a government lab in the U.S. or a professor at an Indian university. The world suddenly became very flat after the year 2000.[19]

## The Many Faces of Open Innovation

Open innovation has been implemented in a variety of ways in different companies. Here are some examples (the text box shows useful tools for open innovation):[20]

*Air Products and Chemicals:* The company's "Identify and Accelerate" initiative identifies internal needs and the role that external partnering can play to accelerate the innovation process.[21] Most of the emphasis is on

## Internet Services Help Open Innovation

NineSigma has a new business model for open innovation, and has built a targeted global innovation network that can identify and connect the talents and capabilities of today's most prepared minds. NineSigma works with clients to prepare a request for proposal for projects, and then distributes this request to many open networks of global technology and R&D providers.[20]

Yet2.com lists technologies for sale or license, and now allows clients to post their technology needs.

Innocentive tenders technical assignments on behalf of its clients (mostly companies in the process industries) on the Internet, and rewards the best solution submitted by the web community with sums ranging from $10,000 to $100,000. In return, the inventor hands over the rights to the solution to Innocentive's client, who pays Innocentive a fee for its confidential tendering services and evaluation of the solutions.

securing outside R&D resources to work on the company's own development projects. The external partnering methods include:

- In-sourcing R&D and technology by partnering with global suppliers of R&D and also via global partnering within the company ("in-sourcing" is the term used by Air Products; the more normal term is "outsourcing" or "off-shoring" of R&D"[22]).
- Using Internet-based commercial providers to provide the connections (more later in this chapter).
- Partnering with the government (which Air Products has been doing for 60 years, notably with the U.S. government). Efforts include: funding R&D at federal laboratories, being a contractor to perform R&D for the government, and acting as a consultant to third parties accessing government funding.
- Licensing-in to accelerate product development by accessing

already-developed technology (versus beginning an in-house project to invent around the existing technology).

*Nokia Venturing:* Nokia has moved beyond "not invented here" and is embracing the best ideas wherever they are, using a multi-faceted approach:[23]

- Nokia's Venturing Organization undertakes venturing activities designed to identify and develop new businesses for the renewal of the corporation.
- Nokia Venture Partners invest exclusively in mobile and intellectual property related start-up businesses.
- Nokia's Innovent group directly supports and nurtures nascent innovators with the hope of growing future opportunities for Nokia.

*Spalding:* In this commodity category, Spalding is reinvigorating the company through innovation, including technology developed externally. Spalding introduced the Infusion, the first basketball with a built-in pump, which led to a 32 percent increase in sales.[24] More recently, Spalding introduced the "Never-Flat" basketball, technology developed by Primo Innovations, a small invention company founded by two PhDs from NASA and DuPont.

*Technology out-licensing:* Caterpillar, Sharp, Dow Chemical, Kimberly-Clark, Philips, and P&G are examples of companies that out-license internally developed intellectual property. The benefits include the value derived from otherwise unused knowledge, and also useful strategic partnerships are developed. For example, P&G's licensed the underlying technology to Clorox that resulted in Glad Press'n Seal Wrap. Thus P&G was able to leverage the value of the patents and enter a successful joint venture with Clorox, whose Glad brand was already a leader in the category.[25]

## The Benefits of Open Innovation

The obvious benefit of open innovation is the much larger base of ideas and technologies from which to draw to drive internal growth.[26] Additionally, the risk of developing truly innovative products is reduced through a shared risk model. For example, one is able to leverage internal R&D using another company's resources. And the firm can conduct strategic experiments at lower levels of risk and resources with the opportunity to extend core business and create new sources of growth. Over time, a more innovative culture is created – from the "outside in" – through continued exposure and relationships with external innovators. Finally, by licensing-out or selling unused products, technology and IP, companies not only capture economic value from the ideas, but also create a sense of urgency by internal groups to "use it or lose it" when it comes to internally available technologies.

Collaborative approaches, joint ventures and strategic alliances are on a growth path because companies' prosperity and growth depend upon them. "Much like an ecosystem, companies are recognizing their successes depend upon a delicate balance of interdependencies within a much broader network of potential partners", according to Docherty[27]. The great majority – 64 percent of U.S. executives surveyed – indicate that they plan to increase their use of strategic alliances during the next two years;[28] and almost 70 percent of the executives said that strategic alliances help companies reach growth objectives in part because they promised attractive returns and shared risk. "Open-market innovation" was included for the first time among twenty-five key management tools studied in a major management practices study, where it is reported to be employed by more than 24 percent of respondents.[29]

## Words of Caution About Open Innovation

Partnering and external collaboration in innovation is not new and it's certainly no panacea! Note that many of the recent books and articles that promote open innovation have been based on only a handful of companies and a few case studies; but they fail to draw on the long tradition of research into the field of collaboration and partnering in innovation – studies that provide many insights into its benefits and pitfalls.

One comprehensive study of 88 development projects (half partnering, the other half in-house) revealed that there are no real performance differences between partnerships and in-house projects on any performance metric.[30] Regardless of the performance measure – financial outcomes, adherence to the budget and time-line, or whether the new product opened up new windows of opportunity – partnership projects do not yield better (or worse) results compared to in-house ones. Some useful conclusions from this study:

- Recognize that external relationships do cost time and effort to establish and maintain. The appropriate type of new product development model should be determined in light of a careful evaluation of its potential benefits, and managers must carefully scrutinize development projects to ensure that partnering really does suit the nature of the project.
- Be alert to the *potential costs of partnerships.* For example, the payback in years was found to be considerably longer for partnerships than for in-house projects. Partnership projects may also consume more resources because of the additional costs and time of managing the complexities of cooperative initiatives.
- Finally, have *realistic expectations* about the outcomes of innovation partnering, for example, about how value gets shared between partners before committing to a new product development partnership.

In a similar vein, other studies over the last few decades on collaborative or externally-focused innovation reveal weaknesses that the proponents of open innovation fail to mention:

- Uncertainties exist when involving external partners in new product development. These arise from issues such as: partner selection; determining the timing and intensity of the involvement and commitment of each partner; the partner's ability and willingness to provide the right kind of knowledge; and the nature and extent of the knowledge to be embodied.[31]

- Tension between the logic of new product development and partnering may offset possible economic and technological advantages;[32] for example, difficulties may arise because of disagreements on the allocation of intellectual property rights.[33]

- In the case of manufacturing partnerships, a cooperative manufacturer risks ending up as nothing more than a subcontractor for key customers.[34]

- In the case of customer-partnering, such co-development with customers may result in ineffective new product development due to the customer's limited domain of expertise – focusing only on a single customer, rather than on the entire market.[35]

The results from these studies serve as a cautionary note to those who see partnering as the single solution to innovation and ignore the diversity of alternatives which not only exist but may be more appropriate in different contexts. The conclusions of many studies underscore the point that innovation and external partnering is no magic bullet for success.

## Procter & Gamble's Connect + Develop

Open innovation has had one of its most successful implementations at P&G. The entire world has now become the main source of innovation ideas for the company through P&G's highly successful Connect + Develop initiative.[36] Using IT and a well-crafted and user-friendly website, P&G opens its doors to would-be innovators, idea people, inventors, collaborators and problems solvers around the world.

## From R&D to Connect + Develop

What P&G realized is that the traditional model of innovation and invention from an internal bricks-and-mortar R&D lab would not yield the innovative products needed in the future. At P&G for example, it was clear that their "invent-it-ourselves" model was not capable of sustaining high levels of top-line growth.[37] The law of large numbers had caught up with P&G and is catching up with too many businesses: For example, if the goal is 30% of sales from new products launched in the previous five years, this means every year a $70 billion business such as P&G must generate $4 billion worth of new products!

The theory underlying Connect + Develop is that great innovations come from looking at the same things as everyone else and connecting them in different ways.[38] What P&G is looking for are those illogical, unpredictable and non-obvious connections, and also combinations of technologies that go well beyond their intended use. Linking technologies in unexpected ways is at the heart of innovation. When conceiving of the Connect + Develop model, P&G's management recognized that their best innovations had come from connecting ideas across internal businesses.[39] A study of the performance of the limited number of products acquired beyond their own labs revealed that external connections could produce highly profitable innovations too. Betting that these connections were the key to future growth, the CEO made it a goal to acquire 50 percent of innovations from outside the company. The strategy was not to replace the capabilities of their 7,500 researchers and support staff, but to better leverage them. The authors of the new system note:

> "We needed to move the company's attitude from resistance to innovations [that are] 'not invented here' to enthusiasm for those 'proudly found elsewhere.' And we needed to change how we defined, and perceived our R&D organization – from 7,500 people inside to 7,500 plus 1.5 million outside, with a permeable boundary between them."[40]

P&G's goal is simple: to be known as the company that collaborates – inside and out – better than any other company, and the absolute best at spotting, developing and leveraging relationships with best-in-class partners in every part of their business. Log onto the website and find out more about Connect + Develop at P&G: www.pgconnectdevelop.com (refer to Exhibit 5.5 for sample content). The website invites ordinary people and companies to submit ideas and proposals for ready-to-go products, packaging, technologies, processes and commercial connections that will result in game-changing innovation to address unmet consumer needs. Different categories of submissions are asked for, including:

- A game-changing technology or package, which is proven and can be quickly applied to a P&G consumer need.
- A ready-to-go product or device, which is already in use and has evidence of consumer interest (the product should offer a new consumer benefit to an existing company category or brand, has been demonstrated, and is patented or a patent is pending).

The webpage then walks the inventor or submitter through a number of questions and fields, including agreeing to some legal requirements, in order to submit their idea, product or technology. If the submission is a technology, then the submitter is directed to a different webpage and to a set of questions and fields specifically designed for technology submissions.

Connect + Develop also has components other than the externally focused webpage.[41] For example there is InnovationNet that acts as a global lunchroom where company researchers can trade information and make connections across the company. The target audience is 18,000 potential innovators within the company. Additionally, the company uses NineSigma software to link external scientists who log onto the webpage with those in the company best positioned to exploit the technology. Another tool is Innocentive, a web-based connection linked to thousands of scientists worldwide that are ready to submit solutions to technical problems that the company posts. The success rate here is about 50 percent.

*P&G* °ρ connect + develop

| PG.com | Connect + Develop Home | Search Technologies | Submit Product/Technology |

- We are currently looking for ready-to-go products, packaging, technologies, processes and commercial connections that will result in game-changing innovation to address unmet consumer needs.
- Do you have a game-changing technology or package?
  - This technology is proven and can be quickly applied to a P&G consumer need
  - This is a game-changing technology or approach
- Do you have a ready-to-go product or device?
  - This product is in use and has evidence of consumer interest
  - This product offers a new consumer benefit to an existing P&G category or brand
  - This product has been demonstrated and is patented or a patent is pending

EXHIBIT 5.5 Some excerpts from P&G's Connect + Develop webpage illustrate how the page provides a detailed but user-friendly process for people and companies to input their ideas, products or technologies.

## Does it work?

The proof is in the examples of successful innovations that have been developed or marketed by the company using this approach. Today, more than 35 percent of P&G's new products in market have elements that originated from outside the company, up from about 15 percent in 2000.[42] And 45 percent of the projects in their current product development portfolio have key elements that were discovered externally. The company's innovation success rate has more than doubled, while the cost of innovation has fallen: R&D investment as a percentage of sales is down from 4.8 percent in 2000 to 3.4 percent today. And, in the last two years, P&G had launched more than 100 new products for which some aspect of execution came from outside the company. Here are some examples:[43]

- By acquiring the newly introduced SpinBrush, P&G was able to bring a superior oral care product to market quickly without undertaking the time and expense of developing an entirely new product.

This allowed the inventor to benefit from connecting their product to an existing market leading brand.

- Several of Olay Skin Care products now utilize new pump dispensers originally developed by a European packaging products company. This connection allowed the developer to realize a greater return by leveraging the volume of an established global brand.
- P&G found the perfect complement to the Swiffer brand in a hand-held duster developed by a Japanese competitor. This connection allowed the smaller firm to leverage markets where they previously had no presence, and create an on-going win-win partnership with P&G.

## Positioning Your Company to Acquire Ideas, Concepts and Products From External Sources

One problem with open innovation is that it has become an all encompassing term that includes almost everything the company does with someone or something outside that company – from outsourcing R&D and marketing to soliciting ideas from private inventors. Note the great diversity in how the term "open innovation" is interpreted and implemented in the different company examples above. So where does one begin?

### The Role of Open Innovation

This book is primarily focused on getting ideas, concepts and inventions to feed your development funnel or pipeline. So here's how open innovation should play a role:

- Search for new product or new service ideas from a wide variety of sources outside your company, well beyond the traditional internal and external idea sources.
- Seek developed products (or products already in the market) ready

for launch by you (for example, in-licensing or marketing agreements).

- Hunt for technologies – those under development or fully developed – that could spawn new products for you.

Now, here are some tips and hints on how to proceed to integrate open innovation into your product innovation efforts:

## Design and Implement a Process

Processes are not a total answer, but they are a start. Identify your potential sources of innovative ideas, and then *map out a process for how ideas and technologies will be acquired*, handled, processed, evaluated and moved forward. It's a fairly complex process! And you are also likely looking at some investment in IT – a webpage to solicit ideas and technologies from external sources (as in P&G's case); a method to get ideas and technologies to knowledgeable people within your company (or even to outsiders) for evaluation and review; and a system to track each idea and its progress; and an easy-to-access electronic vault that stores inactive ideas with potential.

> *Example:* For some years, P&G has relied on a robust idea-to-launch process, or Stage-Gate® system, to drive internal development projects to market.[44] P&G's model, called SIMPL, has been a very important tool in P&G's successes in product innovation over the last decade. But in this new world of open innovation, SIMPL has been modified, so that the latest version of the process – SIMPL 3.0 – now incorporates external Connect + Develop projects as well.

## Work On the Needed Culture Change

Recognize that open innovation is here to stay. In spite of this evident truth, *grassroots resistance from the internal technical community* is certain to occur, as your technical people feel a threat to their job security, egos and importance.[45] Communication to and with your internal technical community is vital, so that they understand the new model and its rationale, and can better appreciate that their role is more important than ever. Appropriate rewards and recognition will also be required in order to help overcome resistance – for example, rewards that are made to the internal group regardless of the source of the idea or solution.

## Put the Resources in Place – a "Search, Connect and Develop" Team

Open innovation is not free! Indeed, it takes significant effort to access multiple external sources for ideas and technology, then review and evaluate the many opportunities or ideas, and work with partners on specific projects. Most of the example companies cited have put together a formal organization or team to make open innovation work: Nokia's Venturing Group, P&G's Connect + Develop team and Air Products Corporate Technology Partnerships Group. There is a lot of legwork needed in order to solicit, review, assess, evaluate and flesh-out the ideas, concepts and technologies that come in from outside the company – ask any venture capitalist who is used to looking at dozens, sometimes hundreds, of ideas before investing. Thus, you must organize and staff up for the effort – *put in place a "Search, Connect and Develop" team*. Also, recognize that an increasing proportion of the R&D or traditional development budget must be allocated to open innovation efforts.

## Know Where to Search

Put in place *the right people with the right mindset* in this quest for innovative ideas and to undertake the initial screening or filtering of these concepts.[46] If the people you select to staff your "Search, Connect and Develop" team are too narrow-minded – for example, they search and connect only in traditional or obvious places, such as other large companies or on Internet bulletin boards – then you'll miss many of the opportunities. And if they lack a creative mind, and cannot imagine

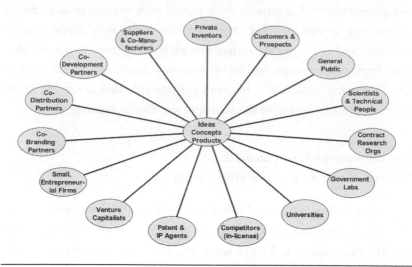

EXHIBIT 5.6 In your search for new and innovative ideas, concepts and fully developed products, practice open innovation. Have an open mind-set and reach out to multiple sources.

possibilities for the future, then they will surely filter out all but the most conservative ideas, and again you miss the game-changers.

Instead, put in place creative people with an open mindset to access and evaluate non-traditional sources of ideas and inspiration for your innovations – inventors, universities, entrepreneurial start-ups, small businesses, government labs, both domestically and abroad – that can give you your next aha (see Exhibit 5.6).

## Learn to Live With and Deal With the Risk

Do not apply your traditional thinking and criteria to these venturesome and innovative projects! *Too rigorous a filter will kill all but the sure-bets!* In most companies, traditional R&D projects are subjected to intensive scrutiny as they pass from stage-to-stage and gate-to-gate in the typical Stage-Gate innovation process. At each gate, they must meet certain criteria in order to secure resources and move forward. Many of these criteria are financial. If you apply the same rigorous financial criteria to many of these open innovation concepts or potential projects, however, they will not make the grade – there is just too much uncertainty, too many unknowns, and it's too early to say just what the numbers will look like.

Dealing with risk means changing your culture and being prepared to gamble a certain percentage of your portfolio resources on more venturesome projects. And it means adopting criteria other than your traditional ones for evaluating such venturesome and higher-risk projects. For example, consider using a scorecard approach in lieu of traditional tools to evaluate these would-be projects.[47]

## Practice Discipline

Just because open innovation may be a relatively new business model for you does not mean that you throw out all your effective business practices and discipline, and start winging it! Learn from the venture capitalists – they practice discipline, and have developed a number of best practices designed to filter, review, scrutinize and move forward solid ideas and concepts. Use a Stage-Gate process, but *a different one* than what you use for traditional projects – an example is the Stage-Gate process designed for high-risk technology developments.[48] More on project evaluation and moving projects forward in Chapter 7.

# Beyond Open Innovation: Other Sources of External Ideas

Other valuable external sources of ideas for new products and services exist, and may fall outside the accepted definition of open innovation. Many of these are well-known sources, so we don't spend as much time on them in this book. But do not dismiss these sources just because they have been known for a number of years. They are tried-and-proven external sources of exceptional ideas for new products.

## Patent Mapping

Patents are an outstanding but all too often overlooked source of valuable information, including ideas for new products.[49] The amount of knowledge contained in patents is enormous but somewhat overwhelming to access and interpret. For example, as of May 2005, there were almost 42 million patents filed in total globally, and these are increasing at a rate of about 4% annually.

Patent mapping involves the distillation and interpretation of large amounts of often complex patent data into one or more high-value representations useful in making business decisions.[50] The goal is to generate actionable intelligence from raw patent information, enabling timely, informed decisions. Usually the maps are visual, as in Exhibit 5.7, and are usually prepared by an external patent mapping firm or internal expert in patent mapping.

For innovators, patent mapping helps the user to conceptualize the intellectual property space and serves as a trigger for new product

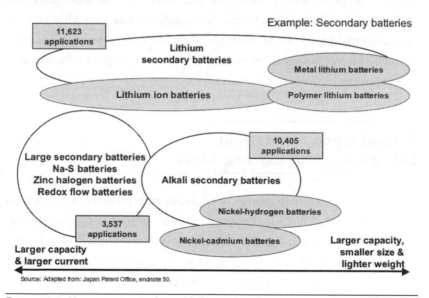

Source: Adapted from: Japan Patent Office, endnote 50.

EXHIBIT 5.7  Use patent mapping to define areas of strong competitive activity. This is a signal that a field is "hot" and worth focusing on for ideation.

ideation and selecting development areas to focus on. For example, if considerable patent and filing activity is noted in a particular field or area, that is a signal – a signal that technologists somewhere are onto something and, more importantly, that management sees that this area is sufficiently interesting to spend the time and money to file a patent.[51] Thus *hot areas in technology* can be spotted – emerging areas, and areas that are seen as having potential. Note that forecasters and futurologists often use the methodology of counting the citations in a field – for example the number of times something is mentioned in magazines or newspapers – as a means of predicting a trend or event; for example, Naisbitt's *Megatrends* book was based on spotting the number of times something was cited in print.[52]

> *Example:* One major chemical company takes patent mapping even further. By accessing the online patent offices (for example, the U.S. Patent Office), patent mappers drill down into a technology area, identify the patents, sort them by competitor, and identify what competitors are working on in their R&D program. The names of the people on the patents are noted, and these names are searched for publications and conference papers, even going back to their days at university and what their PhD thesis was about. In this way, a solid competitive analysis focused on technology activity is possible.
>
> This type of analysis is key not only to understanding where the competitor is heading and what they are working on, but what new products might be anticipated from that competitor. By understanding the competitor's R&D direction and anticipating his product launches, the company is able to identify what new products it will require in order to stay ahead of or at least remain even with the competitor. Hence this methodology becomes a source of strategically-driven ideas for development.

For researchers, patent mapping also deals with the vital question: What do we need to "engineer around" to avoid patent related roadblocks? And for product developers, patent mapping helps to select product components and features to mitigate intellectual property risk and get to market sooner.

## Competitors Trigger Ideas[53]

Competitors represent another valuable source of new product ideas. The objective is *not to copy your competitors* – copycat products have a much lower chance of success – but to generate ideas for new products with competitive advantage. Often the knowledge of a competitive product will stimulate your team in arriving at an even better product idea.

Recognize that being the industry innovator is not the only strategy in product innovation. Indeed there is no clear evidence that being first into a market necessarily guarantees success – there are countless examples of where the pioneer failed, but the number two into the market learned from the pioneer's mistakes, and launched second but much better.[54] Thus being a fast follower is a very viable strategy in product development. But the trick is not being merely a copycat fast follower, but rather a fast follower who seizes upon a competitive idea, and then launches something even better:

> *Example:* Precision Biologics specializes in the development of diagnostic test-kit products for use in hospitals.[55] Being a smaller firm, it does not have the resources to consistently develop revolutionary and unique technologies for diagnostics in this fast-moving field. Rather, its strategy is to watch the more innovative companies with deeper pockets, to observe when a competitive product is selling well, and then to develop and launch something that is "uniquely better" than the competition – "simple innovations that make a significant difference from the customer perspective". Often the key to "uniquely better" is the extensive VoC work that the company undertakes at hospitals. This formula has been a success, and has enabled this smaller firm, started in 1994, to achieve a 26.5% annual compound growth rate in sales over ten years from 1996 to 2006!

Routinely survey your competition. Periodically perform a complete review of competitive products, particularly new ones. Obtain a sample of your competitor's new product. Once obtained, undertake a thorough evaluation of the product from a technical standpoint. Arrange an internal brainstorming session aimed at improving on your competitor's product. Better yet, rip your competitor's product apart using inverse brainstorming – identify everything that's wrong with it! Be sure to determine how well the product is doing in the marketplace from published data or from your sales force and customers. Obtain copies of the advertising and literature for the product: Knowing what the competitor is emphasizing or how it is positioning the product can yield new insights for your own new products. And use VoC to assess your competitors' products' strengths and weakness, and gain insights into how *you can be uniquely better.*

Yet another competitive technique with some promise is to *anticipate your competitor's product roadmap.* That is, assign a team of people in your company to play the role of the competitor in a specific product-market space. They undertake a thorough competitive analysis, look at the competitor's recent and past product launches and the timing and scope of these. They also look at the competitor's patent activities – for example, what he is filing. Based on this and other competitive information (for example, media and PR announcements, annual reports, analysis of its current product line), the team then maps out a series of expected competitive new products in this product-market space – the probable product roadmap, indicating what new products with what performance, and when. An understanding of what the competitors' likely launches will be provides a valuable input to a strategic session to help define new products needed by your company. For example, one strategic question you must address is: "Given that these are our competitor's probable product launches and their timing over the next five years, what new products do we need to stay ahead and even to leapfrog way out ahead of them?"

## Trade Shows – An Excellent Source

Trade shows present the perfect opportunity to uncover dozens of ideas at relatively little expense. Where else can you find all that's new in your field displayed for public consumption? And where else can you find customers ready to give their opinions on new products presented at the show?

Organize a trade show visitation program. Get a list of the relevant trade shows in your industry. Arrange to have at least one person visit each show, even if your firm is not displaying, for the sole purpose of getting new product ideas. This should not be a social event but a serious intelligence mission. Arm your intelligence officer with a sketch pad, a notebook, and a list of key exhibitors. The task is to visit each of the key exhibit booths and to itemize and describe new products on display. Sketches and brochures add detail to this description. At the end of the trip, your intelligence officer's task is to make a formal presentation to the rest of the new products group: "Here's what I found that was new at the show, and here are some product ideas that we might build on."

## Trade Publications Provide Ideas From Around the World

As most intelligence officers will attest, the majority of "intelligence information" is in the public domain – it's just a matter of gaining access to it in a regular and coordinated fashion.

Trade publications report new product introductions via advertisements and new product announcement sections. Like a trade show, these publications provide the stimuli for your group to conceive an even better idea. Do not ignore foreign publications: In some countries, new products may be years or months ahead of yours and may feature unfamiliar competitors who offer products that you've never seen before. So hire an outside search company, domestically and abroad, to gather relevant ads, articles and announcements in selected journals. Alternately, set up an internal search group, assigning different publications to each person in your group. Most publications are now available online making this a much more cost effective technique than in the past.

## Suppliers – An Untapped Source

Suppliers are often a good source of new product ideas and help. This is particularly so when the supplier is a large firm with well–funded R&D and customer applications or technical service facilities. Suppliers too are looking for new applications for their products, and often come up with ideas for their customers. Have your technical and marketing people regularly visit your supplier's lab and technical service facilities; and stay in close touch with your supplier's technical people. Chances are they are working on a development that could lead to your next new product winner.

## Universities – A Brain Trust in Your Back Yard

University professors and researchers are a potentially rich source of breakthrough ideas. Scholars working in science, engineering or medicine can offer a wealth of information on developments in their fields and may indeed have the seeds to your next breakthrough product:

> *Examples:* In the 1960s, the U.S. Defense Department sponsored a project to tie computers together called DARPA (Defense Advanced Research Projects Agency). DARPA had no practical use at the time, but along came a graduate student at Stanford who built a little device to put on the DARPA net and he called it a workstation. He ended up starting a company called Sun Microsystems, which stands for Stanford University Network.
>
> And then there was a husband and wife team, both graduate students, who were building little boxes that moved the data around. They called their devices "routers" and started a little company called Cisco. But it took almost two decades before any of this technology reached the marketplace.[56]

Disparate information and its transmission are keys to innovation, according to a Stanford Business School study.[57] The research shows that the most creative entrepreneurs spend less time than average networking with business colleagues who are friends and more time networking with a diverse group that includes acquaintances and strangers: "Entrepreneurs who spend more time with a diverse network of strong and weak ties... are three times more likely to innovate than entrepreneurs stuck within a uniform network."[58] Not surprisingly, universities with their eclectic diversity are proving to be effective hunting grounds for entrepreneurial companies seeking radically new approaches to problems that can result in game-changing outcomes.

> *Example:* Procter & Gamble conjectured that the solution to their cold-water cleaning problem would be in a laboratory that is studying enzymatic reactions in microbes that thrive under polar ice caps. The University of Auckland, which at the time was one of four universities in the world with an established protocol for working with Procter & Gamble on open innovation, turned out to be a source not only of enzymes from Antarctica but also relevant connections to local business and industry throughout the region.[59]

Researchers at universities may lack an appreciation of the commercial potential of their work or the ability to commercialize it, however. In order to exploit this source, consider establishing contact with key researchers in your field at various universities. Where were the IBMs and AT&Ts when these graduate students, who went on to start Sun Microsystems and Cisco, were playing with their concepts? To help put companies in touch with key researchers, innovation centers and technology transfer centers have been set up at a number of universities in order to help professors commercialize their inventions. So locate these innovation centers and technology transfer centers and make contact with them.

# CHAPTER 6

# Harness the Brainpower of Your Own Employees

The vitality of thought is in adventure. Ideas won't keep.
Something must be done about them.
—ALFRED NORTH WHITEHEAD (1861–1947)
*English logician, mathematician and philosopher*

The need for every employee in your company to be actively engaged in the Discovery or Ideation stage of your innovation process has never been greater. But saying that is not enough! In this chapter, we explore concrete and actionable ways for you to better connect with your employees for innovation ideas and to make them a valuable and productive part of the discovery or ideation process.

## Set Up an Idea Suggestion System – A Potentially Prolific Source

Your employees are an excellent source of new product ideas! Tap into this source on a continuous basis. Whenever we see an organization where employees do not submit lots of new product, new service or even new business ideas, we invariably see…

- *no encouragement to employees*: ideas are not welcome
- *a NIH attitude* – "not invented here"; management rejects anything that is not their own idea, and employees soon get the message and stop submitting ideas
- *no action*: people submit ideas but nothing happens – ideas seem to go into a black hole
- *no incentives*: idea submitters are not rewarded nor recognized, and they are often ridiculed for their off-the-wall or "wild" ideas, and
- *nothing ever comes of the ideas*: management reviews the list of ideas, but their minds are closed – they have already made up their minds as to which projects to do, and these new ideas are just not on the list.

What is surprising is how many companies fail to welcome opportunities and ideas on an ongoing basis from their own employees in a systematic way: Less than one-quarter of businesses have an *active and focused new product ideas solicitation system* in operation – see Exhibit 6.1. But by a four-to-one ratio, best performers do have an idea suggestion system to actively solicit new product and new service ideas from their own people.

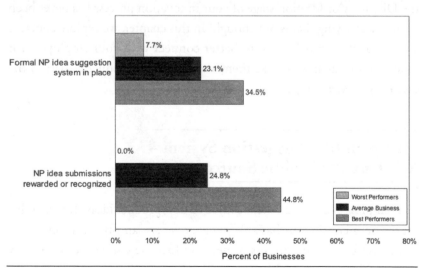

EXHIBIT 6.1 Best performers put a formal new product idea suggestion system in place, and reward or recognize idea submitters.

Implement a new product idea suggestion scheme designed to seek new product ideas from your employees. And make this suggestion scheme a part of your total idea management system pictured in Exhibit 1.14 in Chapter 1.

*A best practice example:* Swarovski, the Austrian crystal and jewelry company, has established a best-in-class idea gathering and handling system as a front end to their Stage-Gate product innovation process – see Exhibit 6.2.[1] Ideas are solicited from employees – they are easily submitted via their new software system, i-FLASH. Ideas go to the i-LAB, an eight-person idea support, handling and management group. This group does a preliminary evaluation of the idea using strategic criteria, and then develops, enriches and enhances the idea to the point where it can be evaluated. These *enriched ideas* are sent to key people in the company via the i-FLASH software for a thorough evaluation, comments and suggestions.

This feedback is then used by the i-LAB to create a full "visualization

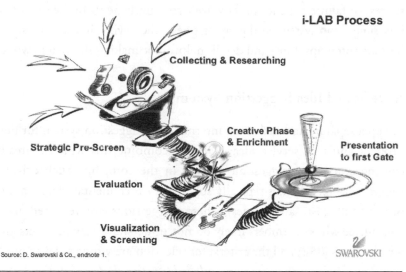

**i-LAB Process**

Collecting & Researching

Strategic Pre-Screen

Creative Phase & Enrichment

Presentation to first Gate

Evaluation

Visualization & Screening

Source: D. Swarovski & Co., endnote 1.

SWAROVSKI

EXHIBIT 6.2  Ideas are solicited from employees globally in the idea system employed at D. Swarovski & Co. Ideas are enhanced by the company's i-LAB while i-FLASH software facilitates the handling and screening of ideas.

of the idea" – a solid concept with drawings or sketches and a description. This visualized idea is then presented to Gate 1 in the appropriate business unit in the company's Stage-Gate process. Note: If the idea does not fit any of the existing business units, but it still is a worthy one, then it goes to Gate 1 in the new business group and potentially becomes an entirely new business for the corporation.

Your electronic suggestion box can be an ongoing scheme, in which ideas are reviewed and awards made on a continuous basis; or it can be a contest over time but with a finite end, with prizes awarded for the top ideas. You can even add a little fun to the contest, awarding prizes for the top ideas in different categories: the "most outrageous idea", the "coolest idea", the "most original idea" and the "biggest money-maker".

Many companies experience great success with their new product idea suggestion systems. However, management in too many firms claim that their idea system does not work – that the ideas are useless – and thus they gave up the scheme after a year or so. Like anything else in business, success or failure depends on how well you implement. In the case of an idea suggestion system, as the saying goes, "the devil is in the details!" So here are some tips, hints and details helpful for making the system work.

## A Dedicated Idea Suggestion System

Set up a separate and dedicated internal idea suggestion system for new product and new service ideas. Do not combine this with an already existing contest or suggestion scheme in the company. Such existing suggestion-box schemes typically solicit very incremental ideas (they're often small cost saving ones); these suggestions are reviewed by a committee whose members likely do not understand new products and new business ideas; and the criteria for selection are wrong for new products. You need a *special, separate and visible internal idea suggestion system* focused only on new products. But be sure to integrate this internal idea suggestion scheme into your total idea management system shown in

Exhibit 1.14 in Chapter 1: Internal ideas are an important, but not the only source of innovation.

## Give Your Idea System a Home – Then Manage It

Idea generation is everyone's job and no one's responsibility! There is no one in the business charged specifically with the responsibility of idea generation. And often when ideas do surface in the business, there is no one to send it to for action. And so good ideas wither and die on the vine.

*Locate your idea suggestion system in an I-Group.* An idea solicitation scheme needs to be managed and it requires some effort to keep it sustained. Do not just launch it, and then cast it adrift! Recall from Chapter 1 that we highlighted the need for idea management and also the need to establish a group to do the work – to capture, screen and move forward robust ideas – namely an *I-Group*. This I-Group is the logical team to manage your internal idea suggestion system.

Part of this management task is to set goals for the number of ideas. Then periodically track the ideas – track what happened to the ideas that passed the first screen and how much value they created for the company – in order to gauge how well the idea suggestion system performs.

Annually review the system and make needed adjustments and improvements. Rarely do idea suggestion systems work perfectly the first time. Invariably there are wrinkles and glitches that need adjustment. For example, most companies' electronic submission forms are too detailed and demanding when first designed, and need simplification to encourage (rather than thwart) creativity. Areas of strategic focus and what constitutes a "good idea" are not clear on the webpage. And the rules for winning or requirements for submission are too restrictive or negative.

*Example:* In one major computer hardware company, the "rules book" for their idea submission system went on for pages and looked like it had been prepared by the legal department. It was more onerous than reading and completing an income tax return. This was a huge turn-off to most employees.

Some rules are necessary, for example rules about ownership of intellectual property (the employee's idea becomes the property of the
company), and rules about how winners are decided in the event of
group submission or when two very similar ideas are submitted at the
same time (don't be a tight-wad; err on the side of generosity). The point
is that your rules, procedures and system may need adjusting from time-
to-time, so annually review and improve the system.

## Publicize the Idea System

Promote the system so that everyone in the business is aware of it – on
posters, bulleting boards, emails and via a webpage. In countless companies
we visit, when we ask, "Do you have an active new product idea suggestion scheme." Half the meeting attendees are not sure!

> *Example:* One major Danish pump manufacturer – considered a
> best-in-class firm in its country – openly and strongly promotes
> creativity and innovation at every opportunity; from the company's
> annual report, which devotes more pages to product innovation than
> to finances, through to its showcase of new products that occupies its
> entire headquarters' front lobby, to its campaign of posters seen
> everywhere on company premises emphasizing innovation and the
> need to submit new ideas. Even the company bus that drives visitors
> to the airport has their motto on the side in big, bold letters: "See >
> Be > Innovate". And guess what, they do – they boast a highly
> motivated staff – both junior and senior people – who are strongly
> committed to product innovation.

## Handle Ideas Promptly

Nothing will kill idea generation more than a lack of timely feedback. In
some businesses, ideas are given an immediate quick strategic screen, and
then get worked on by the I-Group to enhance and visualize the idea, as
they do at Swarovski. Then they are submitted to Gate 1 for a formal

screen. In other companies, the raw ideas go directly to Gate 1 for an immediate screen. Either way, these initial screens must occur quickly and effectively. And be sure to provide timely feedback to the submitter – what the decision was and what the status of the idea is.

## Welcome All Ideas

No idea is a bad one. And do not subject a person's idea to ridicule or create embarrassment for the submitter. Sometimes the craziest ideas spawn others that are brilliant.

> *Example:* The Vice President of Marketing for a manufacturer of garden pesticides and chemicals complained bitterly about how ineffective his recently-launched idea suggestion scheme was. "I think we got more ideas before we had the system in place", he griped. A closer inspection of the electronic submission form revealed that the idea proposer first had to submit the idea to their boss for initial review, before submitting it to the electronic suggestion box. It was this in-between step and the potential embarrassment of a boss being critical of an idea that caused most junior people simply not to submit ideas. When the requirement for a pre-review by the boss was removed, idea submissions soared!

## Provide Guidance

Clearly some ideas are better than others. So, *do provide guidance, direction and assistance* to enhance the quality of ideas submitted. Set up an internal webpage so that idea submitters can log on and gain insights into what types of ideas are being sought, how ideas are evaluated and what criteria are used, and what constitutes a good idea. Lay out your business's areas of focus – your strategic arenas where ideas are especially needed (Chapter 2 showed the importance of defining strategic arenas). And show examples: Often, merely illustrating examples of good ideas on an idea webpage, and explaining why they are good, provides much needed guidance and encouragement.

> *Example:* When Guinness Ireland first implemented its internal idea suggestion scheme in the 1990s, the Gate 1 screening committee – a cross-functional team of mid-level managers – gathered anxiously to review the first batch of ideas. It was not a positive meeting!
>
> Idea #1: Why don't we sell beer-flavored potato crisps (potato chips)?
>
> Idea #2: We should market beer nuts for eating with Guinness stout.
>
> Idea #3: We should have a line of Guinness snack foods.
>
> And the ideas went downhill from there. "Don't these people understand what business we're in?" exclaimed an exasperated product manager after perusing the first dozen ideas. Apparently not. Guinness' management quickly modified the idea system so that when employees logged on they immediately saw the critical areas of focus – a strategic definition of the business, the market segments Guinness was targeting (for example, the female drinker), some information on each key segment, and the types of innovations wanted (for example, innovative packaging concepts).

## Rewards and Recognition

People do what they are incented to do! Thus, consider establishing *rewards or recognition for ideas.* About one-quarter of companies do have a rewards or recognition scheme for new product ideas (see Exhibit 6.1). But by a considerable majority, best performers offer rewards and recognition for ideas, while poor performers do not. Of the two approaches – rewards versus recognition – recognition is the more popular and favored as it tends to create fewer problems and is easier to install:

> *Examples:* At Kraft Foods, recognition for ideas is important. For example, in the Meals division, the Division General Manager

awards employees with squeezable light bulbs for developing ideas and with awards for "Innovator of the Month" and "Innovator of the Year". Recognition at Kraft is typically not monetary, but involves peer praise or pride of ownership, which is viewed as more effective than financial rewards. The company works hard at ensuring people know that new product ideas are important and valued.

Bausch & Lomb uses limited monetary rewards as a method to reward new ideas. The employee can get anywhere from $5 to $5,000, depending on how far the idea progresses through the product innovation process.[2]

Some companies do offer significant rewards for employees who submit breakthrough new product ideas. But great care must be exercised in the design of the system, because often poorly crafted rules can actually thwart ideation.

*Example:* Saint-Gobain in France and its U.S. subsidiary, CertainTeed, have implemented a very professional ideas scheme in which all employees globally can participate. Individuals or groups submit ideas, and receive points as their idea passes from gate to gate in their five-stage, five-gate Stage-Gate product innovation process. If the idea passes the first gate, it receives a token number of points; a pass at Gate 2 merits more points, and so on with more points being awarded at successive gates. And if the idea is so good that the eventual product is launched into the market – it passes Gate 5 – the submitter or submission-team receives a huge number of points. These points are accumulated and are redeemed for prizes, including significant travel and vacation prizes. And when groups of two or three people submit an idea together, the points are multiplied by the number of people – there is no penalty for working collaboratively!

A summary of these tips and hints for making suggestion schemes work is in Exhibit 6.3.

- Set up a separate, dedicated & visible idea system
  - ➢ Focused solely on new products and new services
- Locate the idea system in your I-Group & manage the system
  - ➢ Set goals
  - ➢ Annually review & track ideas
  - ➢ Adjust & improve the system
- Publicize the scheme widely via promotion
- Handle ideas promptly; provide fast feedback
- Welcome all ideas
  - ➢ Make it easy to submit – an electronic suggestion box
- Provide guidance, direction & assistance
  - ➢ Webpage (Intranet)
  - ➢ Lay out areas of focus – your strategic arenas
  - ➢ Define what constitutes a "good idea" & how ideas are evaluated
- Offer incentives or recognition

EXHIBIT 6.3 Get the details right in your idea suggestion system – here are some hints.

## Provide Scouting Time and Resources to Promote Creativity

One reason why 3M has been so innovative over the years is that 3M *pays people to be innovative* and it *gives them the time to be innovative.* One cannot expect employees to suddenly turn on the creative juices at 4:30 on Friday afternoon after a hectic week. A handful of progressive firms encourage select groups of employees to be creative by providing free time – "scouting time" – and some financial help for personal projects – see Exhibit 6.4. But note how much best performers embrace this practice, while poor performing businesses do not allow free time for creative work!

Some divisions at 3M have a day–a–week rule for technical employees: R&D people are encouraged to work on their own "discovery" projects with the hope that some useful idea, for example, another Post–It Notes product will result. According to executives at 3M, some of the best projects come from these Friday projects. Rohm and Haas, Kraft Foods and W.L. Gore (makers of Gore-Tex) allow about 10-15 percent of a technical person's time for scouting work to devote to personal projects. Not only is time available, but many best performing companies also provide financial resources to cover out–of–pocket costs (for example, equipment or materials needs) for informal projects – see Exhibit 6.4. Not every employee takes part in these free time projects, of course. The hope is that a handful of these creative and passionate people will – a self-selected group – and that innovative ideas will be the result.

Using scouting time, it is often possible to progress a project well down the pipeline before asking for formal approval and funding. "Isn't this dangerous?" ask some people. Yes and no – it depends on how far down the pipeline the project progresses. Some companies, that have implemented formal product innovation processes, are happy to see these scouting projects arrive as late as Gate 2 or even Gate 3 (that is, Stage 1 and 2 have been undertaken "outside the system" and using scouting time). We agree. The argument is that highly innovative, embryonic ideas are fragile things; and perhaps a select few should be handled in a special way. But the majority won't follow this route, nor should they. Otherwise you truly *would have chaos!*

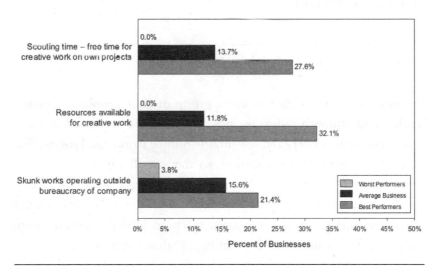

EXHIBIT 6.4 Stimulate internal creativity by providing scouting time (free time for employees' own projects) and resources. Try skunk works. The best performers do!

**Try Skunk Works**

Finally, best performing companies encourage the establishment of skunk works. These are project teams that *operate outside the official bureaucracy and control of the corporation.* Patterned after a WWII model in the aircraft industry, the leader of these self-managed teams reports directly to a senior executive – for example, to the President or General Manager – while the team members themselves do not report in the traditional way to functional bosses, only to the team leader. The team is in effect "outside the company", except for the leader's direct reporting arrangement.

The model is based on a team of engineers who were working on new WWII aircraft designs, housed in a tent, and operating essentially outside the Lockheed company in the 1940s. The organizational design not only allows much greater freedom and creativity – team members are not under direct control of traditional and potentially conservative functional bosses – it also promotes dedication, focus and strong team commitment. While not a dominant organizational design in product innovation, these self-managed teams or skunk works are embraced by best performing companies by a five-to-one ratio when compared to worse performing businesses (Exhibit 6.4).

## Use Group Creativity Methods

Brainstorming is a great way for a group of your people to generate radical and innovative ideas for new products and services. But many managers do not understand how brainstorming works and how to effectively run a brainstorming session, so they are disappointed with the results. Brainstorming is not a group of folks getting together for a casual discussion about what products we need for next year. Nor is it a quick encounter during a break at the coffee machine. Indeed, there exist some very specific do's and don'ts in running a brainstorming session. So here is a quick primer on the theory underlying brainstorming and how to make it work.

Whenever a group of adults get together to try to solve a problem, *two different thought processes* are observed by researchers (outlined in Exhibit 6.5):[3]

1. *Suggesting ideas:* Members of the group make suggestions about what to do: "Let's try this as a solution," someone suggests. This behavior is the act of being creative, free and imaginative; the emphasis is on quantity of ideas – the more the better. It is behavior from the gut and is *childlike behavior.* This divergent process is shown on the left side of Exhibit 6.5.

2. *Evaluating ideas:* The group evaluates or critiques the ideas: "That solution won't work because...". This behavior is analytical, evaluative, intellectual, critical and restrictive. It is typical *adultlike behavior* – what we are trained to do – to have a critical or analytical mind. This convergent process – narrowing down the list of ideas to the better ones – is shown on the right side of Exhibit 6.5.

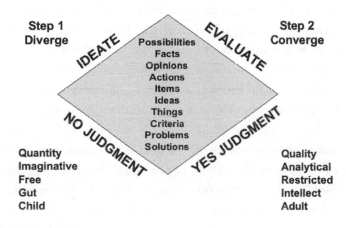

Source: M. Basadur, endnote 3.

**EXHIBIT 6.5** Two modes of management thinking include divergent or creative and child-like behavior (left) and convergent or more adultlike, evaluative behavior (right side). For ideation, operate on the left side.

The dilemma is that when a group of adults meet to solve a problem, guess where they spend most of their time? On the right side of Exhibit 6.5, doing the evaluative, analytical and adultlike work. That's where adults are most comfortable. But the purpose of the meeting is to brainstorm new ideas, to think outside the box and not to spend the entire meeting critiquing ideas.

The solution is this: Deliberately split the two behaviors into two different meetings. For the first session, operate strictly on the creative and imaginative mode – the divergent, left side of Exhibit 6.5. Then, in a later session, regroup and converge – critique, evaluate and rate the ideas – the right side of Exhibit 6.5. Thus, for ideation to work, the two modes of behavior must be kept very separate.

The four rules of good brainstorming are quite simple:[4]

*1. No criticism:* Operate only in the divergent mode, which means that no criticism or evaluation is allowed during the brainstorming or ideation session. The participants focus on making suggestions, generating ideas and extending or adding to each idea; and they reserve criticism for later. By suspending judgment, you create a supportive atmosphere where participants feel free to generate unusual ideas. That means no "yes buts" or "we tried that last year" comments. Show the list of unacceptable phrases listed in Exhibit 6.6 to the group to reveal what is not allowed. Get everyone's understanding and agreement to the rules. Then start. A best-practice set-up for the brainstorming session is shown in exhibit 6.7.[5]

*2. Focus on quantity:* This rule enhances divergent production of ideas. It is based on the premise that *quantity breeds quality.* That is, the greater the number of ideas generated, the greater the chance of producing a radical and effective idea. So do not be timid about keeping the session going for some time – 30 to 60 minutes, and maybe longer in the case of a large group. Even if there are periods of silence, do not give up and quit. It's alright to have silent thinking going on. Indeed, research shows that the frequency of ideas does indeed decrease in the last third of the session, but the quality of ideas does not. Good ideas may still be forthcoming. Exhibit 6.8 shows suggested best-practice procedures for running a brainstorming session, along with some tips on how to make the session more effective.

| | | | |
|---|---|---|---|
| 1. | It's a good idea, but... | 15. | The old-timers won't use it |
| 2. | It's against company policy | 16. | It's too hard to administer |
| 3. | It's all right in theory | 17. | We've been doing it this way for a long time |
| 4. | Be practical | | |
| 5. | It costs too much | 18. | If it's such a good idea, why hasn't someone suggested it before? |
| 6. | Don't start anything yet | | |
| 7. | It needs more study | | |
| 8. | It's not budgeted | 19. | You're ahead of the times |
| 9. | It's not part of your job | 20. | Let's discuss it |
| 10. | It's not good enough | 21. | Let's form a committee |
| 11. | Let's make a survey | 22. | We've never done it that way |
| 12. | Let's sit on it for a while | 23. | Who else has tried it? |
| 13. | That's not our problem | 24. | That won't sell |
| 14. | The boss won't go for it | 25. | Too many technical hurdles |

EXHIBIT 6.6 Here are twenty-five killer phrases that should not be used in your brainstorming session. Show these to remind participants what is not allowed.

### Brainstorming: The Preliminaries

- Invite the right attendees.
- Provide some pre-reading materials to provide background information on the topic and to get attendees thinking.
- When the session starts, define the problem clearly and lay out the criteria to be met. Define your problem or issue as a creative challenge
- Keep the challenge statement concise. Exclude any information other than the challenge itself. For example: "In what ways can we create a solution to this customer problem?"
- Explain the rules of brainstorming. Use the two exhibits – 6.5 and 6.6 – to explain how brainstorming works.
- Get agreement to the rules. Consider agreeing to and imposing a small penalty for anyone that breaks this "no criticism" rule, such as a small fine.
- Run a practice or warm-up session for a few minutes on a randomly selected brainstorming topic. For example: "new ideas for kitchen refrigerators".

EXHIBIT 6.7 The right set up or "preliminaries" is an important part of an effective brainstorming session. Use this list.

During the brainstorm session, if the energy level wanes, the facilitator should boost creativity by posing a lead question, such as: "Can we combine those ideas?" or "How about a look from another perspective?". Prepare a list of such lead questions before the session.

*3. Unusual ideas are welcome:* To generate a robust and long list of ideas, be sure to welcome unusual ideas. They may open new ways of thinking and provide better solutions than regular ideas. Unusual ideas can be generated by looking at the issue from another perspective or setting aside traditional assumptions. If an idea is too "wild" to be feasible, tame it down to a more appropriate idea with additional brainstorming. Often wild ideas stimulate even more creative thinking, which then yield some very good ideas.

*4. Combine and improve ideas:* Good ideas can be combined to form a very good idea, as suggested by the adage: "1+1=3". Also, existing ideas should be improved. This approach leads to better and more complete ideas, and increases the generation of ideas by a process of association.

Brainstorming is a prolific source of creative and imaginative ideas for new products and services, but it must be used with care and be imple-

### Running the Brainstorming Session

- A facilitator should moderate the session – explain the rules, define the topic, and keep the group focused on the problem.
- Encourage enthusiastic and positive participation: All ideas are good ones. Get everyone to participate & suggest ideas, even the quiet participants.
- As ideas are suggested, the facilitator writes these on a flip chart. When the sheets fill, stick these on walls around the room.
- Number the ideas, so that the facilitator can use the number to encourage idea generation: "We have 65 ideas now, let's get it to 75!"
- Enforce the "no criticism & no evaluation" rule!
- The facilitator can ask for clarification of ideas, but should not comment on them. Repeat each idea orally as written to confirm that it expresses the intended meaning.
- After the brainstorming session is finished, take a break. Then reconvene to review and clarify ideas. Do a quick pass and select the best bets – see screening methods in Chapter 8.

EXHIBIT 6.8 The facilitator of the brainstorming session should follow a defined procedure and follow specific guidelines, as outlined here.

mented properly. So employ the guidelines above and in Exhibits 6.5 to 6.8. And as illustrated in Chapter 4 on voice of the customer, you can also use brainstorming methods with your customers and employees co-mingled in the session.

## Run a MRG Event and Utilize the Creative Ability of Your Entire Organization

A *major revenue generator (MRG)* event is an off-site company event designed to produce or scope out at least a dozen MRGs at the end of a few days tough work.[6] It's fun and it works!

The principle is that your own people, including senior people, often have the seeds of great new products within them. By harnessing the creative energy of the entire group, but in a systematic way, unexpected outcomes are often the result. An MRG event is a way to stimulate creativity but in a structured fashion.

Here is how to proceed:

An annual off-site company conference of senior and middle management is the venue. We have all been to these – two or three days of assorted speakers, some from inside the company, others from outside. It is a nice event with some good networking, but not much happens as a result.

This year, make the event yield a different result. Invite fewer speakers and, instead, build in a series of MRG exercises. Let's assume a two-day meeting as an example:

*Morning of Day 1:* After the usual opening speech, participants meet in break-out teams. Here is the first break-out assignment:

"You have 90 minutes to identify the major trends, shifts, changing customer needs, and potential disruptions that are taking place in your marketplace." These trends and needs are recorded on white flip-chart sheets in the break-out meeting rooms. In addition, be sure to challenge teams to answer the money question: "So what? Do these shifts suggest any major new opportunities?" Ask the team to record these aha's and opportunities on a green flip chart. After the break-out session, the teams bring both sets of sheets – white with the trends and green with the aha's listed – and report back to the main meeting.

Note: Some weeks before the session begins, divide confirmed attendees into teams; for example, by product line or market segment. And sprinkle some attendees from corporate functions into each team. Then give some homework assignments in order to give teams a head start:

- Hold a team meeting before the event
- Do a market and technology trends assessment
- Undertake some voice of the customer work.

A little pre-work by each team prior to the conference helps to "prime the pump", and accelerates the sessions at the off-site event.

*Late morning of Day 1*: Use the same break-out teams but a new assignment: This time, they identify the *major technology trends and potential technology disruptions* in their (and their customers') industry that might change the way they do business. Again, teams report back with both white sheets (they identify the trends and disruptions) and green sheets (the major aha's and opportunities suggested by these trends and disruptions).

Other break-out sessions over the first day-and-a-half deal with similar topics, including an assessment of internal company strengths and core competencies that might be leveraged to your company's advantage; and also shifts in the industry and value chain structure – what new players and competition have appeared, what old ones may disappear? But always the challenge to all break-out teams and sessions is: "So what – what opportunities do these changes suggest to you?" Be sure to display both the white and green sheets on the walls of the conference room. And slowly over the 1.5 days, the green sheets begin to reveal dozens, even hundreds, of aha's and opportunities.

*By noon of Day 2*: Shift the challenge from ideation to *opportunity mapping and assessment.* That is, task the teams with mapping out some of the opportunities that their break-out sessions have suggested – this usually means a clustering and sorting of the many new opportunity suggestions made and heard at the event into major opportunities or themes. During the afternoon of Day 2, ask each team to present their list of major opportunities and a brief description of each. Post this list on flip chart sheets on the walls. Then attendees vote. Use a simple scorecard so that each participant scores ideas on four or five simple criteria (see Chapter 8). Then invite attendees to affix "green dots" to the top-scoring ideas from each team presentation. The winners are identified!

If time permits, or if there is a Day 3, the teams take the best-bets – the ideas that scored the highest – and by way of a series of team break-outs-and-report-backs, each team fleshes-out the opportunity further, shapes the product or solution, and begins to map out the path forward or next steps.

It's a great exercise. Sure, it costs money and some time to plan and execute. But the rewards are worth it. The result is usually up to ten major opportunities identified and partially defined, a core of enthusiastic people willing to work on each, and the beginnings of an action plan. See Exhibit 6.9 for a summary.

### Running a Major Revenue Generating (MRG) Event

- Harnesses brain-power of organization in a structured fashion
  - Typically 2 days
- Teams go through rounds with challenge questions in break-out teams:
  1) Market trends assessment
  2) Industry assessment
  3) Company strengths, weaknesses
  4) Technology trends assessment
- What's happening? What are the trends?
- What are the emerging opportunities or aha's as a result of trends?
- Ideas and themes are identified
- Clustered into groups and major opportunities; then presented
- Vote on these – best bets are selected
- Start work on shaping the best bet ideas and formulate next steps

EXHIBIT 6.9 Run an MRG or "major revenue generator" event. Here are the steps, which include running a number of team break-out sessions with challenge questions in the quest for aha's.

*Example:* OMNOVA Solutions of Akron, Ohio had the good fortune of stumbling across a new technology via fundamental research. The new technology enables traditional polymers to have an extremely slippery surface, yet unlike other slippery materials, the resulting polymer retains its usual positive physical properties (for example, abrasion resistance and toughness).

OMNOVA's "slippery polymer" would have remained dormant as a technological curiosity had it not surfaced at a company MRG event. During one of the team break-outs, a scientist mentioned this obscure government-funded research program that had yielded this interesting slippery polymer. Nobody knew what to do with it… until the MRG event! Once the breakout team heard of the technology all kinds of "slippery possibilities" began to emerge! By the end of the two-day MRG event, the best bets had been identified, and a venture team formed. And over time, the resulting projects progressed through the company's stage-and-gate process.

The result: The first product launched is vinyl wall-covering with a difference – it's a relatively low cost, dry-erase whiteboard. Imagine having walls in meeting rooms that everyone can write on; or write-on dry-erasable walls in your child's room at home! And there are more such innovative products in the development pipeline.

## Your Own Employees Have Your Next Breakthrough – Listen to Them

"Only in his hometown and in his own house is a prophet without honor," a famous quotation from the Christian bible, is probably the first reference to the failure to listen to people within one's own organization.[7] You have dozens, hundreds, even thousands of employees. Yes, not all are creative, but many are if given the chance and encouragement. So harness the collective brainpower and creative ability of your own employees. Actively solicit ideas by establishing an I-Group and an idea capture and handling system as in Exhibit 1.13. Put in place a professional new products idea suggestion system, complete with a webpage to provide guidance, and rewards and recognition. Use some of the tools we have outlined in this chapter – brainstorming and major revenue generation events. Utilize these approaches and you will reap the creativity that lies dormant within your own organization.

# Fundamental Research Breakthroughs – Changing the Basis of Competition

Science is organized knowledge. Wisdom is organized life.

—IMMANUEL KANT
*German philosopher (1724-1804)*

Laboratories and technologists around the world have been responsible for some of the most profitable new products in business history. Chemistry labs delivered new synthetic materials and polymers such as nylon, lycra and teflon that changed the world and coincidentally propelled DuPont to greatness; pharmaceutical labs doing fundamental research created new anti-ulcer products, such as Tagamet, and transformed a mid-sized British drug firm into the giant GlaxoSmithKline; and basic research into light at Bell Labs created the laser, which made possible multiple generations of new products – from cutting tools to medical devices, bar codes and even CD players. Today, basic research in the fields of bio-technology, DNA and the human genome, and nanotechnology is creating a new generation of businesses, and potentially the next wave of corporate giants.

If your company devotes resources to fundamental research, then this research unit can and must be an active part of the Discovery phase of your innovation process. It is key to providing the foundation for your

165

next breakthrough new product or family of products that could change the basis of competition. But are you getting good value for money from your fundamental research work?

## Fundamental Research in Difficulty?

All is not well in many corporate research labs today. Sadly, the last decade or so has witnessed the dismantling of the corporate central research laboratory.[1] In many businesses, fundamental research is no longer fashionable, as corporate scientists have been parceled out to the business units. The results are predicable: The research has shifted to a much shorter term focus, and now industry leaders complain that there is nothing great coming down the pipe. Could it be that we've killed the golden goose?

One challenge is that much fundamental research is *undirected and unfocused* and, as a result, *unproductive* – which is why so many CEOs have shut it down or curtailed it. If fundamental research is not yielding the breakthrough projects it should, then consider introducing a little discipline and direction here. Some scientists may scream their disapproval, but remind them that this is not a university where curiosity-based research is the rule – this is a business. Other scientists will welcome the opportunity to become more engaged in value-producing research for the corporation.

## Technology Developments Defined

The term "technology development" refers to a special class of development projects where the deliverable is new knowledge, new technology, a technical capability, or a technological platform. TD projects include fundamental research projects, science projects, basic research, and often technology platform projects. Such research projects often lead to multiple commercial projects – new product or new process development projects.

In this chapter, we show how to provide more direction and focus to your fundamental research and technology development. We introduce the concept of a systematic *stage-and-gate process for technology development projects*. For example, ExxonMobil Chemical has modified its excellent Product Innovation Process to accommodate industrial fundamental research projects.[2] (For convenience, we use the term "technology development" to include all these fundamental research, basic research and knowledge-build projects – see box insert). Specifically, this chapter outlines proven approaches for managing and selecting such science and technology development projects – approaches that recognize that the traditional product development process, such as Stage-Gate, is inappropriate for such projects .[3,4,5]

---

## What's So Special About Technology Development Projects?

---

Technology development (TD) projects are a very different type of development project.[6] Why? First, they are increasingly *rare projects*: We saw in Chapter 1 that the average business's R&D portfolio has shifted dramatically to smaller, short-term projects such as product updates, modifications and fixes over the last 15 years.[7] With the exception of a handful of best-practice companies, gone are the days when portfolios were replete with such science-based, advanced technology and technology breakthrough development projects.[8]

This dearth of breakthrough, innovative technology projects is in part due to management's preoccupation with the short term and immediate financial results, which usually precludes undertaking venturesome development projects.[9] Additionally, the business's inability to handle these projects effectively also contributes to a reluctance to undertake more of them. In short, because these projects are mismanaged, the results are often negative, which creates a real fear of ever undertaking such a project again! Management becomes risk averse.

A second factor that makes these TD projects so special is that they are often *the foundation or platform* for a new product line or an entirely new business. In short, TD projects are important to profitability in that they help to de-commoditize the business's product offerings. They are the breakthroughs, disruptive technologies and radical innovations that create the huge growth opportunities and superlative profits.[10]

> *Example:* ExxonMobil Chemical's Metallocene project is a classic case. Here, a fundamental research study into a new polymerization catalyst yielded some early but "interesting research results", namely polyolefin materials with unusual technical properties. What started out as an early-stage research project in the 1980s ultimately resulted in an entirely new class of polymers with engineering properties and a billion dollar business for ExxonMobil Chemicals!

## Do Not Use Traditional Techniques to Manage Non-traditional Projects

A final reason that TD projects are so special is that they are *fragile*. If one uses traditional management techniques on non-traditional projects, much damage is done. For example, force-fitting a TD project through your normal new product system will create much frustration on the part of the project team, will result in unnecessary or irrelevant work, and could even kill an otherwise high-profit-potential initiative.

> *Example:* ExxonMobil Chemicals was one of the first companies in the U.S. to recognize that such research projects or technology developments required special treatment, and that ramming them through their traditional management processes would do much harm. Thus, by the 1990s, ExxonMobil Chemicals had designed and implemented a special methodology based on stage-and-gate techniques to handle such high-risk technology projects.[11]

***Too ill-defined:*** The fact is that traditional systems just do not work for these special TD projects. Why? Traditional new product processes are designed for fairly well-defined and predicable projects. But technology developments are by their nature *high risk projects with many unknowns* and great technical uncertainties. For example, early in the life of such projects, the likelihood of technical success may be quite low, and a probable technical solution often cannot be envisioned. It may take months or years of lab work to see a technical solution and to gain confidence in a positive technical outcome.

The traditional new product process also requires a full business case and a financial analysis before heavy commitments are made. But in a TD project, often the commercial prospects for the new technology are unclear, especially near the beginning of the project when these commitment decisions are required.

> *Example:* In the ExxonMobil Metallocene project, when experimental work first began, it was unclear whether this would lead to a new plastic, or perhaps a new fuel additive... all the researchers had in the early days was "some gummy stuff with interesting properties"; but the precise direction of the project would not become clear until the researchers had done more work at considerable expense.

Not exactly the reassurance that the short-term, financially-driven executive wants to hear!

*The activities do not fit:* Many of the activities required of most companies' new product processes simply do not fit the TD project. Review any company's new product process and invariably there is a list of activities, such as "undertake a competitive analysis", "do voice of customer work" and "define the product benefits to the user" as required tasks. That's fine when one knows what the market and product are. But how does one undertake such mandatory activities when the market is unknown and the product not even defined? Further, most company's product innovation processes require a list of deliverables at the completion of each stage, deliverables such as a "business case" or "commercialization plan".

Again, these are relatively meaningless concepts when the product and market have not yet been defined. As one frustrated project leader exclaimed:

> "How can I be expected to do a market analysis when I haven't even defined the product, let alone the market. I'm not even sure what this technology is capable of in terms of delivering improved technical performance."

**The wrong Go/Kill criteria:** Finally, the Go/Kill criteria used to rate and prioritize development projects as found in most company's stage-and-gate development processes again assumes a fairly well-defined and close-to-home project. For example, an Industrial Research Institute study revealed that 78 percent of businesses rely heavily on financial criteria to select projects, criteria such as projected annual profits, NPV (net present value) and expected sales.[12] When qualitative criteria are employed, according to the same study, the most popular are leveraging core competencies (for example, the project's fit with the plant, and fit with the firm's base technology), the expected payoff, and the perceived risk level. These quantitative and qualitative criteria are fine for the majority of development projects, but not so good for technology developments. A seasoned R&D executive in a major corporation summarized the situation this way:

> "Using traditional Go/Kill criteria – NPV, ROI [return on investment] and the like – will almost guarantee that new technology projects are killed in our company simply because of the unknowns, uncertainties, risks and the step-out nature of such projects. Our selection rules are very risk averse and geared towards short term projects."

# Use a Development Process Designed for TD Projects

For some years, leading product developers have relied on idea-to-launch processes, such as the Stage-Gate innovation process, to drive new product projects to market.[13] The conclusion at a PDMA Conference that focused on technology developments and fuzzy front-end projects was that "many companies have dramatically improved development cycle time and efficiency by implementing formal Stage-Gate systems" but that the front end remained a mystery.[14] The consensus is that some type of rigorous stage-and-gate process is desirable for TD projects; but the process must be custom-designed for these types of projects.

A recommended and typical TD process, used in numerous companies, is shown in Exhibit 7.1.[15] The TD process in Exhibit 7.1 consists of three stages and four gates:[16]

- *Stages:* These are shown as boxes in Exhibit 7.1. Each stage is comprised of a set of best-practice activities to be undertaken by the project team. These activities are designed to acquire vital information, and thereby reduce the unknowns and hence the risk of the project from stage-to-stage. The outcome of each stage is a specified set of deliverables.
- *Gates:* These are designated by diamonds in Exhibit 7.1, and are the Go/Kill decision points. Here management meets with the project team to decide whether the project merits additional funding and resources to move to the next stage. If a Go, resources are committed at the gate and the project and team move forward.

Here now is a quick walkthrough of a typical TD process (refer to Exhibits 7.1 and 7.2); note that such TD processes, such as SG Navigator™-TD Edition, are also commercially available – a point and click process – for immediate use:[17]

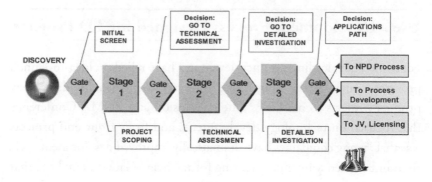

Source: Cooper, *Research-Technology Management*, endnote 6.

EXHIBIT 7.1 The Technology Development Stage-Gate system is specially designed for TD Projects – three stages and four gates including the Applications Path Gate.

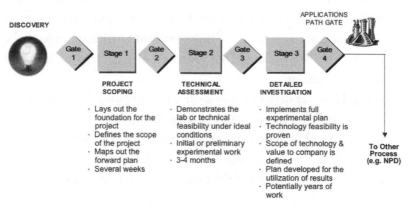

Source: Cooper, *Research-Technology Management*, endnote 6.

EXHIBIT 7.2 The TD project moves from the Scoping Stage – a relatively simple stage – through to the Detailed Investigation Stage, which could entail person-years of experimental and lab work.

## Discovery

The trigger for the process is Discovery or Idea Generation. Quality ideas are essential to a successful technology program in a business, and thus technology ideas from multiple sources must be sought for consideration at Gate 1. Idea generation is often done by scientists or technical people, but can also be the result of other activities, such as:

- A strategic planning exercise, where strategic arenas are identified, and possible TD research directions are mapped out
- Technology forecasting and technology roadmapping
- Brainstorming or group creativity sessions focusing on what might be
- Scenario generation about future market and technological possibilities
- Customer visitation programs and voice-of-customer initiatives
- Active idea solicitation campaigns within the company.

## Gate 1 – Initial Screen

This first gate is the initial screen of the idea, the initial decision to commit a limited amount of time and money to the research project. This gate should be a *gentle screen* which poses the question: Does the idea merit expending any effort at all? Criteria for Go are largely qualitative, are scored at the gate review by the gatekeepers, and should include items such as:

- Strategic fit and impact
- Strategic leverage
- Likelihood of technical success
- Likelihood of commercial success
- Reward or the "size of the prize" if successful.

The Gate 1 gatekeepers or decision-making group is typically comprised of senior R&D people, along with representatives from Corporate Marketing and Business Development to ensure commercial input.

## Stage 1 – Project Scoping

The purpose of this Scoping stage is to build the foundation for the research project, define the scope of the project, and map out the forward plan. The effort is limited, typically not much more than two weeks. Stage 1 activities are conceptual and preparation work (see Exhibit 7.2), and include a technical literature search, patent and IP search, competitive alternatives assessment, resource gaps identification and a preliminary technical assessment.

## Gate 2 – Go To Technical Assessment

This second screen is the decision to begin limited experimental or technical work in Stage 2. Like Gate 1, this gate is also a relatively gentle screen, and poses the question: Does the idea merit undertaking limited experimental work? Gate 2 is again largely qualitative, and does not require financial analysis (since the resulting product, process or impact of TD is still largely unknown). The gatekeepers are the same as at Gate 1.

## Stage 2 – Technical Assessment

The purpose of Stage 2 is to demonstrate the technical or laboratory feasibility of the idea under ideal conditions. This stage entails initial or preliminary experimental work, but should not take more than 1-2 person-months of time, and last no longer than 3-4 months elapsed time. Activities here typically include undertaking a thorough conceptual technological analysis; executing feasibility experiments; developing a partnership network; identifying resource needs and solutions to resource gaps; and assessing the potential impact of the technology on the company.

## Gate 3 – Go to Detailed Technical Investigation

Gate 3 is the decision to deploy resources beyond 1-2 person-months, and opens the door to a more extensive and expensive investigation, Stage 3. This gate decision is thus a more rigorous evaluation than at Gate 2, and is based on new information derived from Stage 2. Gate criteria resemble those listed for Gate 1 previously, but with more and tougher sub-questions, and answered with benefit of better data. The Gate 3 gatekeepers usually include the corporate head of technology (VP R&D or CTO), other senior technology or R&D people, Corporate Marketing or Business Development, and the heads of the involved businesses (for example, General Managers). Note: Because Gate 3 is a heavy commitment gate, be sure to engage senior management of the business units which will likely take ownership of the resulting technology as Gate 3 gatekeepers. Their insights into the commercial viability of the project are essential at Gate 3; further, early engagement ensures a smoother transition to the business unit once the commercial phase of the project gets underway.

## Stage 3 – Detailed Investigation

The purpose of Stage 3 is to implement the full experimental plan, to prove technological feasibility, and to define the scope of the technology and its value to the company. This stage could entail significant expenditures, potentially person-years of work. Besides the extensive technical work, other activities focus on defining commercial product or process possibilities – the expected resulting commercial projects; undertaking market, manufacturing and impact assessments on these; and preparing an implementation business case. Sound project management methods are employed during this lengthy stage, including periodic milestone checks and project reviews. If the TD project veers significantly off-course, or encounters serious barriers to completion during Stage 3, the project is red-flagged and cycled back to Gate 3 for another Go/Kill decision.

### Gate 4 – Applications Path

This is the final gate in the TD process, and is the "door opener" to one or more new product or process development projects (see Exhibit 7.3). Here the results of technical work are reviewed to determine the applicability, scope and value of the technology to the company; and next steps are decided. Note that this Gate 4 is often combined with an early gate in the usual product development process (for example, with Gate 1, 2 or 3 as shown in Exhibit 7.3). Gatekeepers are typically the senior Corporate R&D people, Corporate Marketing or Business Development, plus the leadership team from the relevant business that will assume ownership of the resulting commercial development projects.

## How the TD Process Feeds the Traditional Product Development Process

The final gate of the TD process is the Applications Path Gate, which marks the end of the TD project but potentially the beginning of multiple commercial projects. It is here where the project team presents their conclusions about the commercial prospects for the technology, based upon technical work to date and several quick commercial scoping exercises. At this point, multiple new product projects could be initiated, and feed the typical product innovation process, as shown in Exhibit 7.3. Here, the start points are usually Gates 1, 2 or 3 in the Stage-Gate product innovation system, depending on how well defined the proposed new projects are. Alternately, if the commercial result is a new or improved production process, then the appropriate process development projects are defined here and routed accordingly. The TD project may also result in a licensing opportunity or perhaps even a joint venture with another corporation. The point is that the Applications Path Gate decides the direction for the commercialization of the technology from this point forward.

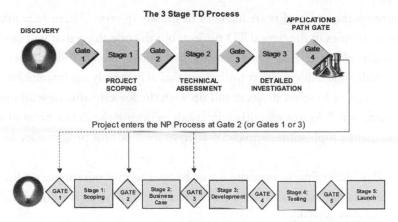

Source: Cooper, *Research-Technology Management*, endnote 6.

EXHIBIT 7.3 The TD process spawns multiple "commercial projects" which feed the Stage-Gate product innovation system at Gates 1, 2 or 3.

# Deciding Which TD Projects to Invest In

Making the resource commitment decisions for TD and fundamental research projects, especially in the early stages, is problematic for many companies. The next chapter (Chapter 8) focuses on evaluation, project selection and project prioritization; however, because TD projects are a special breed of projects, and must be managed and selected in unique ways, we introduce in this chapter some special methods for project selection – for TD projects only.

## Traditional Screening and Evaluation Tools Do Not Work

Clearly, traditional tools, such as financial analysis and profit criteria, are not too useful in the case of these special TD, science or fundamental research projects. In TD projects with much undefined, the level of uncertainty is so great that numerical estimates of expected sales, costs, investment and profits are likely to be grossly in error. There exist many uncertainties in the typical TD project, but the one thing that you can be certain about is that *your numbers are always wrong*. Indeed there is considerable evidence that businesses that rely strictly on financial tools and criteria to select projects end up with the lowest value development portfolios.[18] As one executive declared, in noting the deficiencies of his company's sophisticated financial-analysis methods for project selection:

> "It's like trying to measure a soft banana with a micrometer! Our evaluation tools assume a level of precision far beyond the quality of the data available!"

Not surprisingly, his financial evaluation tool tended to favor predicable and close-to-home projects at the expense of technology development projects.

## Use a Combination of Techniques

Best performers adopt a combination of evaluation techniques and criteria for making Go/Kill decisions on TD projects.[19] The research suggests that no one method works best across the board and can do it all! First consider using a scorecard approach which looks at multiple facets of TD projects, from strategic to technical issues. Note that this TD scorecard is different than the one that should be used for new product projects; a best-practice model for Gate 3 for TD projects is shown in Exhibit 7.4.[20] Scorecards are highly rated by users as a solid decision-making method, and tend to yield superior decisions – more efficient and more effective Go/Kill choices, high value projects and a portfolio of strategically aligned projects.[21]

In the scorecard approach, the project in question is presented by the project team at each gate meeting, and a thorough and facilitated gate discussion ensues. Next, the gatekeepers score the project on zero-to-ten scales as in Exhibit 7.4. The resulting scores are then combined to yield an overall *project attractiveness score*. This scoring exercise and final score

| 1. Business Strategy Fit | Score = Zero | Score = Ten Out of Ten |
|---|---|---|
| Congruence | Only peripheral fit with our business's strategy | Strong fit with several key elements of strategy |
| Impact | Minimal impact; no noticeable harm if project is dropped | The business's future depends on this project |

| 2. Strategic Leverage | | |
|---|---|---|
| Propriety Position | Easily copied; no protection | Position protected through patents, trade secrets, raw material access, etc. |
| Platform for Growth | Dead end; one-of-a-kind; one-off | Opens up many new product possibilities |
| Durability (technical & marketing) | No distinctive advantage; quickly leapfrogged by others | Long life cycle with opportunity for incremental spin-offs |
| Synergy with Corporate Units | Limited to a single business unit | Could be applied widely across the corporation |

| 3. Probability of Technical Success | | |
|---|---|---|
| Technical Gap | Large gap between solution & current practice; must invent new science | Incremental improvement; easy to do; existing science |
| Project Complexity | Difficult to envision the solution; many hurdles along the way | Can already see a solution; straightforward to do |
| Technology Skill Base | Technology new to company; almost no skills internally | Technology widely practiced within the company |
| Availability of People & Facilities | Must hire & build | People & facilities immediately available |

| 4. Probability of Commercial Success (In the case of a TD project with potential for new products) | | |
|---|---|---|
| Market Need | Extensive market development required; no apparent market exists at present | Product immediately responsive to a customer need; a large market exists |
| Market Maturity | Declining markets | Rapid growth markets |
| Competitive Intensity | High; many tough competitors in this field | Low; few competitors; weak competition |
| Commercial Applications Development Skills | New to company; we have no/ few commercial applications skills here; must develop | Commercial applications skills and people already in place in the company |
| Commercial Assumptions | Low probability of occurring; very speculative assumptions | Highly predicable assumptions; high probability of occurring |
| Regulatory & Political Impact | Negative | Positive impact on a high profile issue |

| 5. Reward | | |
|---|---|---|
| Contribution to Profitability | Rough estimate: less than $10M cumulative over 5 years | Rough estimate: more than $250M |
| Payback Period | Rough estimate: greater than 10 years | Rough estimate: less than 3 years |
| Time to Commercial Start-Up | Greater than 7 years | Less than 1 year |

EXHIBIT 7.4 Use a scorecard (0-10 Scales) to rate and prioritize TD projects.

become key inputs to the Go/Kill decision (although many users of this approach claim that it's the process – a senior decision-making group going through a set of key questions, debating their scores, and reaching closure on each – that provides the real value, and not so much the final score itself). Although the sample scorecard in Exhibit 7.4 is for Gate 3, note that most businesses use the *same high-level criteria from gate to gate* for consistency, with the detailed or sub-questions becoming progressively tougher at successive gates.

In addition to a gate scorecard, consider the use of *success criteria* as employed at P&G.[22] Here the project team declares what they hope to achieve in order that the project would be considered "a success". Success criteria for TD projects include, for example, the achievement of certain technical results (for example, positive lab test results) by a given date, attaining a certain technical performance improvement (for example, a certain level of absorption in a new fiber technology), or the expected sales potential to be generated by the new technology (for example, the size of the market that this technology might see potential in, if successful). Success criteria are declared relatively early in the project, and on this basis, gatekeepers approve the project at the early gates. These criteria are reviewed and updated at each successive gate; if the project falls short of these success criteria at the next gate, it may be killed – for example, if certain technical results were not achieved by a given date or gate. The use of success criteria allows the project team to develop customized criteria to suit their project; it forces the team to propose realistic rather than grandiose expectations; and it creates accountability for the project team – something to measure the team against.

## Ensuring the Resources are in Place

How does one ensure that resources will be available to undertake TD projects, especially with today's emphasis on short term projects? Managements in a number of companies have recognized that significant resources have shifted from venturesome projects to small, lower impact

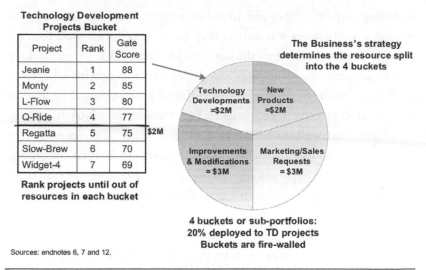

**Technology Development Projects Bucket**

| Project | Rank | Gate Score |
|---------|------|------------|
| Jeanie | 1 | 88 |
| Monty | 2 | 85 |
| L-Flow | 3 | 80 |
| Q-Ride | 4 | 77 |
| Regatta | 5 | 75 |
| Slow-Brew | 6 | 70 |
| Widget-4 | 7 | 69 |

**Rank projects until out of resources in each bucket**

The Business's strategy determines the resource split into the 4 buckets

Technology Developments =$2M

New Products =$2M

Improvements & Modifications = $3M

Marketing/Sales Requests = $3M

**4 buckets or sub-portfolios: 20% deployed to TD projects Buckets are fire-walled**

Sources: endnotes 6, 7 and 12.

EXHIBIT 7.5   Resources are strategically allocated by project type into Strategic Buckets by senior management. In this way, resources for TD projects are strategically decided and then "protected".

efforts. In order to correct this imbalance, they employ strategic buckets as a tool to ensure the right mix of projects – short term versus longer term or TD projects – in their portfolios.[23]

Strategic buckets is a portfolio management method that defines where management desires the development dollars to go, broken down by project type, by market, by geography, or by product area.[24] Strategic buckets is based on the notion that *strategy becomes real when you start spending money*, and thus translating strategy from theory to reality is about making decisions on where the resources should be spent – strategic buckets. In the example in Exhibit 7.5, management begins with the business's strategy and then makes strategic choices about resource allocation: How many resources go to new products or to improvements or to technology developments? With resource allocation now firmly established and driven by strategy, projects within each bucket are then ranked against each other to establish priorities.

Note that projects in one bucket – such as technology developments – do not compete against those in another bucket, such as sales and marketing requests. If they did, in the short term, simple and inexpensive projects would always win out, as they do in most businesses. Instead, strategic buckets build firewalls between buckets. Thus, by earmarking specific amounts to technology developments, the portfolio becomes much more balanced. Note also that different criteria should be used to rate and select projects in each bucket. For example, the relatively qualitative criteria work well in order to rank projects in the TD bucket; but for modifications and improvements or sales requests, clearly financial criteria – profits, savings or expected sales increase – are the best way to rank these projects. More on project ranking and selection in the next chapter.

## Technology Transfer to the Business Unit

A challenge with TD or fundamental science projects focuses on technology transfer – finding a commercial home for the technology within the corporation. The fact is that the initial TD project is usually done by one group (for example, in a Corporate Technology Center), while the resulting commercial projects are executed within another group (for example, by one or more business units). Parachuting a TD project into a business unit is often a *major killer* of great projects. As a seasoned R&D executive declared: "These are not smooth hand-offs. It's more like throwing it over the wall, or very often just dropping the ball."

The problem is that, all too often, the TD project becomes an orphan once it is handed off to the business unit: There is no ownership of the project and no passion in the business unit; the TD project is often incompatible with the business unit's current priorities; there exists no process or mechanism for handling the new project within the business; and the big killer – there is no one to continue the work on the resulting commercial projects within the business unit.

Here are some tips and hints from companies that have successfully implemented a TD process and linked it to their existing businesses.

*Map out the technology transfer process clearly:* Your TD process, which is often housed within a Corporate Technology Center, must be logically linked to the businesses' new product processes. Exhibit 7.3 shows the typical routing. Be sure to map this transfer mechanism out – how it will work, and who does what. Involve the business units in this mapping, and get agreement from them to the proposed transfer mechanism.

If your business units do not have a formal and clearly defined product innovation process, then mapping out the logistics of the transfer (and defining the transfer points) becomes more difficult. Strongly suggest that the business units first need to look at their own idea-to-launch methodology, and implement what best-in-class companies have, namely a well-defined Stage-Gate process. (The traditional Stage-Gate system for new products is shown across bottom half of Exhibit 7.3; for a more detailed view, see Exhibit 1.1).

*Get business unit gatekeepers at the TD gates:* Getting early buy-in to the TD project by senior management from the business unit is key to ensuring a smooth transfer later. One of the complaints we often hear from business unit general managers (or managing directors) is that they

## Some Definitions

For convenience, we use the following terms in this section:

**Corporate Technology Center:** This is the technical group charged with undertaking these fundamental research, science-based or TD projects. Often this is a central group within the corporation.

**Commercial project:** These are the resulting commercial projects undertaken within the business unit that the TD project spawns. They could include new product projects (across the bottom part of Exhibit 7.3) and new process or manufacturing projects.

**Business unit:** The business or commercial group that commercializes or implements the spin-off or commercial projects from the TD project (bottom half of Exhibit 7.3).

were not sufficiently engaged in the early decisions, and thus did not understand the implications, impact and scope of the TD project when it was undertaken in the Corporate Technology Center. This is usually because the general manager (or direct reports) were not closely involved in the decision to undertake the TD project in the first place; and once underway, they were distant from decisions about the formulation and definition of the TD project. Thus, when it came time for transfer, there were many surprises, some disappointments, and not nearly enough commitment on the part of business unit senior management.

*Secure commitment of resources from the business unit:* Technology transfers work a lot better when both sides have some "skin in the game". Thus it is critical that the gatekeepers from the business unit attend the gates in the TD process (most notably Gates 3 and 4 in Exhibit 7.1). And it is equally important that they commit some of their business's resources to the TD project. Thus, even as the project is still in the exploratory research stages, the business unit should provide help and resources, and thereby begin to assume ownership. This makes the transfer all the more seamless.

Resource commitments from the business unit could be funding, but more important, commitment of their people to help with some of the commercial tasks in Stages 2 and 3 in the TD process in Exhibit 7.1. For example, marketing people from the business unit should lead the market analysis tasks, and a small group from the business, working with Corporate Technology people, can prepare the business case. Co-mingle the business unit's staff with the Corporate Technology group, making them part of the TD project team, certainly by Gate 3 in the TD process, preferably earlier.

When the business unit commits its own people to the TD project team, there are three pay-offs: First, key tasks on the TD project – the market analysis and business case – are much more grounded in reality. Second, when the day comes for the project to be transferred to the business unit, some of its people are already up to speed on the project – the transfer is much more seamless. Finally, the business unit already has some commitment to and ownership of the project.

*Strive for some continuity of team members:* Commitment works the other way too. In companies where we witness technology transfer occurring well, typically some people from Corporate Technology, who are working on the TD project, migrate to the business unit. That is, they stay on the project and team as it moves from the Corporate Technology Center to the business unit, thereby bringing commitment, passion and knowledge to the commercial projects once in the business unit.

*The gates must be compatible and harmonized:* Make sure that the gates in the TD process are in sync with the gates in the business's idea-to-launch process – that these gates are not working at cross-purposes or independently of each other. For example, consider merging the final Applications Path Gate in Exhibit 7.2 with Gates 1, 2 or 3 of the business unit's Stage-Gate system, holding the Applications Path Gate meeting for the first 30 to 45 minutes and then shifting to a regular Stage-Gate meeting for the resulting commercial projects within the business unit; the same people attend both parts of the meeting.

A second tip is to ensure that the gate criteria used in the TD process are consistent with the criteria that the business unit uses (but modified for the fact that this is an early stage project), and are agreeable to the business unit people.

*Set up portfolio management for TD projects:* Earlier in this chapter, we recommended the use of strategic buckets to ensure that sufficient corporate resources are reserved and protected for these riskier and larger TD projects. In order to facilitate transfer, try to involve the relevant business unit management in the Corporate Technology portfolio decisions. For example, invite the senior people from key business units to take part in the strategic buckets decisions for Corporate Technology (for example, what proportion of research resources to earmark for TD projects); and which TD projects to do.

Similarly, many business units need a good dose of portfolio management as well. If business units are to provide some of the resources for the TD projects (and all of the resources for the resulting commercial projects) then these resources must be set aside. As we saw in Chapter 1, businesses naturally gravitate to smaller, short-term, low-hanging fruit projects; without the discipline of portfolio management in place, there simply will not be the time or people available within the business unit to do the work on the TD and resulting commercial projects. So encourage the business unit to adopt a portfolio management system, and to use a methodology such as strategic buckets (outlined above and in Exhibit 7.5) to ensure that a certain proportion of the business marketing and technical resources are reserved for these larger and riskier TD projects.

## Make Your TD Projects Pay Off

Technology developments are the engines of growth for many corporations and industries, providing the platforms for the next generation of new products and new processes. With most companies facing constrained resources and having a short term focus, it is imperative that such projects be managed more effectively than in the past so that they truly do achieve their promised results. Adopting a TD Stage-Gate process, using custom-tailored Go/Kill scorecards and success criteria, and employing strategic buckets to ensure resource availability are but some of the approaches that leading companies are adopting to handle these vital TD projects.

# CHAPTER 8

# Picking the Winners

Take calculated risks. That is quite different from being rash.

—GEORGE S. PATTON (1885-1945)
*U.S. General, WWII*

Much like the stock market, picking the ideas and investing in the right projects in product innovation is central to getting more bang for your R&D buck.[1] Sadly, one of the weakest facets of product innovation is effective idea and project selection and resource allocation.[2] As shown in Exhibit 8.1, only 21 percent of businesses' development portfolios contain high value-to-the-corporation projects; only one-in-four businesses effectively rank and prioritize their projects; and less than one business in five has the right balance of projects in their portfolios. These are dismal results, but the story continues: The great majority of businesses (76 percent) have too many projects for the resources available, which means that projects are under-resourced; and only 21 percent have a systematic project selection system in place.

By contrast, companies that are doing well at product innovation – the best performers with the highest R&D productivities – have superior project selection and portfolio management practices (also shown in Exhibit 8.1).[3] These firms recognize that every R&D or new product

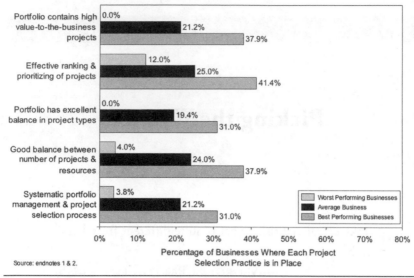

**EXHIBIT 8.1** Project selection practices are among the weakest facets of product innovation. Note how much more effective best performing businesses are at project selection and portfolio management.

project is an investment, and like stock market investing, R&D investments must be scrutinized and selected in a professional and systematic way. Although far from perfect, the best performers effectively rank and prioritize projects and they boast a systematic portfolio management system, much more so than do worst performers.

This chapter explores some of the ways that best performing businesses select new product ideas and make investment decisions in early stage projects. Note that the focus here is on *idea selection* and *early stage projects*, so we do not present every project selection technique known – only those methods most relevant at the *earliest decision points*, namely Gates 1-3 in Exhibit 8.2. These early Go/Kill decisions are particularly challenging investment decisions, because, like venture capital decisions, the project is at a very early stage, and so much is unknown and uncertain. Estimates of sales, costs and profits are little more than guesses, and attempts to apply rigorous financial analysis in these early days are fraught with problems. So read on and see what can be done to improve the effectiveness of these early screening decisions.

## Put a World Class Product Innovation Process in Place: Stage-Gate

The first step to ensuring that you pick the right projects is to install a systematic methodology for evaluating and executing the projects – a stage-and-gate process to select and drive ideas into development and ultimately into the marketplace. A typical Stage-Gate system for major projects is shown in the five-stage, five-gate model of Exhibit 8.2. Such a process is designed to ensure that every new product idea gets a fair, objective and valid hearing and decision, and that these early-stage projects are subjected to increasingly tough Go/Kill decisions at successive gates.

If you do not have such a process or methodology in place, your project selection decisions are certain to be flawed. The process degenerates into a haphazard one: Some projects get properly considered and evaluated, while others – perhaps valuable opportunities – get passed over or fall between the cracks; or worse yet, some projects by-pass the evaluation and screening procedure altogether and slip into the development

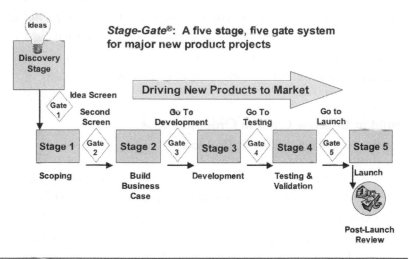

EXHIBIT 8.2 Best performers utilize a Stage-Gate system to drive projects from Ideas through to Launch. The gates weed out the poor projects; the stages provide the essential data for making the Go/Kill decisions.

pipeline by political fiat. And when it comes to making the decision to commit, key information, essential to a Go/Kill decision, is missing.

## A Playbook to Guide the Team to the Goal

A Stage-Gate system is much like a playbook in North American football. This process guides the players or project team stage-by-stage and gate-by-gate from one end-zone down to the goal posts at the other end of the field and to a touch-down. Stage-Gate breaks the innovation process into a series of discrete stages, much like the plays in a football game (Exhibit 8.3). Each play or stage consists of a set of activities and actions, all based on best practices. Early stage activities include, for example, doing a voice-of-customer study, undertaking a technical feasibility analysis, and preparing a preliminary business case. The roles and responsibilities – what each team member is expected to do and is accountable for – are made very clear in the Stage-Gate playbook.

If you do not have a robust, world-class idea-to-launch process, such as Stage-Gate, now is the time to put one in place. Both the PDMA best practices study[4] and our benchmarking study with the APQC[5] find that the great majority of companies have implemented such a stage-and-gate process. Further, the APQC investigation concludes that having a new product process such as Stage-Gate is "just a given – necessary for doing product innovation" for virtually every best performing company.

## Build in Effective Gates in Order to Focus the Resources on the Right Projects

An effective stage-and-gate process is essential in order to help narrow down the field of worthwhile candidate projects to the best bets. The Stage-Gate process, when properly implemented, provides for a *funneling action*, where at each gate, the field of candidate projects is narrowed, and resources become increasingly focused on the best projects.

How does the gating system work?[6] Each stage in your product innovation process is preceded by a gate, starting with the idea screen or Gate 1

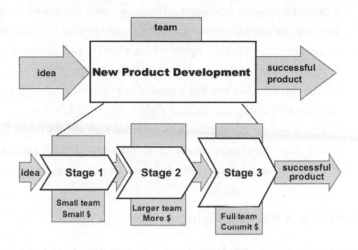

EXHIBIT 8.3 The Stage-Gate system breaks the innovation process into a series of discrete stages. Each stage typically costs more than the one before it – a series of incremental and increasing investments in the project.

in Exhibit 8.2. These gates are the Go/Kill decision points in the process: They provide tough, rigorous project reviews, open or close the road for the project to move on to the next stage, and provide the needed resources for the project to move forward. The weaker projects are killed at each of the early gates to yield the funneling action: The goal here is to skim the cream off the top at each successive gate, focus your limited resources on the high-value ideas and projects, and leave the weaker projects on hold, or kill them. By adopting this gating, screening or culling process, your development portfolio improves, and you maximize your bang for development buck.

*The structure of gates:* Gates are structured as shown in Exhibit 8.4 and feature the following elements:

- Inputs or deliverables – these are the results of actions in the previous stage and contain the information that management needs to make an effective and timely Go/Kill decision at the gate.
- Gatekeepers are the men and women who man the gate and make the Go/Kill and resource allocation decisions. These gatekeepers are

a cross-functional management group, who are senior enough to commit the needed resources for the next stage at the gate meeting.

- Gates also have criteria, upon which the Go/Kill decision is made: Gates are in effect the quality control check points in the process, where you ask two key questions: Are you doing the right project? And are you doing this project right?

- Outputs – these are the decisions (Go or Kill; also Hold or Recycle); and if Go, the commitment of resources – people and money – necessary to move the project forward and through the next stage.

## Get the Gates Working Right

The gates should begin as fairly gentle and tentative gates, with increasing rigor being applied (for example, quantitative or financial criteria) as the project moves through the model in Exhibit 8.2. For example, Gate 1, the idea screen, is largely qualitative with few or no financial considerations. But by Gate 3, there should be a business case on the table, and hence the

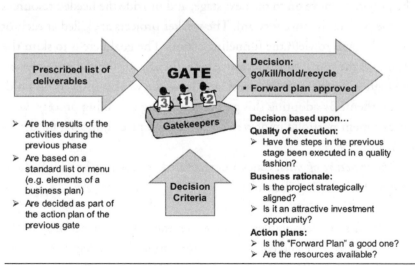

EXHIBIT 8.4 Gates are the Go/Kill decision points in the Stage-Gate system. Gates have inputs (deliverables); gatekeepers with decision criteria; and outputs (Go/Kill decisions and resource commitments).

gate decision and Go/Kill criteria should be much more rigorous, quantitative and financial.

*Incremental commitment:* The way to make investment decisions on bolder, more innovative but riskier projects is to make your innovation process *an incremental commitment* one – much like buying a series of options on a risky property. Stage-Gate is *a risk management model* designed to help you make effective investment decisions when little information is known in the early stages. Each stage involves more commitment and resources than the preceding one, as in Exhibit 8.3. It's much like playing a game of five-card stud poker, where the initial bet or ante is quite low, but more and more money is bet as the hand (or the project) progresses.

The first few gates thus should entail a relatively limited commitment of resources. Commit only enough resources to get the project through the next stage and gather some information, so that it can be reviewed more rigorously at the next gate. At Gate 1, for example, there are simply too many unknowns and too little information to declare an irrevocable "Go" decision. That is, Gate 1 is not an all-or-nothing commitment: Don't ever bet the farm at the early gates!

The problem that some companies create is that they make their major Go/Kill decisions at Gate 1, and then never seriously review the project at successive gates – projects are never killed once past Gate 1. This is wrong. Some projects that pass Gate 1 are probably poor projects, since Gate 1 is far from a perfect decision. As one executive declared, reflecting negatively on his business's approach: "We never kill projects... we just wound them".

*But do not make Gate 1 too tough:* If you try to make Gate 1 a much tougher gate, then you face defeat in another way – you reject all but the "sure bets" and end up with a timid portfolio of small, low-value projects. In short, you kill all the innovative but somewhat risky ideas. And that's the problem many companies have created for themselves.

*Example of how not to do it:* In one major electronics firm, once a project passes Gate 1, it is entered into the business's product roadmap. This means that resources are earmarked for the project, and that the project's sales estimates become part of the business's sales forecast and plan. Things are cast in concrete! What management has in effect done here is to ensure that once projects are past Gate 1, they are never killed – even if they are bad projects.

The issue management now faced was: How can we make Gate 1 more effective and predicable – "toughen it up"? Of course, if they do toughen Gate 1, then they kill their most imaginative projects. This box that management finds itself in is solved by adopting a more incremental or options approach, with gentler early gates, and avoiding full commitments at the early gates.

Recognize that, since Gate 1 is not a perfect decision, you must be prepared to make some tough calls at successive gates – at Gate 2 and 3 – and kill projects if and when the information starts to paint a negative picture. Some management forget that *a correct kill is a success!* That a correct Kill decision "just saved you a bag of money and a heap of trouble!", as a senior executive put it.

Once past Gate 3, the funnel should narrow, and start to look more like a tunnel – *"a funnel leading to a tunnel"* as one R&D V.P. suggested.[7] That is, the majority of your Go/Kill decisions should be made at Gates 1, 2 and 3 in the model of Exhibit 8.2. Kill decisions made after Gate 3, while sometimes necessary, are "late kills" – these are painful decisions since considerable resources have been expended by this point in the process.

## Practice Discipline in Executing the Stages

The playbook is there for a reason – to guide players on what expected and best-practices actions and activities are. So follow it! Too often we find that companies have a well-mapped product innovation process, but that the project teams and management break discipline – they don't follow what the process dictates. That's like a football team ignoring the playbook and winging it on the field – it works on occasion, but most of the time, they lose the game. Discipline matters!

A lack of discipline in product innovation is a major problem for many companies.[8] Key activities – for example, the market study – are left out in the interest of saving a little time; vital actions are abbreviated or not done very well, for example, the preparation of a business case is often substandard and too frequently boils down to pulling numbers out of thin air.

***Better data:*** There are many benefits to having and following a Stage-Gate system (these benefits have been well-documented[9]), but one clear pay-off is that the *quality of information you have is much better.* Review your business's Stage-Gate or idea-to-launch system: The stages should dictate what activities are required, when they are required in the life of the project, and what deliverables are the result. Recall that the deliverables are the results of activities, and consist of a package of information. For example, your Stage-Gate process may demand an activity such as "conduct a competitive analysis" early in the project; the resulting deliverable would be "a competitive analysis which includes competitive pricing, a knowledge of competitive product features, an assessment of competitive strengths and weaknesses, and insights into likely competitive reaction to your launch" – all vital pieces of information. And if you do practice discipline and really do follow the process, the quality of market, technical and business information is much better.

***Yields better decisions:*** With better information on projects, your Go/Kill and project selection decisions will be much improved. No matter how sophisticated your project selection tools are, and no matter how intelligent your gatekeepers are, without good information, your project selection decisions will be in error – you'll end up picking the wrong projects! True, you have little or no information at Gate 1, and so you must use project selection tools that do not require much information; but by Gates 2 and 3, where resource allocations are much heavier, you should have much better information, and be able to spot the winners, and weed out the losers.

The message is clear: Execute the stages well, and you will acquire much better information on your projects. And this superior information enables you to make much more astute Go/Kill decisions, focus your limited resources, and do the right projects. Sadly, many companies seem to practice the reverse philosophy: They cut corners on their projects in the front-end or homework stages and execute key activities in haste; they end up with limited or unreliable market, technical and business information on their projects; as a result, their Go/Kill decision meetings are not fact-based, decisions are ineffective, and the wrong projects are selected. With negative new product results, there is increased pressure to "do more with less" and so even more corners are cut. And the business spirals downward.

## Use Scorecards – An Effective Selection Method for Early Gates

Leading companies have adopted methods or techniques to improve the effectiveness and efficiency of their gate meetings. They've tried to go beyond merely having a meeting of senior managers, who fight it out over which projects to do. Rather, these progressive companies have introduced techniques and methods that take the senior management group through a logical discussion and enable them to make the right Go/Kill decisions in a more objective fashion.

One of the most effective gate tools is the *scorecard* or *scoring model* method. Whenever the scorecard method is used, it receives high marks in terms of both effectiveness and efficiency; but it is not as popular as it should be. So let's drill down into the method, understand why it works, and see some examples of the scorecard approach in action.

### Qualitative Factors Predict Success

Scoring models are based on the theory that *qualitative factors predict new product project success* and project value better than do quantitative or financial factors. There are very few things that one can be sure about in product innovation, except one thing: Your numbers are always wrong...

and often by orders of magnitude. This is especially true in the early stages of a project, when the key investment decisions must be made; and is also true for more innovative projects, where very limited information is available. The advocates of the scorecard approach argue that if you insist on relying on financial and quantitative analysis in the early gates for innovative projects, you will get bad decisions. As a seasoned executive noted: "It's like measuring the dimensions of a room with a rubber yardstick".

## Identify What Drives Success

A number of characteristics of new product projects are strongly correlated with success, and hence become excellent predictors or proxies for success and profits.[10] Over the years, many investigations have probed what makes a winning new product: These studies have compared and contrasted hundreds of successful new products with failures and, in so doing, have identified the critical success factors.[11] Some of the more important success factors – things which are correlated with the profitability of the new product – include:

- *Having a unique superior product* – one which is differentiated from competitors, offers unique benefits, and provides superior value to the customer
- *Targeting an attractive market* – one that is growing, is large, has good margins, weak competition and low competitive resistance
- *Leveraging internal company strengths* – products and projects which build from company strengths, competencies and experience in both marketing areas and technology fare much better.

Note that all of these characteristics are reasonably "known" or can be estimated relatively early in the project. Further, the correlations between some of these success factors and ultimate profitability are far stronger than the correlation between the NPV calculated prior to the Development Stage and the product's eventual profits, according to one major study.[12]

## Use These Factors as Predictors of Success!

Why not use some of these known and strong predictors of success as a tool for selecting projects? As one executive put it, "If you can explain success, then you can predict success!". Thus some progressive companies have developed scoring model systems which incorporate these qualitative factors and success proxies to help them rate and rank proposed new product projects.

*The proof is in the results:* Although not the most popular tool, scoring model users indicate that they work: According to a study of Industrial Research Institute (IRI) firms, those companies that rely on scoring models as their portfolio selection method achieve a superior portfolio of projects on several vital performance dimensions. Scoring models are rated highest of all selection models in terms of efficiency (making decisions in a time efficient manner) and effectiveness (making the right Go/Kill decisions). They also result in a portfolio of high value projects (better than the other methods) and strategically aligned projects. Finally, scoring models fit with management's style more so than the other tools.[13] Thus many leading companies, such as Emerson Electric, ITT Industries, Johnson & Johnson, Kennametal and Procter & Gamble have crafted scorecards to assist in the early gate decisions: For example, an article explaining P&G's success in product innovation notes that: "...a number of businesses have developed screening tools using scorecard methods for early decisions and to select ideas to enter the SIMPL™ process."[14] (SIMPL is the acronym for P&G's Stage-Gate process).

## How Scoring Models Work

In a scoring model system, a list of criteria is developed to rate projects – criteria that are known to discriminate between high-profit, high success-rate projects versus poorer projects. A scorecard is developed from these criteria, complete with anchor phrases, and typically using 1–5 or 0–10 scales for each criterion.

At the gate meeting, the project is presented by the project team or idea presenter. The gatekeepers then score or rate the projects or ideas on the scorecard criteria. The scores are collected from each gatekeeper and displayed, ideally on a large screen. These rating scores are added – weighted or unweighted – across all criteria to yield *a project attractiveness score* for each project. Differences of opinion among gatekeepers become very evident once the scores are displayed, so that a focused discussion and debate can take place; disagreements are resolved and closure is reached. The Go/Kill decision is made and resources are committed.

Scoring models can be used at gate decision points to make Go/Kill decisions on individual projects (by comparing the project attractiveness score to some cut-off criterion); and their results can also be used at portfolio reviews and in portfolio management to help prioritize projects (for example, by ranking projects by the project attractiveness score until there are no more resources).

## Illustrations of Effective Scorecard Systems for Project Selection

One key to making scoring models work is the construction of an appropriate list of scoring criteria – factors that really do separate winners from losers. A number of firms boast excellently constructed scoring models; some sample first-rate scoring models are outlined here for you to consider using:

*The Real-Worth-Win System:* The real-worth-win system is an effective scoring method for early-stage project selection and has been around for many years.[15] The handful of companies that we have observed using the model are highly supportive of the approach for its simplicity, elegance and effectiveness. The system relies on three fundamental questions:

- Is the project real – for example, is there a market need?
- Is it worth it – for example, what's the size of the prize?
- Can we win – for example, do we have the resources or capabilities needed to do the project?

1. **Is it real?**
   - Is there a market need, want or opportunity?
   - Is it technically feasible?
2. **Is it worth it?**
   - How large is the external opportunity – what is its value to the company? (sales & profits)
   - How much will it cost to execute? What resources are required to do it?
3. **Can we win?**
   - Do we have competitive advantage here?
   - Do we have the necessary resources and capabilities to undertake this project (or can these be acquired readily)?
   - How tough is the competition – will they defend? Can they defend?

---

EXHIBIT 8.5 The "Real-Worth-Win" system is a simple yet effective tool for helping gatekeepers decide on very early-stage projects. Consider this as a tool for idea screening.

At the early gates, there are a few sub-questions under each of the three main Real-Worth-Win questions. (Exhibit 8.5 shows sample Real-Worth-Win questions for Gate 1, the idea screen). At successive gates, the number of sub-questions and the degree of rigor increases.

*The PRISM System:* PRISM is an acronym for Product Idea Screening Model, and is a combination scoring model and bubble diagram for use at Gate 1. The model, shown in Exhibit 8.6, was developed by Precision Biologics, a company in the health products field (diagnostics and testing equipment targeted at hospitals).[16]

The model consists of two major factors:

- Arenas of Opportunity – which captures the relative attractiveness of the market or strategic arena that the new product will target
- Business Strength – which captures the ability of the business to undertake the project.

Arenas of Opportunity is further broken down into five questions that gauge market size and growth potential; the competitive situation; and

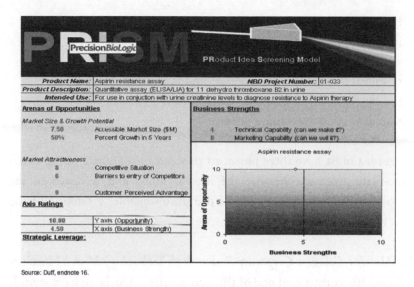

EXHIBIT 8.6 Precision Biologic's PRISM idea screening model relies on seven scaled questions. Ideas are scored by gatekeepers, and the results displayed as "bubbles" on the chart.

degree of competitive advantage the product has. The questions are shown in Exhibit 8.6. Also, the factor Business Strength is further broken down into marketing strengths and technical capabilities.

Management scores the project on these seven questions, which are combined to yield values on the two dimensions or axes. The various ideas are then plotted on the two-dimensional PRISM diagram in Exhibit 8.6, and management can easily see the most attractive ideas.

*The Minus-Zero-Plus System:* A novel scoring model is shown in Exhibit 8.7, again for the idea screening gate in the product innovation process. This was developed by an instrument company, now a division of Siemens, for scoring major new products (as opposed to line extensions or modification projects). There are eight screening questions or criteria, which were carefully developed and tested; each is based on a literature search to identify those factors found to be most important to new product success.

In use, management scores the project on the eight criteria using a "minus, zero, plus" scoring scheme. Here:

- minus (-) denotes "definite No" and is an automatic kill
- zero (0) denotes neutral or "don't know"
- plus (+) denotes "strong positive".

An idea must have three pluses to proceed into Stage 1 in the firm's Stage-Gate process; otherwise the idea is killed and is stored in the company's Idea Vault. The sum of the pluses enables a ranking of the ideas for prioritization.

*The Hoechst-Celanese Corporate Research & Technology Model:* Hoechst-Celanese has constructed one of the best scoring models we have seen. It was designed for advanced technology projects and took several years of refinement; the eventual model is so well conceived that we report it in

1. **Strategic Fit:**
   - The proposed project is aligned with the Company's strategy and vision
2. **Technical Feasibility:**
   - There are no obvious reasons why the product cannot be developed or manufactured
3. **Competitive Rationale:**
   - A competitive reason exists to undertake the project: either it is a necessary defensive or strategic product; or the product likely has at least one element of competitive advantage (e.g., is a unique, superior product)
4. **Market Attractiveness:**
   - The market (existing or potential) is large and growing; the need for the product is significant
5. **Sustainable Competitive Advantage:**
   - The product has a protectable advantage; or raises barriers to entry to competitors (only 0 or +)
6. **Synergies:**
   - The project leverages (or builds from) our core competencies or strengths (marketing, technical, manufacturing) (only 0 or +)
7. **Commercial Attractiveness:**
   - There is potential for profit or positive financial impact – we can make money here
8. **Show-stoppers:**
   - There are no evident show-stoppers or potential "killer variables" at this point (only - or 0)

EXHIBIT 8.7 The Minus-Zero-Plus model relies on eight criteria which gatekeepers use to rate and rank ideas at Gate 1. The eight criteria are all proven discriminators between successes and failures.

this book (refer to Exhibit 7.4 in the previous chapter).[17] The model relies on five factors and 19 scored criteria. These factors are:

1. Business strategy fit – how well the project and technology fits the business's strategy; and how important strategically it is to do
2. Strategic leverage – how much technology can be leveraged by the corporation (how strongly; how broadly; for how long)
3. Probability of technical success – whether or not the project can be done; and whether the company has the resources or capabilities to successfully undertake it
4. Probability of commercial success – market attractiveness, competitive intensity, and external factors, and availability of commercialization skills and resources
5. Reward – a handful of estimate questions on the size of the opportunity, its timing, and payback.

The model has the advantage that it has been extensively validated by the company: That is, scores from the model were compared to eventual results in projects. This model is best applied to larger, advanced technology projects and even platform developments, the type of project highlighted in Chapter 7.

***The ExxonMobil Chemical PIP Scoring Model:*** An effective scoring model for project selection has been part of ExxonMobil Chemical's version of Stage-Gate, their PIP (Product Innovation Process) since the late 1980s.[18] The scoring model for use at gates has been consistently refined and improved over the years. It is based on eight themes that flow from Gate 0 to Gate 4:

1. Strategic fit
2. Market and customer attractiveness
3. Technical feasibility and risk
4. Supply and entry capabilities
5. Competitive advantage

6. Legal, SHE (safety, health and environment) and public policy compliance

7. Absence of potential killer variables (project showstoppers)

8. Existence of a Plan to Proceed.[19]

Although the themes remain the same from gate-to-gate, the nature and toughness of the questions under each heading or theme increase as one moves through ExxonMobil's five-stage, five-gate Stage-Gate PIP model.

In an effort to promote more innovative projects and more fundamental research projects, ExxonMobil Research and Engineering Company has designed and attached *a rigorous front end* onto their traditional PIP system.[20] It is similar in concept to our three-stage Stage-Gate-TD model outlined in Chapter 7. Again, very similar criteria-themes are used in this model, but with slightly modified questions to reflect the more innovative nature of these projects. Exhibit 8.8 shows the criteria used to help make Go/Kill decisions in the early gates of the research model.

1. **Strategic Fit**
   – Fit with business strategy & needs
2. **Market/Customer**
   – The market, business customers & potential breadth of application
3. **Business Incentive & Risks**
   – Economic attractiveness, key business issues & uncertainties
4. **Technical Feasibility & Risks**
   – Science or technical hurdles & uncertainties
5. **Competitive Advantage**
   – Technology or business advantage relative to competition
6. **Killer Variables**
   – Absence of technical or business show-stoppers
7. **Legal/Regulatory Compliance**
   – Safety, health, environmental, operational integrity
8. **Critical Factors for Success**
   – Resources, events, timing or other factors for success
9. **Plan to Proceed**
   – Plan for achieving goals, including objectives, milestones, date for next gate, resources & costs

Source: endnote 20.

EXHIBIT 8.8 ExxonMobil Chemical's Technology Development scorecard uses eight factors, which are scored by gatekeepers. Note that this model is for technology developments, basic research and science projects.

*The SG Navigator™ Model – a best-in-class scoring model for early gates:* What we present now is an integration of the best elements of scoring models found in a number of leading companies. It is also a part of the SG Navigator™ product innovation system.[21] To be a first rate model, the scoring system must...

- use valid criteria – criteria that make sense, and also have been validated (have been proven to really make a difference between winning and losing projects)
- be user friendly – easy to use and understand
- be operational – ask questions that are clear and well-defined
- be realistic in light of the decision context – for example, not demand information or answers that are difficult to get, or simply not available for that stage of the project.

There are six factors in the best-in-class model, all based on studies into what makes new products a success. The model is designed for innovations and genuine new products (and not for improvements, modifications and fixes), and for the first few gates of the Stage-Gate process (Gates 1, 2 and 3 in Exhibit 8.2). The six factors are:[22]

1. Strategic – does the product fit the business's strategy? And how important is this product to the strategy?
2. Product and competitive advantage – is the product unique, superior and differentiated? Does it have a compelling value proposition?
3. Market attractiveness – market size, growth and competitive intensity?
4. Leverages core competencies – does the project build on company strengths in marketing, operations and technology?
5. Technical feasibility – what's the size of the technical gap? How complex is the development? What's your technical track record with projects like this?
6. Return-versus-risk – can you make money here? At what risk? How sure are you of your assumptions?

**1. Strategic:**
- Alignment with Business's strategy
- Strategic importance of project

**2. Product & Competitive Advantage:**
- Unique product benefits to users
- Differentiation vs. competitors' products
- Meets customer needs better
- Value for money

**3. Market Attractiveness:**
- Market size
- Market growth
- Competitive situation

**4. Leverages Core Competencies:**
- Marketing & distribution leverage
- Technological leverage
- Manufacturing/Operations leverage

**5. Technical Feasibility:**
- Size of technical gap
- Technical complexity
- Track record & technical uncertainty

**6. Return versus Risk:**
- Size of prize – estimate potential for profit if successful
- Versus cost-to-do – estimate amount ($) to be risked
- Payback period – roughly how long before cash recovery (guess)
- Certainty of revenue, cost & profit estimates – "fairly sure" to "wild guess"

- The six factors in bold are scored by gatekeepers at Gate meeting
- Factor scores must clear minimum hurdles otherwise an automatic Kill
- Factors are added (weighted or unweighted) to yield Project Attractiveness Score

Source: endnote 21.

Exhibit 8.9 Consider this best practices Scorecard, as found in the SG Navigator model, for early gates. All six factors are based on studies into what makes for a winning new product.

The details of these questions are shown in Exhibit 8.9. Note that only the six factors in bold are scored (use 0-10 scales). A scorecard with anchor phrases should be used to facilitate scoring by gatekeepers at the gate meeting. Scorecards are collected, data entered, and the results displayed. While the detailed questions in Exhibit 8.9 are for the idea screen, namely Gate 1, similar questions are used at Gates 2 and 3 but with increasing rigor. For example, by Gate 3, the Return-versus-Risk questions focus on NPV and payback period, since financial data are presented as part of the business case at that gate.

Once the scoring and data display are complete, the project is plotted on a bubble diagram along with other projects, much as in the PRISM model. Here the scores on the six factors in Exhibit 8.9 are added in a weighted fashion to create the two dimensions in Exhibit 8.10 (see box insert). The two dimensions are:

- Magnitude of the Opportunity (vertical axis): This factor combines Product and Competitive Advantage, Market Attractiveness and Return-versus-Risk in a weighted fashion.

## Calculating the Two Dimensions

To compute the dimension Magnitude of the Opportunity for Gate 1, statistical analysis shows that placing almost equal weights on all three factors is approximately correct (with Product Advantage weighted slightly more). But by Gate 3, place more weight on the financial Return-versus-Risk factor). The factors for Gate 1 with approximate weightings are:

Magnitude of Opportunity = .40 * Product Advantage + .30 * Market Attractiveness + .30 * Return-versus-Risk

And to compute Fit with Business/Business Leverage, use the following weights at Gate 1:

Fit & Leverage = .33 * Strategic Fit + .33 * Leverages Competencies + .33 * Technical Feasibility

- Fit with Business/Business Leverage (horizontal axis): This factor captures how well the project leverages the firm's capabilities, resources and strength, how feasible the project is, and whether it fits the strategic direction of the firm.

Note that a single low score on any one factor automatically kills the project. For example, if Technical Feasibility is rated very negatively, it really doesn't matter that the project scores high on some of the other factors – it's dead!

## The Strengths of the Scorecard Approach

The major strength of the approach is its simplicity – it is easy to use and understand. Scorecards also capture many facets of a positive project, and not just financial aspects. For example, the model builds in strategic, competitive advantage and technical considerations. And it can deal with multiple goals. Additionally, the scorecard model yields a project score,

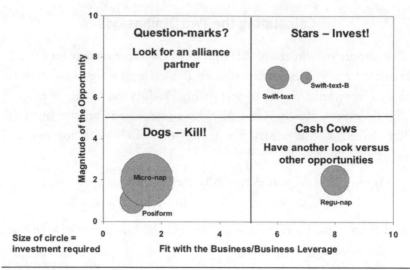

EXHIBIT 8.10 Plot the ideas and opportunities on the two-dimensional grid. The values are determined from the SG Navigator scoring model factors in Exhibit 8.9 and using the combining formula given in the text box.

and not just a list of ticks in boxes. This score can be used to rank projects or ideas, and helps in the prioritization decision. Finally, and as noted above, the model works. It yields the right decisions and in a timely fashion more so than do other approaches.

Perhaps the greatest strength is that the model engages senior management in the decision process in a positive and constructive way. The scoring procedure requires that senior management arrive at the gate meeting properly briefed and prepared, that they take part in an enlightening discussion of the project, and finally – privately and independently of each other at the meeting – they score it. Scores are displayed, debate ensues, and a decision is made. It's an excellent way to get a group of senior people to walk through the pros and cons of a project on a variety of important criteria, focus their discussion, and get closure and a decision. Most important, in companies where the approach is used, senior management seems to like it – it fits their management style.

## The Weaknesses of the Scorecard Approach

The greatest challenge is getting compliance. Some people see the process as a little burdensome at gate meetings, as it adds a little time. True, but with a capable and strong gate facilitator keeping the discussion focused, and the right electronic aids, the scoring and display can be quite time-efficient.

A second concern focuses on the fact that scoring is sometimes very subjective. This too is true; sadly, whenever you have real people in a room making decisions, there is bound to be some degree of subjectivity. Nonetheless, subjectivity can be minimized by ensuring that the questions and scales are carefully crafted; that a robust scorecard with clearly-defined anchor phrases is used; and that the project team is in the room to answer questions of clarification with facts.

A final issue is that, while using the scorecard system might be easy, developing such a system is not. Indeed, we have witnessed many score-card systems that were abysmally designed – bad questions, wrong questions, poorly worded questions, too many questions, double-barreled questions, and so on. One of the most consistent weaknesses is using criteria that have not been found or proven to be markers for highly profitable projects. Designing such a system is no task for an amateur, so get help here from someone who is expert at scorecard design, and has a thorough understanding of what the key Go/Kill criteria should be.

## Compute the Risk-Adjusted Economic Value: Expected Commercial Value

Although the Idea Screen or Gate 1 is usually too soon to apply a financial or economic approach, by Gates 2 or 3, an attempt must be made to assess the economic value of the project. The Expected Commercial Value (ECV) method is a recommended approach to determining the economic value on early-stage projects when often the data are limited and very uncertain. The key word here is "expected".[23] One weakness of traditional financial tools, such as the NPV or payback period, is that they fail to consider risks and uncertainties: Probabilities of technical and commercial success are simply not effectively or correctly factored in.

The ECV method overcomes this weakness, and is one of the more well-thought-out financial models. It is an extension of traditional financial models, such a NPV, but features several new twists that make it particularly appropriate to early stage projects – for example, at Gates 2 and 3 in Exhibit 8.2. ECV handles *risk and uncertainty of data and outcomes* effectively by introducing the prospect of multiple possible outcomes of projects, and their probabilities of occurring. The method also captures the notion of *incremental commitment* – the fact that one "buys options" on a project, and that the project could be cancelled at any point.

## An illustration – How ECV Works

Let's use an example to illustrate how the ECV works. English China Clay (ECC, the world's largest producer of clay and clay-related products) determines the value or commercial worth of each project to the corporation,

| Project Name | PV | Prob Tech Success | Prob Comm Success | Dev Cost | Comm Cost | NPV | ECV |
|---|---|---|---|---|---|---|---|
| Alpha | 30 | .80 | .50 | 3 | 5 | 22 | 5.0 |
| Beta | 63.8 | .50 | .80 | 5 | 2 | 56.8 | 19.5 |
| Gamma | 8.6 | .75 | .75 | 2 | 1 | 5.6 | 2.1 |
| Delta | 3 | 1.00 | 1.00 | 1 | 0.5 | 1.5 | 1.5 |
| Echo | 50 | .60 | .75 | 5 | 3 | 48 | 15.7 |
| Foxtrot | 66.3 | .50 | .80 | 10 | 2 | 54.3 | 15.5 |

EXHIBIT 8.11 The ECC company is considering six early-stage risky projects. It calculates the Expected Commercial Value of each from the Decision Tree model in Exhibit 8.12.

## An Example: Project Alpha in Exhibit 8.11

- Project Alpha has an income stream – future profits forecast five years into the future. When these future earnings are appropriately discounted to the present (discounted cash flow), the Present Value (PV) of these future earnings is $30 million (column 2 in Exhibit 8.11).

- The probability of technical success – being able to successfully develop the product to meet the technical performance requirements and at the target cost – is quite high, estimated to be 80 percent likelihood (column 3).

- The $30 M cash flow is far from certain, however. In fact, the probability of commercial success is estimated to be 50:50 or 50 percent, a very risky project (column 4).

- The Development costs are $3 million (column 5).

- And the Commercialization cost is $5 million – largely capital equipment (column 6).

One can quickly calculate the NPV or net present value – simply the PV less Commercialization and Development costs. This is $22 million (column 7).

namely, its expected commercial value. The company is considering a number of fairly large and high-risk early-stage projects, listed in Exhibit 8.11, whose expected incomes, development and commercialization costs, and estimated probabilities of success are shown. We use the first project in Exhibit 8.11 as an example of the determination of the ECV. For the facts on Project Alpha see the text box insert.

The NPV shown in Exhibit 8.11 ignores risks and probabilities and obviously overstates the value of each project. Question: What is the true value – what is the Expected Commercial Value or ECV of each project?

A decision tree is used to compute the Expected Commercial Value of each project. Decision trees map out the chain of events in a project much

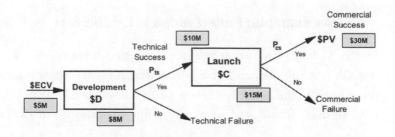

$ECV = Expected Commercial Value of the project
$P_{ts}$ = Probability of Technical Success
$P_{cs}$ = Probability of Commercial Success (given technical success)
$D = Development Costs remaining in the project
$C = Commercialization (Launch) Costs
$PV = Present Value of project's future earnings (discounted to today)

EXHIBIT 8.12 The ECV of Project Alpha is computed using a Decision Tree approach. Start at the right and work toward the left, and follow the calculation in the text box insert.

like a tree (as shown in Exhibit 8.12), and show the possible outcomes of different events or decisions as the branches of the tree. Also shown on the branches are the financial consequences of each outcome, as well as the probabilities that various outcomes will occur.

Let's again use Project Alpha as the illustration, and follow the decision tree shown in Exhibit 8.12 to see how the Expected Commercial Value is calculated.

Note that the decision tree shown in Exhibit 8.12 is based on a convenient two stage model. You may elect a three or a four stage model, with each stage having its own costs and probabilities of success. For example, an extra stage may be Validation, with the likelihood of success of the Beta tests or Field Trails being the relevant probability. And you can also have an array of possible commercial outcomes – from "huge success" to "disaster", each with its financial consequences and probabilities of occurring (we showed just two branches or outcomes in Exhibit 8.12, success or failure).

See how different the ECV is from the simple NPV in Exhibit 8.11 –

## The ECV Solution: Let's walk through the decision tree in Exhibit 8.12

- Start on the far right side of the exhibit. There you see the Present Value or PV of the project of $30 million.

- But this PV income stream assumes commercial success, which is 50%. Thus PV must be multiplied by the probability of commercial success, Pcs. So the ECV is now PV x Pcs or $15 M – that is, the day before the project goes commercial, the firm has 50:50 odds of earning $30 M or nothing: The project is worth $15 M.

- But to get to market, the firm must commercialize the project (represented by the Commercialization box in the exhibit). Thus the firm must spend C dollars or $5 M on Commercialization costs. Thus the ECV is now $(PV \times P_{cs}) - C$, or $10M.

- But before commercialization can occur, the product must be a technical success. Thus the ECV value above must be multiplied by the probability of technical success, Pts or 80%. The ECV equation is now $[(PV \times P_{cs}) - C] \times P_{ts}$ or $8 M.

- But to get to a technical success, the firm must spend money on Development, designated by the Development box in the exhibit. Development costs D dollars or $3 M, and so the ECV must be reduced by that amount.

- The ECV or Expected Commercial Value of Project Alpha is thus $5 M (shown in the far right column of Exhibit 8.11).

The ECVs for the other projects in Exhibit 8.11 are calculated in the same way, and are also shown in the far right column (column 8).

compare columns 7 and 8. For example, Project Alpha's NPV, after subtracting development and commercialization costs, is $22 million. Thus, at first glance, one might be tempted to place a commercial worth of $22 million on Project Alpha. But not so, according to the ECV method: The real value of the project when adjusted for risk is only $5 million – a major difference from the $22 million! The point is that merely rating or valuing projects according to NPV could be very misleading.

## Ranking the Projects Using the Productivity Index

The Expected Commercial Value places an economic worth on each of a number of early-stage projects in Exhibit 8.11 with uncertainties and risks considered. Now, how does one determine which projects to fund and which to place on hold? Usually there are more would-be projects than there are resources to do them.

In order to arrive at a prioritized list of projects, we use the Productivity Index and consider resource constraints.[24] The Productivity Index is based on *the theory of constraints*. Whenever you wish to maximize something (for example, the expected value of the development portfolio) but subject to a constraint, the rule is simple:

> Rule: Take the ratio of what you are trying to maximize (the ECV) and divide this by the constraining resource (for example, R&D resources required to do the project).

This rule translates into the Productivity Index:

$$\text{Productivity Index} = \frac{\text{Output}}{\text{Input}} = \frac{\text{Project Value}}{\text{Constraining Resource}} = \frac{\text{ECV}}{\text{Development Cost per project}}$$

*The illustration from English China Clay:* Recall from Exhibit 8.11 that the ECC Company is considering a number of projects. The ECV has been computed for each project in Exhibit 8.11 using the decision tree approach in Exhibit 8.12. All are good projects with positive ECV values (a negative ECV would have signaled a Kill decision).

Here is the next challenge: The company has a Development

budget of $15 million. Since these are all approximately one year projects, you cannot do all of them. Note that adding up the Development costs in Exhibit 8.11 gives a total of $26 million, almost double the budget.

In order to determine which are the top priority projects and should be funded versus put on hold, the Productivity Index is determined for the six projects in Exhibit 8.11, The Productivity Index is computed using the equation above (the ECV/ Development Cost ratio) and results are shown in column 4 in Exhibit 8.13.

Projects are now rank-ordered according to this Productivity Index, thereby ensuring the greatest bang for buck; that is, the ECV of the portfolio is maximized for a given R&D budget. Exhibit 8.13 shows the final prioritized list, with a horizontal line noting the point where the budget of $15 million is exceeded. Projects above the line are designated "Go"; those below the line are placed on hold.

Note that had the company's projects simply been rank-ordered according to the Expected Commercial Value alone (rather than the Productivity Index or the ECV/Development-Cost ratio), the prioritized list would

| | Project Name | ECV | Dev Cost | Prod Index = ECV/Dev | Sum of Dev |
|---|---|---|---|---|---|
| **(Note: Development Budget constraint of $15 M)** | Beta | 19.5 | 5 | 3.90 | 5.0 |
| | Echo | 15.7 | 5 | 3.14 | 10.0 |
| | Alpha | 5.0 | 3 | 1.67 | 13.3 |
| | Foxtrot | 15.5 | 10 | 1.55 | 23.0 |
| | Delta | 1.5 | 1 | 1.50 | 24.0 |
| | Gamma | 2.1 | 2 | 1.05 | 26.0 |

$$\text{Productivity Index} = \frac{\text{Output}}{\text{Input}} = \frac{\text{ECV}}{\text{Development Cost}}$$

EXHIBIT 8.13 To maximize the value of the portfolio, determine the Productivity Index (PI = ECV/Dev Cost) and rank projects by this index until out of resources.

have been quite different. And, most important, the value of the total portfolio would have been inferior: That is, the resulting project list would have yielded a lower total ECV value for a given R&D budget!

## Strengths of the ECV Approach

The greatest advantage is that the ECV method does indeed account for project risks and probabilities – both commercial and technical – which the usual NPV calculations do not. And for most innovative and early-stage projects, the probabilities of success are less than 100 percent. Ignoring this fact, as do traditional NPV approaches, tends to overvalue projects. And the differences are often large – the huge differences between the traditional NPV numbers and the EVCs for the same projects in Exhibit 8.11. Thus ECV is a method that does introduce some discipline and financial rigor but in a way that is most appropriate to higher risk projects with many unknowns.

A second major but more subtle benefit is that the method recognizes the incremental or *options nature* of investing in projects – that projects are "purchased a piece at a time"; and that management has Go/Kill options along the way. Note that if a project is halted partway through, certain expenses are not incurred. This options approach thus reduces the risk of a project. So the "correct valuation" of a project should be via an options or decision tree approach as in Exhibits 8.11 and 8.12. (The ECV is also a close approximation to other and more complex options methods such as "options pricing theory" or the "real options" method).[25]

## Favors the Right Kinds of Projects

A careful review of the method in Exhibit 8.12 and the rank-order list in Exhibit 8.13 reveals that certain types of projects will be appropriately driven to the top of the priority list by this ECV model:

- those projects that are closer to launch
- projects that have relatively little left to be spent on them – all

money spent so far is a sunk cost, and hence not relevant to the ranking decision

- projects with higher likelihoods of success (commercial and technical probabilities) and a higher stream of earnings
- projects that utilize less of the scarce or constraining resource (in the example, projects with lower Development costs).

## Words of Warning Too

The major weakness of the method is its *dependency on financial and other quantitative data*. For example, data on all projects' future streams of earnings, on their probable commercialization (and capital) expenditures, on their development costs, and on probabilities of success must be available. Often these estimates are unreliable, or they are simply not available early in the life of a project; hence the method can only be used for projects past a certain point in the process (for example, after a financial business case has been developed).

A second weakness is the treatment of probabilities: How does one quantitatively estimate probabilities of success? Estimating probabilities of success amounts to little more than pulling numbers out of the air in some companies; yet the impacts that these probability estimates have on the valuation of projects is high. These probability numbers are in effect multiplied by each other, and then multiplied by the present value of projects. Modest errors in these probability estimates can produce huge errors in project valuation figures!

## Estimating Probabilities

Three methods are available for estimating probabilities of success. Some companies have developed data tables (based on past projects) which show the likelihoods of success for different types of projects.[26] A second approach is to impute probabilities of success from some of the factors in the scoring model. For example, when using the Hoechst-Celanese model, the 0-10 scores for two factors – probability of technical success and probability of commercial success in Exhibit 7.4 – can be directly translated into a percent probability (again based on historical data the company has collected).[27]

*Modified Delphi Method:* The third and perhaps the most powerful method to estimate probabilities is a modified Delphi approach. Delphi is a technique designed to assemble the collective wisdom of a group of knowledgeable people into a well-informed conclusion (in this case, an estimate of the probability of commercial or technical success).

First, a group of experts or knowledgeable people discusses a topic (in this case, the probability of technical success of an innovative idea facing significant technical challenges). A moderated discussion takes place, with the moderator priming the pump with leading questions throughout the discussion, such as:

- Can anyone identify the technical barriers in this project?
- What might be some possible solutions?
- Does a solution already exist in the outside world?
- What other technical barriers or roadblocks might we encounter? Is there a way around these?

Towards the end of the discussion session, each expert is asked to privately indicate his or her estimate of the probability of technical success (write a number between zero and one hundred). The estimates are collected and displayed anonymously on a flip chart to the group. Very often, there will be significant differences of opinion, so the moderator directs the next round of discussion to probe the reasons for these differences. After two or three rounds of dialogue, each round followed by private voting, a consensus is reached.

The method is subjective, but has proven to be an effective way of capturing both qualitative and quantitative views from groups of experts. And in many studies over the years, the method consistently yields "answers" that are very close to the truth!

# Picking the Winners Early – A Summary

Selecting winning new products early in the game is no easy task. In this chapter, we have identified some of the approaches that leading firms use to make early-stage decisions on innovative ideas and projects when relatively little is known. The main recommendations are:

*1. Install a robust idea-to-launch process:* This process should be based on stage-and-gate methodology to guide your ideas and projects from idea through development and into market launch (Exhibit 8.1). By following this process, you get the benefit of tough gates that weed out bad ideas and weak projects early; and you should also benefit from better information gleaned in the stages so that subsequent gates can be fact-based and more effective.

*2. Use a scorecard approach:* Scorecards are particularly suitable for the first few gates – Gates 1 to 3. Scorecards used by gatekeepers right at the gate meeting work! And they are most appropriate when data on projects are limited. A number of different scorecards were presented here, and each has its merits. Do consider using *different scorecards* for different types of projects, for example:

- A scorecard such as the Hoechst-Celanese model (Exhibit 7.4) for advanced technology, technology platform, and technology development (TD) projects
- A scorecard such as the best-in-class SG Navigator scorecard for innovative new products (as in Exhibit 8.9)
- Perhaps a simpler scorecard for the idea gate, such as the Real-Worth-Win system (Exhibit 8.5) or the PRISM model (Exhibit 8.6)
- And for development projects that are not really innovative or new products – line extensions, modifications, customer or salesperson requests – a quick financial analysis or cost-benefit index combined with a tailored but simple scorecard designed for these types of projects.

And use graphics, so that the scorecard results can be displayed on several dimensions, as in the PRISM and SG Navigator models (Exhibits 8.6 and 8.10).

*3. Determine the risk-adjusted economic value of early-stage projects:* Introduce financial analysis, but not too early in the process. Overuse of financial tools may prematurely kill innovative projects, and besides, the early-stage financial numbers are largely fictional. So Gate 2 in Exhibit 8.2 would be the earliest a financial analysis should be considered (after a preliminary business case is on the table), and certainly at Gate 3, where there is a full business case available.

When using a financial analysis, employ a method that recognizes that the revenue and cost estimates are uncertain – that they have less than a 100 percent chance of occurring – and that these projects are risky. Thus deal with probabilities and risks through a method such as the Expected Commercial Value, which relies on a decision-tree approach (Exhibit 8.12). And when ranking projects at Gates 2 or 3, don't just rank them by ECV; rather, introduce the notion of constrained resources, and use the Productivity Index to rank projects as in Exhibit 8.13. This ensures maximum bang for buck for your R&D spending.

**A final thought:** We began this chapter with a quotation from U.S. General George S. Patton, imploring us to "take calculated risks." But to do so, one must indeed *calculate the risk* – push the numbers and do the math. So use the ECV method as a way of calculating the risk-adjusted value of projects; and use scoring models, another proven tool for helping senior managers make Go/Kill decisions under conditions of uncertainty and risk.

# Some Final Thoughts –
# Seeking Game-Changing Innovations

He is the best man who, when making his plans, fears
and reflects on everything that can happen to him, but
in the moment of action is bold.

—HERODOTUS (c. 484–424 B.C.)
*Greek historian. The Histories, 7.49*

## Work the Innovation Diamond

How do the best performing companies make generating a steady stream
of great new product winners seem so easy? Four major drivers underlie a
business's performance in product innovation. That is, best performing
businesses have *four common denominators* in place, according to our
benchmarking study introduced in the first chapter. We call these the *four
points of performance* that comprise the *Innovation Diamond* (see Exhibit
9.1).[1] While companies such as Procter & Gamble use the Innovation
Diamond to guide their product innovation efforts,[2] so to can you
employ the Innovation Diamond as a framework to guide your quest for
game-changing and breakthrough new products.

Consider the four points or facets of the Innovation Diamond in
Exhibit 9.1, starting at the top or north point:

# 1. A Product Innovation and Technology Strategy for Your Business

Best performing companies put a product innovation and technology strategy in place, driven by the leadership team and the strategic vision of the business. We saw in Chapter 2 how critical having a product innovation strategy is to direct your business's innovation efforts. Such a strategy defines the hunting grounds – what's in bounds and out of bounds – and helps to focus your search for new product ideas.

Perhaps more important than the plan itself is the process that your leadership team goes through when they work together to develop an innovation strategy. As Dwight D. Eisenhower, the Supreme Allied Commander at D-Day, declared: "Plans are nothing; planning is everything". Thus, the development of a product innovation strategy helps to energize the Discovery Stage: By undertaking the various analyses – industry, market, technology, value chain and core competencies – you are almost certain to identify new opportunities in the form of new markets, new products and even new businesses to consider. This exercise is *strategic ideation*, and is also a major input into the development of a strategic product roadmap. And in Chapter 3 we saw how three related strategic approaches – developing peripheral vision, identifying disruptive technologies, and employing scenarios of the future – are a huge potential source of visionary new product ideas and even new businesses.

Finally, a product innovation strategy helps your leadership team to screen and evaluate your ideas and early-stage projects. Note that in every scoring model used by best practice firms in Chapter 8, the first question is always a strategic one: Does this project align with your strategy? And how important strategically is this project? Without a product innovation strategy well articulated, the questions cannot be answered.

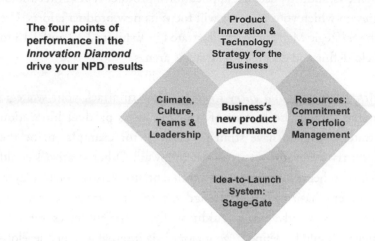

The four points of performance in the *Innovation Diamond* drive your NPD results

Product Innovation & Technology Strategy for the Business

Climate, Culture, Teams & Leadership

Business's new product performance

Resources: Commitment & Portfolio Management

Idea-to-Launch System: Stage-Gate

EXHIBIT 9.1 Four major themes – the four points of performance – impact most strongly on businesses' performance in new product development. Use the Innovation Diamond to guide your product innovation efforts.

## Key Element in an Innovation Strategy

The message for senior management is that, if your business is one of the many that lacks a product innovation strategy, then the time is ripe to develop and install such a strategy. Recall the key elements and steps from Chapter 2 and summarized in Exhibit 9.2:

- *Goals and role:* Start by defining your goals – the goals of your business's total new product effort, and the role that product innovation will play in enabling your business to achieve its business objectives. Then ensure that the role of new products in achieving the business's overall goals is clear and communicated to everyone in your business.

- *Arenas and strategic thrust:* Focus is the key to an effective product innovation strategy. Map out where you will attack, or perhaps more importantly, where you will not attack: The concept of strategic arenas is at the heart of a new product strategy – the markets, industry sectors, applications, product types or technologies on which your business will focus its new product efforts. Use the Strategic Map approach illustrated in Exhibits 2.12 and 2.13 to help define and decide your strategic arenas.

- *Attack strategy and entry strategy:* How to attack your strategic arenas should also be part of your business's product innovation strategy. You do have strategic choices: for example, to be the industry innovator versus a "fast follower". Other strategies could focus on being low cost versus a differentiator versus a niche player; or on emphasizing certain strengths, core competencies or product attributes or advantages. Additionally, entry strategies for new arenas should be defined: "go it alone" via internal product development, versus seeking alliances through licensing, partnering and joint venturing.

- *Deployment – spending commitments, priorities and strategic buckets: Strategy becomes real when you start spending money!* Your product innovation strategy specifies how much to spend on product innovation; and it should indicate the relative emphasis, or strategic priorities, accorded each arena of strategic focus. The concept of Strategic Buckets is introduced in Chapter 7 as a powerful tool to ensure the right allocation of resources across strategic areas and to different types of development projects.

- *The strategic product roadmap – the major initiatives and platform developments:* A strategic roadmap is an effective way to map out a series of major development initiatives in an attack plan. A roadmap is simply a management group's view of how to get where they want to go or to achieve their desired objective (as shown in Exhibit 2.15). So be sure to map out your major development initiatives over a five to seven year timeframe, and establish tentative placemarks for these developments. Inputs to this road-mapping exercise are shown in Exhibit 2.16.

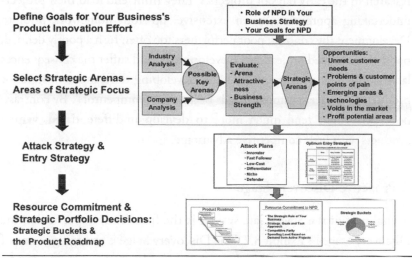

EXHIBIT 9.2  Define your Product Innovation Strategy for your business – start with goals and work through to define strategic buckets and your roadmap.

## 2. An Effective Idea-to-Launch System

An idea-to-launch framework for product innovation is one solution to what ails many businesses' new product efforts.[3,4] Such a framework is also one of the four points of performance in the Innovation Diamond in Exhibit 9.1 – it is tactual and is shown at the south point of the diamond.

Facing increased pressure to reduce the cycle time, yet improve their new product success rates, companies implement Stage-Gate systems to manage, direct, and control their product innovation initiatives (an example of Stage-Gate is in Exhibit 8.2). That is, these businesses have developed a systematic process – a playbook, game plan or framework – for moving a new product project through the various stages and steps from idea thru to launch.

While many companies claim to have an idea-to-launch process, the best performers *seem to get it right more often.* Best performing businesses build in a strong customer-focus and rely heavily on voice-of-customer research in the early days of projects.[5] They front-end load their projects undertaking appropriate, often extensive, up-front homework prior to Development (by contrast, poor performers too often rush a poorly defined, poorly investigated project into Development, and suffer the consequences later!). And best performers focus on developing differentiated, superior products that meet customer needs better than competitors'. By contrast, poor performers tend much more to develop undifferentiated, vanilla products with little competitive advantage.

## A Proactive Discovery Stage

A vital part of the Stage-Gate system is the front end, in particular, the Discovery Stage in Exhibit 8.2. The Discovery Stage is emerging as one of the most pivotal but neglected stages in the idea-to-launch process – it feeds the innovation funnel. Your Discovery Stage should include a number of methods and approaches to generating, capturing and stimulating new product ideas – see Exhibit 9.3. Here is a quick summary:

- *An idea capture and handling system:* Best performing companies build an idea capture and handling system into their product innovation process, as in Exhibit 1.14. Swarovski models the way as shown in Chapter 6: The company has established an i-LAB to handle and flesh out the in-bound ideas, and employs its i-FLASH software to solicit ideas, and then to secure quick idea evaluations. Your idea capture system should include an entrance way or "on ramp" to a focus person or I-Group that handles the ideas. Ideas may be enhanced and fleshed out by this group and, when sufficiently defined, are submitted to Gate 1 for a review. There should also be an idea vault or repository of inactive ideas that is open to the company.
- *Customer-focused:* Voice of customer is fundamental to discovering great new product opportunities. But the key here is to go beyond what customers indicate that they want, and to seek real insights into their unmet and unspoken needs. This can only be accom-

plished by face-to-face interactions with customers, and using techniques such as camping out or day-in-the-life-of (ethnography) and customer visits with in-depth interviews. Working with lead users, employing focus groups to identify problems and points of pain, and crowdsourcing are other VoC methods, recommended in Chapter 4, that might better suit you.

- *Open innovation:* Leading companies have recognized the need for *open innovation* – for a balance between internally- and externally-generated ideas and new products. And they have put in place the processes, IT support, teams and culture to *leverage external partners and alliances* in the quest for new ideas, inventions and innovations from outside the firm (as illustrated in Chapter 5). In the quest for new product and new business ideas, look not only externally for customer problems to be solved or unmet needs to be satisfied, but now also to inventors, start-ups, small entrepreneurial firms, partners, and other sources of available technologies that can be used as a basis for internal or joint development. And acquire

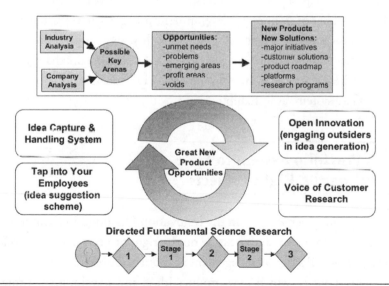

EXHIBIT 9.3  The Discovery Stage in your Stage-Gate system must be proactive and managed. It includes multiple activities that converge to generate great opportunities for product innovation.

external innovations that have already become productized or even commercialized by others.

- *Internal ideas:* Do not forget your own employees as vital sources of innovation ideas. When you set up an idea capture system, be sure to build in an idea suggestion schema that welcomes ideas from employees, using the tips and hints in Chapter 6 as a guide. Hold off-site Major Revenue Generating events once a year and engage your creative people in the ideation process in a structured fashion. And use brainstorming sessions within your organization periodically and with customers to encourage creativity.

### Stage-Gate-TD

While the Stage-Gate system has proven to be an effective way to guide new product projects through to launch, recognize that such a system may not be appropriate for technology development and fundamental research projects. So we outline a special version of Stage-Gate for such projects in Chapter 7 – see Exhibits 7.1 and 7.2. If your business undertakes a number of technology development projects where the deliverable is new knowledge or a technological capability, then consider setting up this special version, namely Stage-Gate-TD. And make sure that these TD projects bear fruit by firmly linking this TD process into your regular Stage-Gate system, as in Exhibit 7.3.

## 3. A Portfolio System to Help Focus on the Right Projects

A *third point of performance* in the Innovation Diamond in Exhibit 9.1 is resource commitment and focusing on the right projects, namely *portfolio management*.[6] Portfolio management is about resource allocation in your business. That is, which new product ideas and development projects from the many opportunities should your business fund? And which ones should receive top priority and be accelerated to market?

## Employ Strategic Buckets

Strategic allocation of resources is an important facet of portfolio management. And Strategic Buckets is an effective strategic approach to ensure that R&D or development resources – people and money – are allocated properly. In this method, the leadership team of the business translates their strategy into reality by making strategic choices about where the development resources are to be spent: They set up *buckets of resources*, sort projects by bucket, and then rank projects within each bucket until they run out of resources. Although we introduce Strategic Buckets in Chapter 7 as a way to direct resources to major and riskier projects (Exhibit 7.5), the method can be employed to yield optimal resource splits not only across project types, but also across strategic arenas, across markets and by product lines; the method is the same, but the resulting splits and pie diagrams are different.

## Install the Right Project Selection Methods

Two project selection methods are recommended for making Go/Kill decisions on ideas and early-stage projects. Such projects are usually characterized by many unknowns, uncertainties and risks, rendering traditional investment-and-return financial models somewhat ineffective. Indeed, overuse of traditional financial tools too early in the game will result in killing your most venturesome and imaginative projects, so you end up with a development portfolio of low-hanging fruit projects – the opposite of game-changers and breakthrough initiatives. The methods we suggest are:

- *Scorecards or scoring models:* Here gatekeepers evaluate the idea or proposed development project on a scorecard comprised of about 6-10 carefully chosen and well-crafted criteria. These criteria should have basis in fact (for example, are known discriminators between winning and losing projects, or have been validated; examples are given in Exhibits 8.5 to 8.9). The scoring is done right at the gate meeting following a presentation of the idea or project by the I-Group or early-stage project team. Such scorecard methods are particularly suitable for the early gates (Gates 1, 2 and 3 in Exhibit 8.2). Note that different scorecards should be created for different types of projects (for example, TD projects versus new products versus extensions and modifications).

- *Expected Commercial Value and the Productivity Index:* To the extent that some financial analysis is required before entering Development (by Gate 3 for sure, perhaps as early as Gate 2 in Exhibit 8.2), then at least use a financial model that deals with the reality of the situation. The ECV method is a decision-tree approach which incorporates risks, uncertainties and probabilities, and also accommodates the incremental investment nature of the development process (and hence approximates the real options or options pricing approaches). The decision-tree maps out the events and decisions in the life of a project, and defines the probable outcomes and consequences of these events, and their likelihood of occurring (as shown in exhibit 8.12). Building in the Productivity Index enables you to rank-order a list of solid projects, and then select the ones to invest in when you have resource constraints (as most businesses do).

Use both selection methods to help you, and your leadership team, make the first few decisions on game-changing ideas and breakthrough development projects.

## Fact-Based Go/Kill Decision Making

Installing an idea-to-launch system such as Stage-Gate, besides system-atizing the Discovery Stage and then driving projects to market, also helps you with your idea and project selection decisions. A key benefit is that by building in regular and rigorous gates, you weed out the weaker ideas and projects in an objective and deliberate way. Gates have defined deliver-ables (the vital information needed to make the decision); gate criteria (ideally in the form of a scorecard); and gatekeepers (those executives who own the resources needed to progress the project). It's a visible process, where the leadership team of your business can play a positive role as gatekeepers.

A well-crafted Stage-Gate innovation process, when implemented with discipline, has the added benefit of delivering the solid information on your early-stage projects. A robust Stage-Gate process front-end loads projects – it is designed to build the key homework or due diligence activities into Stages 1 and 2 in Exhibit 8.2. These are the critical market, customer, competitor, technical, operations and business studies that get the data that are the basis for constructing a fact-based business case for the would-be project. And a fact-based business case then enables you and your leadership team to make better Go/Kill decisions at Gates 2 and 3 before heavily resource commitments are made going into the Development Stage.

# 4. The Right Climate and Environment for Innovation

People, culture and leadership is the *fourth point of performance* in the Innovation Diamond in Exhibit 9.1. We have not discussed the topic so far, but, clearly throughout this book, having the right climate, culture and leadership from the top pervades the practices that we recommend. Without the right environment within your corporation, innovation simply will not happen! Although difficult to measure, having the right climate and culture, with leadership from the top, proves to be one of the strongest drivers of businesses' product innovation performance results in the Innovation Diamond.[7]

## Senior Management Commitment

Senior executives in best performing businesses lead the innovation effort and they are strongly committed to new product development. An example is at Procter & Gamble, where the CEO, A.G. Lafley (Chairman of the Board, President and Chief Executive), makes it clear:[8]

> "Innovation is a prerequisite for sustained growth. No other path to profitable growth can be sustained over time. Without continual innovation, markets stagnate, products become commodities, and margins shrink."

A significant minority of businesses now make product innovation results part of senior management's performance metrics, and in some cases tie executive variable pay and bonuses to the business's innovation performance. For example, at ITT Industries, new product results (measured by new product sales as a percentage of the business's annual sales revenue) is now a key performance metric for business unit general managers, along with meeting profit and cost targets. Note that while still not widespread, this practice is seen in best performing companies almost four times as often as in poor performers.

## Promote Creativity

Senior management plays a lead role in championing the innovation effort in best performing businesses, much more so than in poor performing businesses.[9] For example, they promote creativity and innovation by allowing time off for scouting or "Friday projects" as in 3M, Kraft Foods and W.L. Gore, as seen in Chapter 6. They are not overly risk averse and do invest in the occasional high risk project; and they encourage skunk works – projects and teams working outside the official bureaucracy of the business. Senior management has installed an idea suggestion scheme for new products that welcomes ideas from employees. And idea submitters, product champions and project team members are openly recognized and rewarded in best performing companies.

## Inspiration or Perspiration?

A great product innovation process coupled with brilliant execution is only half the battle. If the idea was mediocre to start with, then don't expect stellar results. Getting great new product ideas is the first step in a successful new product effort. By focusing on the front-end of your product innovation process – getting your Discovery Stage right – you feed the funnel with game-changing ideas. And that is the first step.

Sadly there are *no magic bullets* to generating and delivering a steady stream of breakthrough new products. But there are concrete steps that you can take, as we outlined throughout this book. It is tough work, however each of the methods and approaches we outlined: defining a innovation strategy, using voice of customer research, seeking external ideas through open innovation, harnessing the creative abilities of your own people, and leveraging fundamental research; is proven to yield great new ideas and potential game-changers. But these methods do take time and effort to set up and follow though on. To paraphrase Thomas Edison, *innovation is ten percent inspiration and ninety percent perspiration.*

The rewards are there, however. Witness throughout this book the strong evidence that best performing businesses do employ these idea generation methods. The pay-offs of success are simply too high, and the costs of failing to act are too great, to ignore the need to feed your development funnel with breakthrough ideas. So take up the challenge of creating that next game-changing innovation!

# ENDNOTES

## CHAPTER 1

1. Stage-Gate® is a registered trademark of the Product Development Institute Inc. See www.prod-dev.com.
2. Cooper, R.G. & Mills, M., "Succeeding at new products the P&G way: A key element is using the "Innovation Diamond", *PDMA Visions*, XXIX: 4, October 2005, pp. 9-13
3. Hamm, S., "The View from the top", *Business Week*, April 3, 2006, pp. 52-54.
4. New products here are defined to include true innovations as well as new items in the product line and significant product revisions and improvements, all launched within the last three years. Source of data: PDMA 2004 study. See: Adams, M. & Boike, D., "PDMA foundation CPAS study reveals new trends", *Visions*, XXVIII: 3, July 2004, pp. 26-29; and: *The PDMA Foundation's 2004 Comparative Performance Assessment Study.*
5. *How Companies Use Innovation to Improve Profitability and Growth.* Arthur D. Little, Innovation Excellence study, 2005.
6. *Fast, Focused, Fertile: The Innovation Evolution*, Cheskin and Fitch: Worldwide, 2003.
7. Arthur D. Little study, see endnote 5.
8. "Smart Spenders: The Global Innovation", Booz Allen & Hamilton, November, 2006.
9. Source of R&D to sales spending data: endnote 8.

10. For 2004 data, see endnote 4. For 1990s data, see: Griffin, A., *Drivers of NPD Success: The 1997 PDMA Report.* PDMA 1997.

11. Cooper, R.G., "Your NPD portfolio may be harmful to your business's health", *Visions,* XXIX: 2, April 2005, pp. 22-26.

12. For 1985 quality-of-execution data, see: Cooper, R.G. & Kleinschmidt, E.J., "An investigation into the new product process: steps, deficiencies and impact", *Journal of Product Innovation Management,* 3:2, 1986, pp. 71-85. For current quality of execution data, see our major benchmarking investigation undertaken by the authors with the APQC (American Productivity & Quality Center): Cooper, R.G., Edgett, S.J. & Kleinschmidt, E.J., *Best Practices in Product Development: What Distinguishes Top Performers,* at www.stage-gate.com and *Improving New Product Development Performance and Practices* by APQC, Houston. Also: Cooper, R.G., Edgett, S.J. & Kleinschmidt E.J., "Benchmarking best NPD practices-3: The NPD process & key idea-to-launch activities", *Research-Technology Management,* 47:6, January-February 2005, pp. 43-55.

13. For current portfolio breakdown data, see our benchmarking APQC study in endnote 12; also: Cooper, R.G., Edgett, S.J. & Kleinschmidt E.J., "Benchmarking best NPD practices-2: Strategy, resources and portfolio management practices", *Research-Technology Management,* 47:3, May-June 2004, pp. 50-60. Source of 1990 breakdown: Kleinschmidt, E.J. & Cooper, R.G., "The impact of product innovativeness on performance," *Journal of Product Innovation Management,* 8, 1991, pp. 240-251.

14. PDMA study. See endnote 4.

15. Our benchmarking-APQC study, see endnotes 12 & 13.

16. This section on root causes is taken from *Visions* article, endnote 11.

17. Cooper, R.G. & Edgett, S.J., "The dark side of time and time metrics in product innovation", *Visions,* XXVI:22, April-May 2002, pp. 14-16. The negative impacts of cycle time were first articulated in: Crawford, C.M., "The hidden costs of accelerated product development," *Journal of Product Innovation Management,* 9:3, September 1992, pp. 188-199.

18. This point is made by: Katz, G., "Not so fast," *Visions,* XXVIII:4, October 2004, p. 8. See also: Cooper, R.G. & Edgett, S.J., "Overcoming the crunch in resources for product innovation," *Research-Technology Management,* 46:3, May-June 2003, pp. 48-58; also endnote 17.

19. See our benchmarking-APQC study; endnotes 12 & 13.

20. IRI portfolio study: Cooper, R.G., Edgett, S.J. & Kleinschmidt, E.J., "New product portfolio management: practices and performance", *Journal of Product Innovation Management,* 16:4, July 1999, pp. 333-351; and: Cooper, R.G., Edgett, S.J. & Kleinschmidt, E.J., "Portfolio management for new product development: results of an industry practices study", *R&D Management,* 31:4, October 2001, pp. 361-380.

21. Arthur D. Little study, see endnote 5.

22. Arthur D. Little study, see endnote 5.

23. IBM, *Expanding the Innovation Horizon: The Global CEO Study,* 2006.

# CHAPTER 2

1. Parts of this chapter are taken from a previous book by one of the authors: Cooper, R.G., *Product Leadership: Pathways to Profitable Innovation*, 2nd edition. New York: Perseus Publishing, 2005. www.stage-gate.com.

2. Our benchmarking study with the APQC: see Chapter 1, endnotes 12 and 13.

3. Luck, D.J. & Prell, A.E., *Market Strategy*, Englewood Cliffs, Prentice Hall, 1968, p. 2.

4. Ansoff, I.H., *Corporate Strategy*, New York: McGraw-Hill, 1965.

5. Corey, R.E. "Key options in market selection and product planning," *Harvard Business Review*, September-October 1978, pp. 119-128.

6. Some sections in this chapter are taken from a book by the authors: Cooper, R.G., Edgett, S.J. & Kleinschmidt, E.J., *Portfolio Management for New Products*, 2nd edition. Reading: Perseus Books, 2002.

7. *New Product Management for the 1980s*, New York: Booz-Allen & Hamilton Inc., 1982.

8. Menke, M.M., "Essentials of R&D strategic excellence," *Research-Technology Management*, 40:5, September-October 1997, pp. 42-47.

9. Our benchmarking study: see endnote 2.

10. Our benchmarking study: see endnote 2.

11. Parts of this section are taken from an article by one of the authors: Cooper, R.G., "Maximizing the value of your new product portfolio: Methods, metrics and scorecards", *Current Issues in Technology Management*, published by Stevens Alliance for Technology Management, 7:1, Winter 2003, p. 1. Also, this section is based on a book by one of the authors, endnote 1.

12. See: Cooper, Edgett & Kleinschmidt, endnote 6; also: Cooper, R.G., Edgett, S.J. and Kleinschmidt, E.J., "Optimizing the *Stage-Gate*, process: What best practice companies are doing – Part II", *Research-Technology Management*, 45:6, November-December 2002.

13. See: Albright, R.E. & Kappel, T.A., "Roadmapping in the corporation", *Research-Technology Management*, 46:2, March-April, 2003, pp. 31 40; also: McMillan, A., "Roadmapping – agent of change", *Research-Technology Management*, 46:2, March-April, 2003, pp. 40-47; and: Myer, M.H. and Lehnerd, A.P., *The Power of Product Platforms*, New York: Free Press, 1997.

14. Source: Albright, R.E., "Roadmaps and roadmapping: Linking business strategy and technology planning," *Proceedings, Portfolio Management for New Product Development*, Institute for International Research and Product Development & Management Association, Fort Lauderdale, January 2001.

15. Day, G.S., "A strategic perspective on product planning," *Journal of Contemporary Business*, Spring 1975, pp. 1-34.

16. Porter, M.E., *Competitive Advantage: Creating and Sustaining Superior Performance*. New York: Free Press, 1985.

17. Christensen, C.M., *The Innovator's Dilemma,* New York: Harper Collins, 2000.
18. See success drivers in, for example: Montoya-Weiss, M.M. & Calantone, R.J., "Determinants of new product performance: A review and meta analysis", *Journal of Product Innovation Management,* 11:5, November. 1994, pp. 397-417; and: Cooper, R. G., Chapter 1 "New products: What separates the winners from the losers" in: *The PDMA Handbook of New Product Development,* 2nd Edition, New York: John Wiley & Sons, 2004.
19. Hamel, G. & Prahalad, C.K., *Competing for the Future,* Cambridge: Harvard Business School Press, 1996.
20. Corey: see endnote 5.
21 Abell, D.F., *Defining the Business,* Englewood Cliffs: Prentice Hall, 1980.
22. Crawford, C.M., "Protocol: New tool for product innovation", *Journal of Product Innovation Management,* 2, 1984, pp. 85-91.
23. Based on: Cooper, R.G., "Defining the new product strategy," *IEEE Transactions on Engineering Management,* EM-34, 3, 1987, pp. 184-193; Cooper, R.G., "Identifying and evaluating new product opportunities" in: Day, G.S., Weitz, B. & Wensley, R., *The Interface of Marketing and Strategy,* Vol. 4 of the series: *Strategic Management Policy and Planning: A Multivolume Treatise.* Greenwich: JAI Press Inc, 1990. See also: Cooper, R.G., "Product innovation & technology strategy", reprinted in *Succeeding in Technological Innovation,* Washington: Industrial Research Institute, May 2001, pp. 14-17.
24. Some of this section on roadmapping is taken from Lucent Technologies (Bell Labs). See endnote 14. See also: Meyer, M.H. & Lehnerd, A.P., *The Power of Platform,* New York: The Free Press, 1997.
25. Source of technology roadmap definition: see Albright, endnote 14.
26. The PDMA definition of "platform" in the sidebar is found in the Glossary of: *The PDMA Handbook of New Product Development,* M.D. Rosenau Jr., editor. New York: John Wiley & Sons, 1996.
27. See: Meyer & Lehnerd, endnote 24.

# CHAPTER 3

1. For an excellent description of the principles and method of peripheral vision, see: Day, G. & Shoemaker, P., "Scanning the periphery", *Harvard Business Review,* November 2005, pp. 135-148. Parts of this section on peripheral vision are based on this article.
2. Fuld-Gilad-Herring Academy of Competitive Intelligence, cited in endnote 1.
3. Source of Mattel example: Day & Shoemaker, see endnote 1.
4. Source of DuPont example: Day & Shoemaker, see endnote 1.
5. *No Relationship Between R&D Spending and Sales Growth, Earnings, or Shareholder Returns,* Booz Allen & Hamilton, October 2005.

6. Taken from Day & Shoemaker, see endnote 1.
7. Parts of this section originally appeared in: Cooper, R.G., Edgett, S.J. and Kleinschmidt, E.J., *Portfolio Management for New Products,* 2nd edition. New York: Perseus Publishing, 2002; and: Cooper, R.G., *Product Leadership: Pathways to Profitable Innovation,* 2nd edition. New York: Perseus Publishing, 2005.
8. For an excellent review of the impact of disruptive technology and what to do about it, see: Paap, J. and Katz, R., "Anticipating disruptive innovation", *Research-Technology Management,* September-October 2004, pp. 13-22. Parts of this section on disruptive technologies are based on this article.
9. The plight of leading firms when faced with a new technology is outlined in research by: Tushman, M.L. and O'Reilly III, C.A., *Winning Through Innovation: A Practical Guide to Leading Organizational Change and Renewal,* Cambridge: Harvard Business School Press, 1997.
10. Examples taken from Paap and Katz, see endnote 8.
11. Meyers, S. and Marquis, D.G., *Successful Industrial Innovation,* Washington: National Science Foundation, 1969.
12. Foster, R.N., *Innovation: The Attacker's Advantage,* Summit Books, 1988.
13. Christensen, C.M., *The Innovator's Dilemma,* New York: Harper Collins, 2000.
14. Adapted from Getz, G., "Looking ahead at the front end," *Proceedings, Portfolio Management for New Product Development,* Institute for International Research and Product Development & Management Association, Ft. Lauderdale, January 2001 and Christensen, see endnote 13.
15. These types of disruptions are from Paap and Katz; this section is based on their article – see endnote 8.
16. Example taken from Paap and Katz, see endnote 8.
17. See Christensen, see endnote 13.
18. Parts of this section on scenarios are taken from: Schwartz, P., "The official future, self delusion and value of scenarios," *Financial Times,* Tuesday, May 2, 2000, *Mastering Risk,* section, pp. 6-7. See also: Schwartz, P., *The Art of the Long View,* New York: Bantam Doubleday Dell Publishing, 1996.
19. Parts of this section originally appeared in: Cooper, R.G. *Winning at New Products: Accelerating the Process from Idea to Launch,* 3rd edition. Reading: Perseus Books, 2001.

## CHAPTER 4

1. For additional reading on the topic of VoC, see: McQuarrie, E.F., "Customer visits", *The Marker Research Toolbox: A Concise Guide for Beginners.* Thousand Oaks: Sage Publications, 1996, pp. 51-65. A summary of many customer analysis techniques is given in: The University Libraries, "Customer analysis teams" in: *Customer Analysis: A Manual of Techniques,* University of Southern California, 1997. Also; two VoC

approaches are outlined in detail in: Burchill, G. and Brodie, C., *Voices into Choices: Acting on the Voice of the Customer*, Center for Quality Management: Joiner Publications, 1997; and Ulwick, A., "Turn customer input into innovation", *Harvard Business Review*, January 2002.

2. Success factors in NPD are outlined in: Cooper, R. G., "New products: What separates the winners from the losers." Chapter 1 in: *The PDMA Handbook of New Product Development*, 2nd Edition, New York: John Wiley & Sons, 2004.

3. Cooper, R.G., Edgett, S.J. & Kleinschmidt E.J., "Benchmarking best NPD practices-3: The NPD process & key idea-to-launch activities", *Research-Technology Management*, 47:6, January-February 2005, pp. 43-55.

4. An excellent outline for a customer visit program is given in Appendix B of the book: McQuarrie, E.F., *Customer Visits: Building a Better Market Focus*. Newbury Park: Sage Publications, 1993.

5. For more information on the use of lead users in idea generation see: von Hippel, E.A., *Democratizing Innovation*, Cambridge: The MIT Press, 2005; Lilien, G.L., Morrison, P.D., Searls, K., Sonnack, M. and von Hippel, E.A., "Performance assessment of the lead-user idea generation process for new product development", *Management Science*, 48:8, August 2002, pp. 1042-1059. Also: von Hippel, E.A., Sonnack, M. and Churchill, J., *Developing Breakthrough Products and Services: The Lead User Method*. Minneapolis: LUCI Press. Also: Herstatt, C. and von Hippel, E.A., "From experience: developing new product concepts via the lead user method: a case study in a 'low tech' field", *Journal of Product Innovation Management*, 9, 1992, pp. 213-221. Also: Urban, G.L. and von Hippel, E.A., "Lead user analyses for the development of new industrial products", *Management Science*, 34:5, May 1988, pp. 569-582. Also: von Hippel, E.A., *The Sources of Innovation*. New York: Oxford University Press, 1988.

6. Adapted from: von Hippel, E.A., Thomke, S. and Sonnack, M., "Creating breakthroughs at 3M", *Harvard Business Review*, September-October 1999, pp. 47-57.

7. For some applications within 3M, see endnote 6.

8. This section on crowdsourcing is based on the article: Boutin, P., "Crowdsourcing: Consumers as creators", *Business Week*, July 13, 2006.

9. Thomke, S. and von Hippel, E., "Customers as innovators: A new way to create value", *Harvard Business Review*, April 2002, pp. 74-81; and von Hippel, E., *Democratizing Innovation*. Cambridge: The MIT Press, 2005.

10. Adapted from: Boutin, P. in endnote 8.

11. Adapted from: Boutin, P. in endnote 8.

# CHAPTER 5

1. Parts of this section are adapted from: Chesbrough, H., "'Open innovation' myths, realities, and opportunities", *Visions*, XXX:2, April 2006, pp.18-19.
2. Examples adapted from: Chesbrough, H., see endnote 1.
3. Source; Chesbrough, H., *Open Innovation: The New Imperative for Creating and Profiting from Technology*, Harvard Business School Press, 2003.
4. Parts of this section are adapted from: Docherty, M., "Primer on 'open innovation': Principles and practice", *Visions*, XXX:2, April 2006, pp. 13-17.
5. Source: Chesbrough, H., see endnote 1.
6. Examples adapted from: Chesbrough, H., see endnote 1.
7. Tao, J. and Magnotta, V., "How Air Products and Chemicals identifies and accelerates", *Research-Technology Management*, September-October 2006, pp. 12-18.
8. Roberts, E.B., "New ventures for corporate growth", *Harvard Business Review*, 1980, pp. 3-17; see also: Roberts, E.B. & Berry, C.A., "Entering new businesses: selecting strategies for success", *Sloan Management Review*, Spring 1983, pp. 3-17.
9. These definitions include some adapted from: Docherty, M., see endnote 4.
10. Adapted from Docherty, M., see endnote 4.
11. Example adapted from: *Open Innovation*, QuickMBA, www.quickmba.com/entre/open-innovation.
12. Adapted from Docherty, M., see endnote 4.
13. Clusman, P. and Achter, A., "How Kimberly-Clark uses open innovation to enhance NPD success", *Visions* XXX:4, September 2006, pp. 10-11.
14. Early examples are adapted from: Chesbrough, H., see endnote 3.
15. Huston, L. and Sakkab, N., "Connect and Develop: Inside Procter & Gamble's new model for innovation", *Harvard Business Review*, 84:3, March 2006.
16. Both P&G's SIMPL idea-to-launch process and their Initiatives Diamond are explained in: Cooper, R.G. & Mills, M., "Succeeding at new products the P&G way: A key element is using the Innovation Diamond", *PDMA Visions*, XXIX, 4, October 2005, pp. 9-13. Available online at: www.stage-gate.com.
17. These multifold trends which converged in the early part of the 21st century are from several sources; see endnotes 7, 15 and: Friedman, T.L., *The World is Flat: A Brief History of the Twenty-First Century*. New York: Farrar, Straus & Giroux, 2006.
18. Source: Friedman, see endnote 17.
19. Source: Friedman, see endnote 17.
20. Source: Frank Piller's Website on Mass Communication, Customer Integration & Open Innovation: www.mass-customization.de.
21. Tao, J. and Magnotta, V., see endnote 7.
22. Friedman, see endnote 17.
23. Some examples in this section are adapted from: Docherty, M., see endnote 4.
24. "An Idea with Bounce", *Technology Review*, April 2005.

25. Example adapted from: Docherty, M., see endnote 4.
26. Parts of this section on the benefits of open innovation are adapted from Docherty, M., see endnote 4.
27. Quotation from: Docherty, M., see endnote 4.
28. *Collaborating to Grow*, KPMG Study, cited in *Industry Week* article, Aug. 1, 2005.
29. *Management Tools and Trends Survey*, Bain & Company, 2005.
30. Campbell, A.J. and Cooper, R.G., "Do customer partnerships improve success rates?", *Industrial Marketing Management*, 28:5, 1999, pp. 507-519.
31. Leonard-Barton, D., *Wellsprings of Knowledge: Building and Sustaining the Sources of Innovation*. Boston: Harvard Business School Press, 1995.
32. Bidault, F. and Cummings, T., "Innovating through alliances: Expectations and limitations", *R&D Management*, 24, 1994, pp. 33–45.
33. Bruce, M., Leverick, F., Littler D. and Wilson, D., "Success Factors for collaborative product development: A study of suppliers of information and communication technology", *R&D Management*, 11, 1995, pp. 134–145.
34. Johne, A., "Listening to the voice of the market", *International Marketing Review*, 11:1, 1994, pp. 47–59.
35. Schrader, S. and Gopfert, J., "Structuring manufacturer-supplier interaction in new product development teams: An empirical analysis", in *Relationships and Networks in International Markets*, Hans George Gemunden, T. Ritter and A. Walter, eds., Pergamon Press, Elsevier Science, Oxford, 1998.
36. The section is adapted from material on P&G's "Connect + Develop" webpage, as well as from internal private communications. See: www.pgconnectdevelop.com.
37. Adapted from: Huston & Sakkab, see endnote 15.
38. Adapted from: N. Sakkab, "From research and development to connect and develop", in a P&G publication entitled: *Sharing & Caring*, 2005, www.procterundgamble.de/infomaterial.
39. Adapted from: Huston & Sakkab, see endnote 15.
40. Source: Huston & Sakkab, see endnote 15.
41. Adapted from: N. Sakkab, see endnote 38.
42. Performance results are from: Huston & Sakkab, see endnote 15.
43. Adapted from material from P&G webpage, see endnote 36.
44. As outlined in: Mills, M., "Implementing a Stage-Gate® process at Procter & Gamble", Association for Manufacturing Excellence International Conference, "Competing on the Global Stage", Cincinnati, October 2004. See also: Cooper & Mills, see endnote 16.
45. Parts of this section are based on work from: Docherty, see endnote 4.
46. Adapted from: Docherty, see endnote 4.
47. See scorecard for advanced technology projects in: Cooper, R.G., "Managing technology development projects", *Research-Technology Management*, November-December 2006, pp. 23-31.
48. See Stage-Gate-TD in endnote 47.
49. Adapted from: Falco-Archer, *Patent Mining*, 2005, www.falcoarcher.com.

50. An excellent handbook on patent mapping is available from: Japan Patent Office, Guide Book for Practical Use of "Patent Map for Each Technology Field", available as a PDF file at www.okpatents.com /phosita/images /patent_map_JPO.pdf.

51. Note that patent filing is expensive and consumes scarce IP people resources; therefore companies are selective about what they file, thus revealing what they consider important.

52. Naisbitt, J. *Megatrends: Ten New Directions Transforming Our Lives*, Warner Books, 1982.

53. These better-known external methods are from: Cooper, R.G. *Winning at New Products: Accelerating the Process from Idea to Launch*, 3rd edition. Reading: Perseus Books, 2001, Ch. 6.

54. Crawford, C.M., "The hidden costs of accelerated product development", *Journal of Product Innovation Management*, 9:3, September 1992, pp. 188-199.

55. Duff, S., "*Stage-Gate case study: How Precision Biologics has adapted the Dr. Bob Cooper "Stage-Gate®" process to develop new products,*" presented at (Canadian) National Research Council conference, Halifax, June 2006.

56. Both examples from: Holstein, W.J., "Putting bright ideas to work off campus", *The New York Times*, Sunday, November 5, 2006.

57. Parts of this section adapted from: Lee, P., *Open Innovation and the Role of Modern Universities.* Working paper, Auckland University, 2006.

58. Ruef, M., "Strong Ties, Weak Ties, and Islands: Structural and Cultural Predictors of Organizational Innovation", *Industrial and Corporate Change*, 11, 2002, pp. 427-449.

59. Example supplied by Lee, P., CEO of UniServices, The University of Auckland; see endnote 57.

## CHAPTER 6

1. Used with permission. Source: Private communication with H. Erler, VP Innovation, D. Swarowski, Austria, 2006.

2. Both examples are from our benchmarking study. See: Cooper, R.G., Edgett, S.J. and Kleinschmidt, E.J., *New Product Development Best Practices Study: What Distinguishes the Top Performers*, Houston: APQC, 2002. Also: R. G. Cooper, S.J. Edgett & E.J. Kleinschmidt, *Best Practices in Product Innovation: What Distinguishes Top Performers*, Product Development Institute, 2003. See www.prod-dev.com.

3. Source: Dr. Min Basadur (McMaster University, M.G. DeGroote School of Business), a world expert on group creativity.

4. A comprehensive outline of suggestions for brainstorming is provided in: Wikipedia, http://en.wikipedia.org/wiki/Brainstorming#Approach.

5. Source: Mind Tools, http://www.mindtools.com/brainstm.html.

6. Taken from: Cooper, R.G., *Winning at New Products: Accelerating the Process from Idea to Launch*, 3rd edition. Reading: Perseus Books, 2001, Chapter 6.

7. Source: *New International Version of the Bible*, Matthew 13, verse 57.

## CHAPTER 7

1. Parts of this section are from: Cooper, R.G., *Product Leadership: Pathways to Profitable Innovation*, 2nd edition. New York: Perseus Publishing, 2005, Chapter 7; and: Cooper, R.G., *Winning at New Products: Accelerating the Process from Idea to Launch*, 3rd edition. Reading: Perseus Books, 2001, Chapter 5.

2. The ExxonMobil Chemicals process for new science projects is described in: Cohen, L.Y., Kamienski, P.W. and Espino, R.L., "Gate system focuses industrial basic research", *Research-Technology Management*, 41:4, July-August 1998, pp. 34-37.

3. Stage-Gate® is a registered trademark of Product Development Institute Inc. See www.prod-dev.com.

4. The argument that technology projects require a special version of Stage-Gate has been voiced previously; see Koen, P., "Tools and techniques for managing the front end of innovation: Highlights from the May 2003 Cambridge Conference", *Visions*, XXVII, 4, October 2003.

5. Ajamian, G. and Koen, P.A., "Technology stage gate: A structured process for managing high risk, new technology projects", In *The PDMA Toolbox for New Product Development*, ed. by Beliveau, P., Griffin, A., and Somermeyer, S., New York: John Wiley & Sons, 2002, pp. 267-295.

6. Much of the rest of this chapter is from an article by one of the authors; Cooper, R.G., "Managing technology development projects – Different than traditional development projects", *Research-Technology Management*, November-December 2006, pp. 23-31.

7. Cooper, R.G., "Your NPD portfolio may be harmful to your business's health", *Visions*, XXIX, 2, April 2005, pp. 22-26.

8. Cooper, R.G., Edgett, S.J. and Kleinschmidt, E.J., "Benchmarking best NPD practices – II: Strategy, resource allocation and portfolio management", *Research-Technology Management*, 47:3, May-June 2004, pp. 50-59, Exhibit 2.

9. The reasons for the shift in portfolios are explored in Chapter 1 and in endnote 7.

10. See for example: Christensen, C.M., *The Innovator's Dilemma*. Harper Collins Publishers, 1997; and: Foster, R.N. and Waterman, R.H., *Innovation: The Attacker's Advantage*, Summit Books, 1998.

11. See ExxonMobil Chemical's process, endnote 2.

12. The IRI study on portfolio management methods employed by industry is reported in: Cooper, R.G., Edgett, S.J. & Kleinschmidt, E.J., "Best practices for managing R&D portfolios", *Research-Technology Management*, 41:4, July-August 1998, pp. 20-33; and is summarized in: Cooper, R.G., Edgett, S.J. and Kleinschmidt, E.J., *Portfolio Management for New Products, 2nd edition*. New York: Perseus Books, 2002.

13. See: PDMA studies: Adams, M. & Boike, D., "PDMA Foundation CPAS Study reveals new trends", *Visions* XXVIII, 3, July 2004, pp. 26-29; and: Cooper, R.G., Edgett, S.J. and Kleinschmidt, E.J., "Benchmarking best NPD practices – III:

Driving new-product projects to market success", *Research-Technology Management*, 47:6, November-December 2004, pp. 43-55.

14. Source of quotation: Koen, P. in endnote 4.

15. An early version of a technology model is described in: Eldred, E.W. and McGrath, M.E., "Commercializing new technology – I", *Research Technology Management*, 40:1, January-February 1997, pp. 41-47; see also the model outlined in endnotes 4 and 5.

16. An earlier version of this model is outlined in: Cooper, R.G., *Product Leadership: Pathways to Profitable Innovation*, 2nd edition. New York: Perseus Books, 2005, Chapter 7.

17. SG Navigator™-TD Edition is a commercially available Stage-Gate® process for TD projects. It contains all the stage and gate descriptions, deliverables, templates, scorecards, and how-to instructions – in short, all you need to implement a Stage-Gate-TD process. See www.stage-gate.com for more information.

18. See endnote 10 and 12; see also: Cooper, R.G., Edgett, S.J. and Kleinschmidt, E.J., "New product portfolio management: practices and performance", *Journal of Product Innovation Management*, 16:4, July 1999, pp. 333-351.

19. See endnote 12; also: Cooper, R.G., Edgett, S.J. and Kleinschmidt, E.J., "Portfolio management: Fundamental to new product success", In *The PDMA Toolbox for New Product Development*, ed. by Beliveau, P., Griffin, A. and Somermeyer, S., New York: John Wiley & Sons, 2002, pp. 331-364.

20. See endnote 12, portfolio book.

21. See IRI study endnote 12, and also endnote 18.

22. Cooper, R.G. and Mills, M., "Succeeding at new products the P&G way: A key element is using the Innovation Diamond", *Visions*, XXIX, 4, October 2005, pp. 9-13.

23. IRI study, endnote 12.

24. This section is based on endnote 7; strategic buckets are explained in portfolio book in endnote 12.

# CHAPTER 8

1. This section is taken from an article by the authors: Cooper, R.G. and Edgett, S.J., "Ten ways to make better portfolio and project selection decisions", *Visions Magazine*, XXX, 3, June 2006, pp. 11-15.

2. Results from our major benchmarking study with the APQC (American Productivity & Quality Center). See: Cooper, R.G., Edgett, S.J. & Kleinschmidt, E.J., *Best Practices in Product Innovation: What Distinguishes Top Performers*, Product Development Institute, 2003, www.stage-gate.com. A summary is reported in a three-part article series: Cooper, R.G., Edgett, S.J. & Kleinschmidt, E.J., "Benchmarking best NPD practices", *Research-Technology Management*, 47:1, January-February 2004, pp. 31-43; Cooper, R.G., Edgett, S.J. & Kleinschmidt, E.J., *Research-Technology Management*, 47:3, May-June 2004, pp. 50-60; and: Cooper, R.G., Edgett, S.J. &

Kleinschmidt, E.J., *Research-Technology Management, 47:6,* January-February 2005, pp. 43-55.

3. Source: Our benchmarking study, see endnote 2.

4. Source: PDMA best practices studies: Adams, M. & Boike, D., "PDMA foundation CPAS study reveals new trends", *Visions,* XXVIII: 3, July 2004, pp. 26-29; and: *The PDMA Foundation's 2004 Comparative Performance Assessment Study (CPAS).* Similar results were reported in the mid 1990s data, see: Griffin, A., *Drivers of NPD Success: The 1997 PDMA Report.* PDMA 1997.

5. Source of data for Stage-Gate: Benchmarking study with the APQC, see endnote 2; and: Cooper, R.G., Edgett, S.J. & Kleinschmidt, E.J., "Benchmarking best NPD practices-III: The NPD process & key idea-to-launch activities", *Research-Technology Management, 47:6,* January-February 2005, pp. 43-55.

6. For a detailed description of the authentic Stage-Gate® system, see Cooper, R.G., *Winning at New Products: Accelerating the Process from Idea to Launch,* 3rd edition. Reading: Perseus Books, 2001; updates to the system are available in: Cooper, R.G., "Formula for success", *Marketing Management Magazine,* (American Marketing Association), March-April 2006, pp. 21-24.

7. From: Bull, S., *Innovating for Success: How EXFO's NPDS Delivers Winning New Products,* presentation made to APQC as part of benchmarking study; see endnote 2.

8. Reasons for this lack of discipline and poor quality of execution, and what to do about it, are in: Cooper, R.G., "The invisible success factors in product innovation", *Journal of Product Innovation Management,* 16:2, April 1999, pp. 115-133.

9. The benefits of Stage-Gate have been revealed in a number of studies. See summary in: Cooper, R.G., *Winning at New Products,* see endnote 6. Also, see endnote 1.

10. Parts of this section are from: Cooper, R.G., Edgett, S.J. and Kleinschmidt, E.J., *Portfolio Management for New Products,* 2nd edition. New York: Perseus Publishing, 2002, Ch. 3. See: www.prod-dev.com.

11. A listing of success factors is found in: Cooper, see endnote 8; also: Cooper, R.G., "New products: what separates the winners from the losers", in *PDMA Handbook for New Product Development,* ed. Milton D Rosenau Jr., New York: John Wiley & Sons Inc, 1996.

12. Source: One major consumer goods firm undertook a major study of predictors of new product success. The conclusion: Of six predictors, the NPV calculated prior to the Development phase was the poorest predictor of eventual profitability – there was actually a fairly low correlation between predicted NPV and actual NPV. Other factors, such as product superiority and purchase intent, were more strongly linked to profit performance.

13. See IRI study results in *Portfolio Management for New Products,* endnote 10, Ch 6.

14. Source of quotation: Cooper, R.G. & Mills, M., "Succeeding at new products the P&G way: A key element is using the Innovation Diamond", *PDMA Visions,* XXIX, 4, October 2005, pp. 9-13.

15. The source of the Real-Win-Worth model is unclear but some users attribute it to The Forum Corporation of America; others cite Shirrella.

16. Duff, S., *Stage-Gate Case Study: How Precision Biologics Has Adapted Dr. Bob Cooper's "Stage-Gate®" Process to Develop New Products*, presented at (Canadian) National Research Council conference, Halifax, June 2006.

17. Source: *Portfolio Management for New Products* in endnote 10, Ch 3.

18. Source: Fitzpatrick, C., McAlpin, J., Vannucci, R., Cook, G., Hazel, J. & Johnsrud, D., *New Product Development at ExxonMobil Chemical*, presentation made to APQC, October. 29, 2002; see endnote 2.

19. Based on the ExxonMobil PIP process; source: endnote 18.

20. Cohen, L.Y., Kamienski, P.W. and Espino, R.L., "Gate system focuses industrial basic research", *Research-Technology Management*, 41:4, July-August 1998, pp. 34-37.

21. SG Navigator™ is a best-in-class Stage-Gate® system that is commercially available; see www.stage-gate.com

22. From: Cooper, R.G. & Edgett, S.J., see endnote 1.

23. Parts of this section are from: *Portfolio Management for New Products*, Ch. 3, endnote 10.

24. The Productivity Index is described in detail in: Cooper, R.G. & Edgett, S.J., *Lean, Rapid and Profitable New Product Development*, Product Development Institute, Ch. 5, 2005, see www.stage-gate.com, It was first proposed by the Strategic Decisions Group (SDG): Matheson, D., Matheson, J.E., and Menke, M.M., "Making excellent R&D decisions", *Research-Technology Management*, November-December 1994, pp. 21-24: and Evans, P., "Streamlining formal portfolio management", *Scrip Magazine*, February, 1996.

25. For more information on options pricing theory, see: Faulkner, T., "Applying 'options thinking' to R&D valuation", *Research-Technology Management*, May-June, 1996, pp. 50-57; and: Luehrman, T., "What's it worth? A general manager's guide to valuation," *Harvard Business Review*, May-June, 1997, pp. 132-142.

26. Sample probability tables are found in: *Portfolio Management for New Products* in endnote 10, Ch 8.

27. Tables to translate scoring model scores into probability of success are found in: *Portfolio Management for New Products* in endnote 10, Ch 8.

# CHAPTER 9

1. The four major drivers of innovation performance highlighted in the Innovation Diamond were uncovered in our benchmarking study with the APQC; see Chapter 1, endnote 12. Parts of this section are taken from: Cooper, R.G., *Product Leadership: Pathways to Profitable Innovation*, 2nd edition. New York: Perseus Publishing, 2005. www.stage-gate.com.

2. See how P&G uses the Innovation Diamond is explained in: Cooper, R.G. and Mills, M., "Succeeding at new products the P&G way: A key element is using the Innovation Diamond", *Visions*, XXIX, 4, October 2005, pp. 9-13.

3. Parts of this section are taken from: Cooper, R.G., *Winning at New Products: Pathways to Profitable Innovation*, Microsoft whitepaper, www.microsoft.com, 2005. Also available at www.stage-gate.com.

4. This section is based on material from many sources; see for example: Cooper, R.G., "Doing it right – winning with new products", *Ivey Business Journal*, July-August 2000, pp. 54-60; Cooper, R.G., *Winning at New Products: Accelerating the Process from Idea to Launch,* 3rd edition. Reading: Perseus Books, 2001; Cooper, R.G., "Stage-Gate new product development processes: A game plan from idea to launch", in: *The Portable MBA in Project Management*, ed. by Verzuh, E., Hoboken, New York: John Wiley & Sons, 2003, pp. 309-346.

5. Source: our benchmarking study, endnote 12 in Chapter 1.

6. Parts of this section are taken from the Microsoft whitepaper in endnote 3, and are based on: Cooper, R.G., *Product Leadership: Pathways to Profitable Innovation*, 2nd edition. New York: Perseus Publishing, 2005. See: www.stage-gate.com.

7. Source of this section – see endnote 6.

8. Source of P&G quotation: Cooper, R.G. and Mills, M., *Visions*, see endnote 2.

9. Source: our benchmarking study, endnote 12.

# INDEX

## Additional Resources

More resources are available to help companies achieve innovation success through our sister company, Stage-Gate Inc.

Visit the website www.stage-gate.com to order books and reports, to register for our executive innovation seminars, or to learn how to invite Dr. Cooper or Dr. Edgett to keynote at your next critical business event.

Subscribe to the Stage-Gate® knowledge community at www.stage-gate.com and receive our e-newsletter for innovation executives, the latest research articles, and updates.

*Presented through the Product Development Institute's
sister company, Stage-Gate Inc., seminars and workshops are
offered at varying times and locations throughout the year.*

# Attend Our Public Seminars

*Led by World-Renowned Innovation Experts
Dr. Robert G. Cooper and Dr. Scott J. Edgett*

## Successfully Designing and Implementing the Stage-Gate Process:
*How to Accelerate Your NPD Results*

The Stage-Gate® Innovation Process is the world's most widely used method for taking new product ideas from inception through to successful launch – because it works! The critical challenge is not in the decision to adopt Stage-Gate but in how you implement it so it becomes engrained in the very fabric of your organization. Join Dr. Robert Cooper and Michael J. Wiebe, Principal Consultant at Stage-Gate Inc., and learn how to implement the Stage-Gate Process in your organization to realize its fullest potential.

## Lean, Rapid and Profitable New Product Development:
*Improving Your Productivity*

Although many companies have introduced a new product process they are still struggling to get the financial results they expected. Productivity – the profit achieved versus the cost and time to do projects - is far below what it should be. Projects continually take too long, and the development pipeline is clogged with too many projects. With time-to-market so critical, can you really afford to have so many time-wasters in your system? Streamline your NPD process – a faster, more scalable and flexible innovation process. Join Dr. Cooper for solid insights into accelerating your new product process, learning what best practices top-performing businesses have already discovered and are successfully applying.

## Developing a Product Innovation Strategy and Deciding Your New Product Portfolio:
*Making Strategic Choices and Picking the Winners*

Picking the right projects and platforms to invest in is at the heart of successful product innovation. But effective project selections or portfolio management hinges on having a clearly defined and articulated Product Innovation and Technology Strategy for your business; the markets, technologies or products you should focus your efforts on and a strong link to portfolio management. Most businesses lack an effective and clearly articulated product innovation strategy; yet having this strategy is one of the important common denominators of successful businesses. Join Dr. Cooper and learn how to ensure scarce resources are consistently allocated to the most meritorious and strategic projects.

## Generating Breakthrough New Product Ideas:
*Feeding the Innovation Funnel*

Product innovations are the life blood of the modern corporation. But product innovation is in trouble – R&D productivity is down – there is less bang for buck. Game-changing or blockbuster product innovations are absent in most firms' development portfolios. And the key role of innovation has not gone unnoticed by the financial community – their message is clear – organic growth based on product innovation is paramount, with Wall Street placing increased pressure on CEOs to deliver. Join Dr. Edgett for this critical seminar on sustaining organic growth through innovation.

## Portfolio Management for New Products:
*The Blueprint for Effective Project Selection and Prioritization*

Almost 50% of all product innovation dollars are spent on losers – products that never make it to market or ultimately fail in the marketplace. Companies typically attempt too many projects with too few resources, fail to align project selection with strategies and neglect to balance their portfolio. Join Dr. Edgett for this intensive 3-day seminar and learn how to improve your return on product innovation investment by implementing a high quality portfolio management program.

## Technology Developments, Platforms & Fundamental Research Breakthroughs:
*Managing For Profitable Results*

Developments that build capabilities – new platforms, new technology, and fundamental research – lay the seeds for a family of winning new products, or a much improved manufacturing process. These are your "tomorrow projects" and potential game-changers that give your business sustainable competitive advantage. Technology Development projects are the foundation for new products and new processes and thus are vital to the prosperity of the modern corporation.

**Visit us online at www.stage-gate.com
for more information and to register.**

# Other Best Selling Books and Reports by Dr. Robert G. Cooper and Dr. Scott J. Edgett

## LEAN, RAPID AND PROFITABLE
## NEW PRODUCT DEVELOPMENT

Although many companies have introduced product innovation processes, they are still struggling to achieve the financial results they expected. Dr. Robert Cooper and Dr. Scott Edgett explain how to leverage the principle of lean, maximize the value of a new product portfolio, streamline the product innovation process, and achieve growth that is both profitable and sustainable. Discover the seven principles to *Lean, Rapid and Profitable New Product Development*.

## PRODUCT LEADERSHIP
## Pathways to Profitable Innovation (Second Edition)

*Product Leadership*, Second Edition, is the advanced course – a comprehensive guide for executives and senior managers who have a mandate to grow their businesses and impact performance through product innovation. *Product Leadership* goes beyond explaining what strategies are helpful to a company's success. It explores how to chart a competitive strategy and foster a culture that encourages product innovation. This book showcases examples of how companies such as Microsoft, GE, Nike and many others consistently prosper and it provides the reader with a wealth of practical knowledge.

## BEST PRACTICES IN PRODUCT INNOVATION
## What Distinguishes the Top Performers

*Best Practices in Product Innovation* is a breakthrough study that reveals the impact of performance drivers at the business unit level. Authored by Dr. Robert G. Cooper, Dr. Scott J. Edgett and Dr. Elko J. Kleinschmidt, the foremost world experts in product innovation, this report provides five in-depth case studies of top performing companies, isolates the drivers of innovation strategy, outlines metrics used to measure new product process and practices, and much more.

### PORTFOLIO MANAGEMENT FOR NEW PRODUCTS (Second Edition)

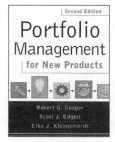

*Portfolio Management,* Second Edition, forces the reader to take a look at "the big picture" and question whether their organization is meeting its new product goals. This ground-breaking book presents a rigorous and practical approach to managing an organization's product portfolio and provides true examples of companies' portfolio strategies. It provides a wealth of knowledge, including how to pick the right approach for your organization and how to balance and maximize the value of your portfolio. This book is an essential resource for any company whose profitability, and very existence, relies upon the products it chooses to develop and the speed with which they are brought to market.

### WINNING AT NEW PRODUCTS (Third Edition)

For over a decade, Dr. Robert G. Cooper's book has served as a bible for product developers' world-wide. In this fully updated and expanded edition, Dr. Cooper demonstrates with compelling evidence why consistent product development is so vital to corporate growth and how to maximize your chances for success. With *Winning at New Products,* you will learn methods for developing a Stage-Gate® process, screening and prioritizing new product projects, incorporating customer input into product design, and much more to accelerate your speed-to-market.

### PRODUCT DEVELOPMENT FOR THE SERVICE SECTOR

In *Product Development for the Service Sector,* a comprehensive approach to product development tailored specifically for the dynamics of the service industries is presented, leveraging the extensive research and consulting experiences of Dr. Robert Cooper and Dr. Scott Edgett. Their experiences with companies such as Sprint, the Pennsylvania Energy Company, Marriott, VISA and the Royal Bank of Canada are highlighted.

**All Books are Available for Online Purchase at**
**www.stage-gate.com**